The
LEFT BRAIN
SPEAKS

The
RIGHT BRAIN
LAUGHS

The
LEFT BRAIN
SPEAKS

The
RIGHT BRAIN
LAUGHS

A Look at the Neuroscience of Innovation
& Creativity in Art, Science, & Life

Ransom Stephens, PhD

VIVA
EDITIONS

Published in the United States by Cleis Press, an imprint of Start Midnight, LLC, 101 Hudson Street, Thirty-Seventh Floor, Suite 3705, Jersey City, NJ 07302.

Printed in the United States.
Cover design: Scott Idleman/Blink
Cover photograph: iStock
Text design: Frank Wiedemann
Illustrations: Ransom Stephens

First Edition.
10 9 8 7 6 5 4 3 2 1

Trade paper ISBN: 978-1-63228-046-6
E-book ISBN: 978-1-63228-047-3

"There's more to it than that."

—MILES DYLAN,⋆
FROM HIS BOOK *EVERYTHING*

⋆Miles Dylan is a fictitious philosopher invented by college roommates Michael (Miles) Vinson and Chris (Dylan) Young. Miles Dylan's lack of actual existence (and consequential lack of actual publication) renders tremendous freedom in attributing tidbits of wisdom that, unattributed, might be taken less seriously. For a complete reference, see *The Toilet Papers* by Miles Dylan.

TABLE OF CONTENTS

1

YOU & ME

IT STARTS WITH ON/OFF.

As Starla wakes up, the light seeping through her closed eyelids tells her that the room is no longer dark.

Before we can understand anything about visual awareness, we have to understand the difference between light and dark. Let's call our humble detector of day or night, shadow or illumination, "first-order vision." By growing higher orders of visual consciousness from this simple starting point, we trace the complex from the simple.

Besides, we have to start somewhere; it might as well be morning.

Now, with the alarm clock playing a wakeful tune like "Enter Sandman," Starla opens her eyes, stretches, and drags her sleepy ass out of the sack.

She hears rain tapping on the window and puzzles over how such bright light can leak around the curtain on a rainy day.

Pulling aside the curtain, she beholds the magic of coexisting rain and sunshine. A heavy, gray cloud lumbers past. The late morning sun shines from behind her, working its rays under the cloud and lighting the hills across the valley from her window. At first, the colors look wispy, but then she sees a rainbow arcing over the horizon and, having seen it, she can't unsee it: red at the top followed by orange, yellow, green, blue, indigo, and violet at the bottom.

Perhaps the mnemonic device Roy G. Biv comes to mind; or maybe she muses on the magic and wonders if it's a metaphor come to life: Is she somewhere over the rainbow? Maybe she pictures light entering the spherical raindrops, bending into the component colors as in a prism or on a Pink Floyd album cover, and then reflecting off the other side of the raindrops back to her eyes, or maybe she jumps into her clothes and heads out in search of the pot of gold at the end of that rainbow.

We'll see how the story ends, but we know that it begins with a dichotomy: light and dark, a dichotomy that expands into a spectrum of colors when she pulls the curtain open. So it is with the left-brain/right-brain dichotomy. And so it is with every scientific endeavor. We don't start with the simplest situation because it's a good idea; we start at this first-order, on/off level of understanding because we're dumb apes who don't have a hope of understanding something complicated if we don't start with something easy. Okay, I'm a dumb ape; you're a glorious human.

Let's back up and take a closer look at Starla's experience. Her first-order visualization was light and dark. Then, with her light detectors wide open, her second-order visualization brought a spectrum of colors; a spectrum that can be divvied into an infinite number of colors between red and violet or, for that matter, between red and orange.

If she's into it, maybe she starts assigning the colors names like atomic tangerine and razzle-dazzle rose, dividing the colors into categories, subcategories, and sub-subcategories. This sounds boring to me, sort of like stamp collecting. A lot of science *is* like stamp collecting, but that's not the kind of science we're doing in this book.

After zoning out on the rainbow, Starla goes into the kitchen to fire up the coffeemaker. Still thinking about the infinite variations of color within the rainbow, she notices the Metallica black-light poster over the microwave. Rather than question the ridiculousness of her roommate's interior-decorating choice—having just woken up, after all—she fixates on the artificially bright fluorescent colors of the fire-breathing, dragon-demon, heavy-metal poster; mostly gonzo green and electric lava. She realizes that these colors are not among the infinite number of colors in the rainbow.

"What the hell?" she thinks to herself.

Scooping coffee into a filter, she recalls that human eyes detect only three colors, and that every color we see is a combination of red, green, and blue—she thinks the three colors might have fancier names, maybe like the overpriced ink cartridges in the printer that came "free" with her laptop: magenta, yellow, and cyan. The thought causes her to pour an extra scoop into the filter.

She figures that those black-light colors must be a combination of the three fundamental colors or she wouldn't be able to see them. And since the colors in a rainbow come from separating the yellowish-white light of the sun into its spectrum, black-light colors must be some sort of combination of red, green, and blue, but in a way that emphasizes the separate components differently than sunlight does in rainbows.

She hits the power button and hopes the coffee starts dripping soon. It occurs to her that too much thought in the morning could be lethal, a thought that brings to mind the color of coffee. She dubs it heavy-metal patina, which gives her a giggle.

As our heroine fixes her morning java, let's note that she has worked her way to a third-order understanding of color. Three layers of complexity: light-dark, the rainbow spectrum, and now fluorescent black-light colors.

Finally sipping her coffee, Starla wonders how her roommate convinced her that a Metallica poster was appropriate kitchen art.

With sufficient caffeine rushing through her veins, Starla accelerates into action, transforming from a color-contemplator into a business professional with meetings to attend in faraway lands. When she's packed tight into a coach window seat staring at the same raincloud, and presumably the same rainbow, she wonders why they're called bows. Shouldn't they be called ribbons? From up here, the rainbow doesn't touch the ground. It's not even an arc; it's a closed circle. Pondering the time wasted by leprechauns searching for pots of gold, she realizes two things: First, the reason why Ireland can never seem to maintain economic prosperity, and second, that there's another rainbow. The secondary rainbow is far dimmer than the primary, and the colors are reversed, with violet on top and red at the bottom. Starla has made a fourth-order discovery.

1.1 PEELING THE IGNORANCE ONION

I opened our book with Starla's rainbow experience because it shows how science progresses. We peel the onion of ignorance one layer at a time.

Just as there is a lot more to light than bright and dark, there's a lot more to how brains work than left and right, but that's where we're going to start. Then, building on that somewhat false dichotomy, we'll toy with others.

Yes, it's all a ruse.

In this book, you and I will investigate how innovation leads to discoveries, how art and science are totally different (yet also damn near the same), why we're never really alone even though we can't seem to get together, how analysis and intuition can't live without each other, why talent can't be distinguished from skill or vice versa, how life is built from death, and why the death of a friend feels so incomprehensible.

You will notice that each chapter heading combines two concepts that we often think of as separate but turn out to be deeply interrelated. Yes, even life and death; before you throw a yellow flag (or hold up a yellow card) on the seemingly obvious absurdity of that last statement, wait until you see what I mean. Then throw the flag, mark off the fifteen yards (or take a penalty kick), and we can talk.

By the way, I'm going to convert all measurements from American vernacular to metric, including football references.

With the preamble out of the way, let's get rolling.

Consider that instant of puzzlement when Starla heard rain tapping on the window and wondered how it could be so bright on a rainy day. Without that quandary, she'd never have boarded the train of thought that led to her analysis of rainbows and her discovery of how color works. That surprise, that instant when awareness of something out of the ordinary boiled up from her senses to her conscious mind, was the key to her whole discovery process. Had it never happened, Starla would probably still have the Metallica poster in her kitchen.

1.2 LEFT & RIGHT

Before the dawn of modern neuroscience, back when the first tentative insights came from people like Freud and Jung as they tried to reverse-engineer the brain, studies of anatomy demonstrated that, along with arms, legs, eyes, ears, nostrils, hands, and feet, people had what appeared to be two copies of their brains: a left hemisphere and a right hemisphere. The first-order insight—the dark-light level of understanding—was that the left brain controls the right side of the body and the right brain controls the left side. Like the vast majority of information on how the brain works, this insight came from doctors observing patients with injured brains.

Take Graham for instance. We travel to a South African bar during the Boer War, a mere 110 years ago. Seated a few stools down, Graham, a surly English officer, refers to a conscripted Scot as a cheap drunk. The Scot objects to being called cheap and rises in anticipation of a jolly brawl. Graham reaches for a sidearm. Disappointed that there won't be a tussle, the Scot pulls out his pistol too. The two men stare at each other. At this point, you and I get the hell out of the bar. We hear a gunshot from inside followed by silence. Peeking through the door, we see that the bullet has destroyed the left side of Graham's brain. We rush in and recommend that pressure be applied to the wound. Recognizing the uncharitable nature of his actions, the Scot stops the bleeding and, after months of care, Graham's injury heals.

With no left brain hemisphere, Graham can't see through his right eye or hear in his right ear; he has no control over his right arm or leg, though he can smell through his right nostril but not his left. With half a mind to work with, Graham provides first-order evidence that the two sides of the brain control opposite sides of the body. The gap in that observation, that nostrils don't share the asymmetry of the other senses and motor functions, indicates higher-order subtleties still to be understood. Among the less subtle distinctions was that Graham also couldn't speak or understand language.

While the left and right brains look quite similar, they assume distinct roles in sensory and language processing. The obvious generalization is that the left and right lobes play different roles and perform separate tasks. The legend of your left brain as the inner accountant and your right brain as the inner artist emerged in 1960 and turned out to be a gross oversimplification.

Don't be too harsh on the neurologists of the day. They didn't propagate the left-right myth; the press did. And don't be too harsh on them either. Two ingredients go into misinformation: First, people overreact, it's one certain assumption you can make about human behavior; and second, science progresses through incremental discoveries one layer of the ignorance onion at a time.

The right brain does play a big role in creativity, but so does the left brain. The left brain breaks things down into little, understandable pieces, but the right brain makes sure that those pieces still fit a greater whole.

The title of our book—I wrote it and you bought it, so we both own it—*The Left Brain Speaks, the Right Brain Laughs*—is a glaring example of a mythic oversimplification. In nineteen out of twenty right-handed and four out of five left-handed people, the left brain does the speech-production-and-recognition heavy lifting, and, without the right brain, your sense of humor is all but lobotomized. However, your left brain produces the actual hahahas of laughter. So our title serves as an example of mostly-but-not-completely false dichotomies. Just between the two of us, if you prefer, we can call it *The Left Brain Tells the Joke, the Right Brain Gets It, and Then the Left Brain Laughs.*

1.2.1 A new and improved left-right oversimplification

To update the roles of your left and right hemispheres, we begin with a guiding principle and then assemble a bunch of nuances. In the pages that follow, the roles will fit a larger pattern and make more sense.

Through the miracle of fiction, please don a pith helmet, and the two of us can hike into the savannah of one hundred thousand years ago. We come upon a young man named Butch as he emerges from the cave he shares with his community of ten to thirty cave people— he doesn't know how many because he can't count past three.

With his torn lion-skin loincloth and a plethora of scars across his torso, Butch emits quite an aggressive vibe, so we hide behind some reeds. You point out a bloat of hippos in the pond. I start to laugh at the word bloat, and you remind me that hippos are huge, gnarly critters and I shut up.

Butch notices the hippos too and ducks behind a boulder. He looks down and finds a nice rock. He watches the hippos for several minutes and then stands, steadies his right foot, goes into a windup, and lets the rock fly. Wham! Right into the hippo's eye and through its brain. We look at each other and agree that the kid's got a hell of an arm. If he was left-handed and, you know, born one hundred thousand years later, he could have gone pro.

Now let's look at it in slow motion.

Butch spots the herd. His left brain examines individual hippos, looking for one that appears sedentary enough so that it's not likely to move, is meaty enough to feed the whole tribe, is standing in water shallow enough for him to retrieve it, and is close enough for him to get a good shot. Meanwhile, back in his right brain, someone's keeping an eye out for trouble.

In order to reproduce, Butch must both survive the hunt and eat. The left brain focuses on the task at hand. The right brain keeps a lookout for anything that might require attention. The left brain ferrets out the details, while the right brain keeps those details in check by making sure they don't contradict the big picture. The right brain also tries to tell the left brain that Butch can't carry a hippo back to camp, but his left brain suppresses that warning with a cheerful but delusional reply: "It's okay, as soon as I kill the hippo, I'll invent the wheel!" His right brain sighs.

Your left brain is the one that takes you out on crazy fantasies, and your right brain reels you in. Your left brain can't see the forest for the trees; your right brain can't see the trees for the forest. Your right brain takes in the whole grand mystery, and your left brain sifts out the fine details. And when they come together, you create beauty and understanding. You can't ring the bell without both, but sometimes, in their efforts to keep you alive and having sex, they suppress each other when you might prefer that they collaborate.

Instead of thinking of your right brain as an underutilized creative genius and your left brain as an overworked analyzer, here are two choices for your new and improved oversimplification:

(a)   Your left brain is a fascinated child, and your right brain is an indulging parent.
(b)   Your left brain is a delusional idiot, and your right brain is a judgmental asshole.

Like all oversimplifications, you can get some mileage out of the concept, but if you take it too seriously, you'll make mistakes. So let's dig down another couple of layers.

1.2.2 Sorting out the left-right dichotomy

Your neocortex, the wrinkly, pinkish-gray outer layer of your brain, is about a tenth of an inch thick (about three millimeters) when peeled off and spread out on a table. The left and right versions look pretty much the same, though the right side is a bit bigger and whiter. The color contrast occurs because the left side has lots of local processing centers, more gray neurons, and the right side has broader connectivity with longer, better-insulated wiring. The two hemispheres communicate through a cluster of nerve connections called the corpus callosum—don't worry about all this jargon; I'll remind you what it means when it comes up again.

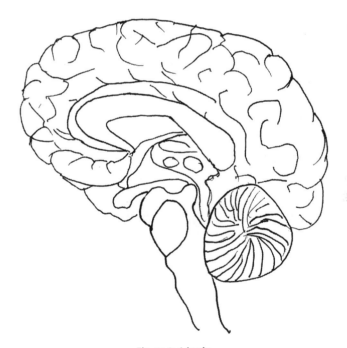

Figure 1: A brain.

The interior of your brain, called the limbic system, is composed of a bunch of nodule-like things, each of which has both left and right versions, except for your pineal gland. The left and right sides of the interior are connected by the anterior commissure, another pack of nerve fibers.

The point of this exercise in physiology is that the left and right lobes *really are* separate. Most of our left-right symmetries play both collaborative and redundant roles. You have two arms; if one gets cut off, you have a much better chance of survival with one than with none, even if you no longer have a fastball. It's the same deal with your brain, sort of.

The most pronounced effect of the two hemispheres is that if your right brain were somehow turned off, no one around you would notice for several hours, and you might not notice at all; but if your left brain were turned off, you'd seem like an imbecile, not just because you'd lose all command of spoken or written language, but also because you wouldn't be able to care for yourself or others.

To get an idea of how the left and right sides compete, collaborate, and provide a level of redundancy, I listed some distinctions in Table 1.

I assembled Table 1 from everything I've read and the experts I've talked to, but please don't take it verbatim. Instead, realize that these distinctions are just the layers of the ignorance onion beneath the one that insisted your right brain is creative and your left brain is analytical. If some of the entries make you uncomfortable, but you can't figure out why, it's because your right brain disagrees with my left brain.

ATTRIBUTE	RIGHT	LEFT
General	How?	What?
	Immediate hunches	Deliberate predictions
	Problem identifier	Problem solver
	Looks for inconsistencies	Keeps grinding away into never-never land
New experience	Excited by novelty, new information, developing skills	Integrates new information and skills into existing context
	Takes over when expectations break down	Assumes expectations will play out
	All at once, "aha!" insight	Gradual understanding
	Keeps explanations consistent with facts	Concocts descriptions, rationalizes
Attention	Broad, flexible, easily distracted, literal	Highly focused on parts, develops abstract context, can get obsessed
Facial identification	Facial identification with a mild racial bias	Lesser facial identification but without the built-in bigotry
Facial expression	Involuntary, honest	Voluntary, capable of deception
Emotion	Empathic, recognizes emotional responses of others	Recognizes complex emotions but doesn't take things as seriously
	Intense, tends toward pessimism, negativity, fear, mourning, grief	Cheerful, optimistic, amused
Symbolism and abstraction	Sees "7" and gets the idea but can't make sense of "seven"	Can deal with either numeric symbols or spelled-out numbers
	Mostly literal but tunes in to metaphors	Removes concepts from context, makes them abstract, creates fantasies
	Overlays expectation of the whole	Finds and separates common elements of the whole

Table 1: Contrasts of the right and left brain hemispheres—use these as indicators, not absolutes. The science has a long way to go (notice how I put the right on the left and the left on the right so that your eyes associate the information in each column with the correct hemisphere).

1.3 THE PICTURE WITHIN A PICTURE

Using a mind to figure out how a mind works is nothing if not self-referential.

In considering the Great Questions, philosophers tend to get caught in traps. Descartes's *cogito ergo sum* (which is all the Latin I know and means something like "I think, therefore I am"), though fun to ponder with a rum buzz while staring at the stars on a late summer night (mojito *ergo sum*), doesn't deliver the goods. Science, at least in the past two hundred years, delivers the goods by making a few simple assumptions and running with them.

Philosophers from Lucretius to Sartre have debated whether the mind and the brain are the same thing. Is the mind a metaphysical object tenuously linked to the mass of white and gray wetware in your skull? Or is the mind something that the brain does?

Isaac Newton laid down the bedrock of the scientific method in his first rule of reasoning: "We are to admit no more causes of natural things than such as are both true and sufficient to explain their appearances." In other words, we make the simplest assumptions possible until they're derailed by observable, repeatable contradictions. Assuming that the mind results from purely physical, material interactions within the brain begs fewer questions than positing a metaphysical mind in a physical body. Keep in mind that the whole point of experimental science is to trash reasonable-seeming assumptions. So if you favor a spiritually linked mind and body, keep a close eye on the data; if you're right, the purely physical assumption will fail, and you can tweet "in your face, @ransomstephens!"

In this book, we'll make as few assumptions as we need to go forward, and we'll tread carefully and consciously as we make them. For example, we'll assume that the universe exists, that there is an external reality, that we know the difference between being asleep and being awake, beer is more desirable than wine, and that rock 'n' roll is superior to jazz.

1.4 WHAT ARE WE DOING HERE?

...And why are we in this basket?

I don't know what you're doing here, but I want to understand how brains work for the same reason that I want to know how anything works—for the buzz of understanding, and so I can put that understanding to work. By studying the neuroscience of why people value certain things, how talent and skill feed on each other, and how the whole emerges from the parts, we'll develop intuitions for how to be better at everything we do.

Okay, hold on a second.

You're not reading a self-help book. I'm not pretending to have all the answers; I don't deal in secrets; and I have no interest in selling you anything other than fine reading material. The only answers you'll find here come from a baby science that's just starting to reveal how brains work. But when you understand how something works, you develop intuitions about what it can do well, what it can't do well, and how to position it to be successful. You and I can be better: better partners, better friends, and better constituents of planet Earth. We face problems individually and together, and our brains are the only tools we have to create solutions. We only get a few decades of awareness; we should put our heads to work.

That's what we're doing here, in the best-case scenario. In the worst case, we have a few laughs. So here's to creating and appreciating, understanding and empathizing, more love and less fear, all that sort of crap.

In *The Left Brain Speaks, the Right Brain Laughs*, we will pay a lot of attention to creativity because the brain itself is an instrument for creating.

We'll investigate the neuroscience processes that lead to amazing feats in the arts and sciences, what happens in the brain when we get those "aha!" lightbulb moments, as well as when we derive a solution/invention/masterpiece through the deliberate process of hard work.

We'll keep the jargon to a minimum. Check the bibliography if you want maps of all the folds, grooves, and ridges in your brain—

called sulci and gyri by the pros—functional magnetic resonance images (fMRI), positron-emission tomography (PET) scans, and so forth. That said, we won't shy away from brain physiology when we need it, or when it's too irresistibly fascinating (or funny) to pass up.

My background is in experimental particle physics, technology development, and science and fiction writing. As a physicist, I'll provide some scientific insight into how physical systems work. As a veteran researcher of a mature science I'll try to see beyond the preliminary results of this brand-new science, I'll try to provide guidance as to where neuroscience is probably headed, when we should be skeptical, and what's not likely to change as the field matures. As a fan of neuroscience, I'll sit next to you on this tour and, together, we'll try to make sense of it.

One last thing, instead of sequential info-dumps, we're going to circle around concepts and build on them in subsequent chapters. It's easier to learn when you encounter something more than once at increasing levels of complexity. Each time a subject returns, I'll remind you what we already covered so you won't need to look back. I hope this level of repetition will help more than it annoys.

You're about to meet my grandfather. Gird your loins!

2

ANIMALS & PEOPLE

FRANK RANSOM'S MOTHER DIED IN 1893 WHEN HE was three years old. He was sent to an orphanage in Oakland that operated by providing children as free labor to families who agreed to train and feed them. The potential for abuse was, shall we say, insane.

Frank Ransom never said a negative word about his childhood. He described a youthful paradise on ranches in the temperate hills of Northern California spent driving cattle, milking cows, and working the fields under the guidance of a series of extraordinarily generous patrons.

Frank was nine years old when he went to apprentice with Mr. Smith on a ranch near Santa Rosa, about sixty miles north of San Francisco. He told stories about living in a barn and sleeping on hay in a stall with horses for roommates. When quizzed a bit, rather than admitting that the Smiths didn't let him inside their house, he said that he never wanted to leave the horses.

On Christmas Eve, Mr. Smith came out to the barn and gave Frank an orange. Frank described that orange as though it were the Holy Citrus Grail. His eyes lit up as he pantomimed peeling that orange. Its juice burst forth, ran down his chin, and made his straw bed sticky. He spoke with such sincere joy that his grandchildren—four middle-class kids growing up in the suburbs, including me—yearned to spend Christmas Eve in a drafty barn sleeping on muddy hay with an orange. An orange.

Frank Ransom was the most positive man I've ever known. He never spoke ill of anyone.

Armed with a third-grade education and confidence born of naïveté, Frank built a successful business during the Great Depression. Over the course of his life, he counted governors, presidents, professional athletes, and even a Supreme Court justice among his closest friends. Of course, he thought of everyone he knew as one of his closest friends. One could say that Frank Ransom had a positive outlook.

One of his favorite sayings came from the first lines of an Ella Wheeler Wilcox poem: "Laugh and the world laughs with you; weep and you weep alone." The world spent a great deal of time laughing with Frank, and the only time anyone saw him cry, he shed tears of joy.

2.1 DIFFERENT PERSPECTIVES ON REALITY

That melancholy phrase packed with implications for human behavior, "Laugh and the world laughs with you; weep and you weep alone," stuck with me. How often did Frank Ransom weep alone? How did such a happy man emerge from that world?

Frank's positive outlook, wherever it came from, found the positive in every event and built on that positive, reinforcing it no matter what the conditions. He was a smiling lad digging through horse manure, positive that he'd find a pony, a positive pony.

This chapter is about perspective.

Frank Ransom maintained his positive perspective even when the chips were falling. When the Great Depression hit, he and his wife Grace had two children. He figured that rich folks would always have money to spend, but that they wouldn't be spending quite as much on luxury items as they did in the Roaring Twenties. He reconfigured his business to provide less-pricey luxuries. His business improved during the Depression. Frank Ransom found a pony in the manure of the Depression.

To see how Frank managed to grab the positive and toss the negative, we need to understand what gives us different perspectives, how we are plopped into different states of being and how our brains push and pull us before we have a chance to ponder how we'd like to respond. Since they're our window on the world, our senses—touch, taste, smell, hearing, and sight—set the stage for the variety of perspectives we can attain. Our senses and how we process them limit our perspectives just as they limit the perspectives of other animals. Every animal sees the world in a different way with a different physical perspective. We have a lot to learn from other animals. And I mean this in a purely selfish way.

We have a great deal of control over our perspectives, but some perspectives are thrust upon us by the order and speed of the processes our brains use to understand the world around us. Visceral, emotional, and intellectual responses operate at different rates and plop us into certain perspectives that help us survive and get laid. But in the fifteen thousand-plus years since we started to think of ourselves as civilized, we've invented a world where a lot of those automatic responses work against us. Strangling your boss might seem like a good idea at the time, but it rarely gets you a raise.

In everything we do, there's a hierarchy of perspective, from immediate to barely tangible to fully abstract. To understand how we react to challenges, it helps to start with something easy, like the imminent attack of a saber-toothed tiger.

But first, a few words about what makes you so damn smart (and good lookin').

2.2 EVOLUTION

Natural selection is a more descriptive term than Darwin's "evolution" because it indicates how the process works. Random mutations cause random changes over many generations. The changes that benefit an organism's proliferation tend to proliferate.

You know the statement: "Whatever doesn't kill you makes you stronger." It should be: "Whatever doesn't kill you, make you weaker, or leave you the same makes you stronger." The modified version of the cliché serves as a nice description of natural selection. If a mutation makes you stronger, your progeny stronger, their progeny stronger, and so on, that mutation has a good chance of making it into your gene pool. Mutations that make you stronger are adaptations. If a mutation makes you weaker, and by weaker I mean less competent at survival and/or less competent at reproducing and parenting, it's not likely to make it out of the gene pool's shallow end. On the other hand, if it doesn't make you weaker or if it leaves you more or less just as well equipped to survive and spawn as before, it has a pretty good chance of staying in the gene pool, and maybe somewhere down the line, that mutation might team up with another and the combination could make you stronger. Mutations with this sort of delayed gratification are called exaptations—we'll get to them later.

Mutations that make it into the gene pool are "selected" by nature. That sounds nice and tidy, right? Well, random mutations happen to both predator and prey, as well as the landscape itself. Just because a mutation makes you better at reproducing does not mean that it will make it into the pool, because the pool changes too.

Here's evolution's feedback loop: The mutation alters the individual. The individual alters the environment. The environment, including other animals, as well as friends and relatives, determines which mutations benefit a species and which do not. Those that benefit carry on to progeny. The progeny alter the environment, and so on—a picture within a picture.

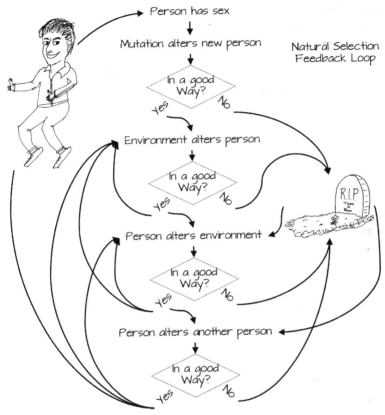

Figure 2: The natural selection feedback loop.

2.2.1 The power of long times and large numbers

People produce new generations about every twenty years, and tiny random mutations occur every time. Looking around, we see very little change across the four or five generations we're exposed to during the few decades we live. So if it takes a thousand generations for a significant mutation to proliferate, how long would it take to crank out a whole different beast? Several hundred thousand years equates to tens of thousands of mutations, so that's the rule-of-thumb timescale for natural selection in humans. The timescale differs for different species. A dog generation is about a tenth of a human genera-tion, so coyotes, wolves, and puppies evolve ten times faster. Most life on earth has a generation that lasts weeks; some bacteria turn over in minutes. With such short generations, biologists and biotechni-cians can see adaptations evolve through natural selection in their labs during their lunch breaks.

Making choices by random chance is no more intelligent than playing the lottery. When a baby is born with a significant mutation, odds are that it will kill him. But with billions of years to work with, millions of random variations easily combine into a hefty list of excel-lent adaptations.

You see, evolution enjoys a relaxed timescale. Seriously, Darwin was in no rush. I mean, he's long dead, but even if he were alive, the dude would still have the long view in mind. We rarely deal with truly large numbers, so it's no more surprising that we have trouble grasping evolution than that we buy lottery tickets.

2.2.2 Evolution predicts what already happened

In physics, theories predict how stuff works. If you kick a football and tell me its direction and speed, I can calculate where it's going to land. Quantum electrodynamics, while a mouthful, predicts the behavior of hydrogen atoms to a greater precision than anything else human beings have measured.

Evolution doesn't predict which mutations will happen. It's not that kind of theory.

When presented with a vat of bacteria and details of the chemical soup where it lives, temperature, humidity, and all the other condi-tions, evolution won't predict what comes out after one hundred thou-sand generations. It tells you that whatever survives will be better suited for those conditions than what you started with. It doesn't predict which mutations will occur, only that the survivors will be better at surviving than their ancestors. Just because a mutation is beneficial doesn't mean it will happen.

Any explanation we serve up for how or why an organism has

a certain characteristic must be consistent with the rules of natural selection. It's in this sense that evolution serves as a judge for biological explanations. However—and watch your step here because this is a minefield for biologists, behaviorists, neuroscientists, psychologists, linguists, and philosophers—just because an explanation makes sense in the light of natural selection doesn't mean it's right.

Before continuing, let me be clear that there is no scientific doubt about the reality of evolution through natural selection. It forms the backbone of biology, biochemistry, bioengineering, and pharmacology. You will not find employees at a biotech firm who deny natural selection, and if you do, I would advise against investing.

2.3 A FROG, A PUPPY, AND RICHARD FEYNMAN WALK INTO YOUR CRANIUM

Our brains evolved from the bottom up, so it's tempting to distinguish the three obviously distinct sections of the brain as prehistoric, primitive, and genius—your inner frog, puppy, and Richard Feynman. Neurobiologists assure us that it's not nearly so simple. At each step in the millions of years of their development, brains have re-optimized their internal wiring. There wouldn't be much point in putting a Corvette engine in a horse-drawn carriage if you didn't disconnect the horses, add a transmission, install a killer stereo, and put on some nice tires and wheels. A steering wheel might be nice too.

We'll use our modified version of this "triune model" of the brain as a metaphor, not a theory, for how the brain works. Metaphors are great for illustrating scientific concepts, as long as we don't let those metaphors grow hooves and trample the concepts.

Starting from where the neck bone connects to the head bone, our inner frog brain is composed of the brainstem and cerebellum. The brainstem is a collection of nerves that controls all the processes we take for granted, like heart rhythm, breathing, and perspiration. The cerebellum, sometimes called the "mini-brain," sits just above the back of your neck and is a bulbous processor composed of more

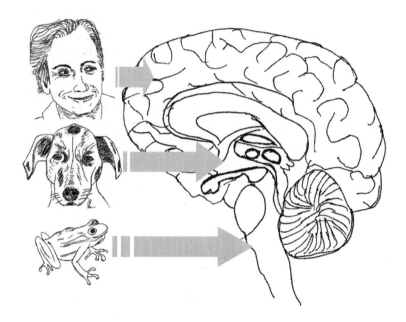

Figure 3: The same drawing of a brain as before, but with different labels.

neurons than you have in the rest of your brain combined. It coordinates your motions from dancing to throwing to raising your beer mug to your mouth on target almost every time.

Your inner frog is, in evolutionary terms, the oldest part of your brain. It delivers and receives information to and from neurons all over your body—tactile sensations of your skin, orgasms, pain, the various biological urges to fill and empty your body and so on.

2.3.1 First dose of jargon: neurons, axons, dendrites, and synapses

We're both pleasantly and painfully aware of the presence of nerves throughout our bodies. Nerves deliver signals to our brains and carry instructions from our brains to our muscles. The spinal cord is the cable through which tactile sensations are received and commands to muscles are transmitted. Every sense has such a cable. The optic and auditory nerves are really bundles of thousands of individual nerves, each carrying a unique signal. It's the same deal with the sense of smell and its olfactory nerve. Taste is altogether nervier, delivering data from tongue to brain through the facial, glossopharyngeal, and vagus nerves.

What we think of as nerves are more accurately called neurons. In addition to carrying signals to and from the brain and body, neurons within our brains form the scratch paper on which we write our thoughts. Like all biological cells, neurons have a cell body that houses the nucleus, chromosomes, and all that stuff from Bio I that we've forgotten.

Axons carry signals from one neuron to another. Your longest axon is the sciatic nerve that runs from your tailbone to your big toe. The shortest are millimeter-or-less connections between neighboring neurons within your brain. Neurons have a single axon for transmitting signals, but they can have a veritable forest of dendrites for receiving signals. One axon can connect to many dendrites, including the dendrites of its own neuron. When a neuron's axon connects to one of its own dendrites, it feeds back its own signal.

The cell body is about 30 microns (0.03 mm) across, a bit smaller than the diameter of a human hair. While axons can be quite long, they are about 1 micron (0.001 mm) in width. Dendrites are a little wider than axons, though rarely longer than 50 microns (0.05 mm). The points where an axon connects to a dendrite are called synapses. With the central body or "soma," the long axon, and the cluster of dendrites about the body, the whole thing looks sort of like a tree.

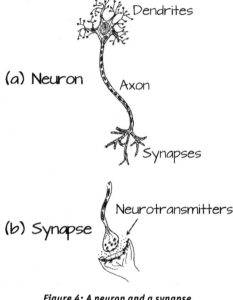

(a) Neuron

Dendrites

Axon

Synapses

(b) Synapse

Neurotransmitters

Figure 4: A neuron and a synapse.

2.3.2 *Your inner puppy and inner Feynman*

The next layer, your inner puppy, called the limbic system, is made of organ-looking things; stuff like the amygdala, basal ganglia, hypo-thalamus, and a mess of other individually discernible doodads.

Your inner puppy is the part of you that likes to play, the part that betrays whether you're happy or sad, afraid or confident. It wags your tail when you're happy and perks your ears when you're fascinated. It's the part of you that feels appetites like hunger, thirst, and carnal lust.

The outer layer, your inner Feynman, where you do mathematical physics, make conscious decisions, recognize faces, speak, plan, and develop goals, is the uniform-looking, wrinkly outer layer called the neocortex.

Richard Feynman was the greatest American physicist of the twentieth century. When he worked on the Manhattan Project he picked locks in top-secret buildings; as a member of the panel assem-bled by NASA to investigate the Challenger space shuttle explosion, he discovered the engineering mistake by questioning bureaucratic dogma; he gave a series of famous lectures on basic physics that have dazzled every physics major in the last fifty years; and he also made physics far more approachable by describing sub-nuclear processes in cartoons called Feynman diagrams—I'll show you some later.

The urge to think of your inner frog/brainstem plus cerebellum, inner puppy/limbic system, and inner Feynman/neocortex as three distinct layers that evolved over different epochs is tempting because, well, it's more or less how it happened. But puppies have a bit of Feynman and frogs a bit of puppy. That is, amphibians and reptiles may not feel anger per se, but they respond to challenges as though they do, and if a lizard looks pissed off and acts pissed off, I'm willing to assume that it's pissed off, and being pissed off is an emotion. Similarly, when my dog Professor Buckley figures out how to unlatch the gate or wakes me up with his leash in his mouth, it's the work of his inner Feynman.

Your brain divvies up the workload to millions of subnetworks that perform the processes that keep you going. Each subnetwork processor is also a building block for other processors. If the left side of your brain just in front of your ear is damaged, you'll lose the ability to speak because you have a speech processing unit in that space. However, that processing unit is part of a broad network. To discuss an orphan growing up on northern California ranches, you associate information from other localized subnetworks including those that process how you feel about the kid and whether or not he wept alone or just let the world laugh with him, plus what you know about citrus, geography, and turn-of-the-twentieth-century history. When you get to the oranges, associations from your visual, scent, and taste processors all affect what you have to say and then, finally, you can associate all that baggage with the lower-level motor cortex processor that blows air through the vocal cords of your inner guitar to produce audible speech.

The vast majority of people, about 95 percent, use the same areas of their brains to perform the same tasks. A guy gets a whack to this part of his head and he can't talk anymore. Look at his brain after he dies, see the part that's wrecked, and it must be the inner talker, right? Well, sort of, but not quite.

Functional nuclear magnetic resonance imaging, fMRI, produces those multicolored pictures of brains that you see in magazines, newspapers, and books, such as those listed in the bibliography. As fMRI techniques have improved, subtle mental processes have been isolated to specific regions of the brain. Reading, writing, and arithmetic processors have been found, though the three Rs require combinations of processors. Facial recognition has been localized to a region of the right brain. And where we store information about movie stars has been narrowed down to several thousand neurons.

The processing centers in your inner Feynman don't have clear-cut boundaries the way that organs do, and this is where our frog-puppy-Feynman metaphor runs out of steam. You could cut open my belly, saw my rib cage apart and yank out my heart, liver, pancreas, stomach, gizzard—all that gooey stuff—cut away the inputs and outputs, arteries and veins, and throw each organ in a separate bucket. But what I call processing centers aren't separate organs. If you cut open my brain, you can't tell my speech processor from my calculus processor because, as we'll see, these two processors share subnetworks.

Your inner Feynman is not composed of individual components that perform separate tasks; it's a network.

The left brain has localized clusters of neurons, processing centers that provide higher-level data for association among other processing centers and the entire network as a whole. The right brain has processing centers too, but on the right, the neurons have longer connections that form fewer but bigger and broader subnetworks.

To color-code it, neuron cell bodies are dark gray. Since the axons that stick out from neurons carry electrical signals, they need insulation just like the wires that go from your MP3 player to your ears. That bio-insulation, called myelin, is white. The left brain is a darker shade of gray than the right brain because it has a larger number of closely packed gray neurons with short axons. The right brain is a paler shade of gray because it has fewer gray neurons with more long-reaching white axons.

The difference in how the left and right brains are wired indicates their functional difference. The left brain's localized subnetworks tend to perform more focused processes, and the right brain's farther-reaching, global subnetworks tend to monitor broad relationships among processes.

2.4 HOW TO GREET A SABER-TOOTHED TIGER...OR CHESS PLAYER

Say you're walking along the street, you turn a corner, and there, towering over you, is a snarling saber-toothed tiger. The sight and smell of it enter your brain and, still barely processed, the data arrive first in your thalamus.

The thalamus is the part of your inner puppy that acts as a way station for incoming data. Our eyes scan far more objects than we notice. The thalamus is the first step in deciding whether or not the thing in view is worth considering. The thalamus immediately sends the data to your amygdala, which is your four-F center: fight, flight, freeze, or "mate."

Your amygdala reacts to the sight, scent, and snarl of the saber-toothed tiger with a blast of fear. The fear triggers an injection of the action hormone epinephrine, which is also known as adrenaline, into your bloodstream. In so doing, the amygdala tells your inner frog to crank up your heart rate, start sweating, and get ready to run, fight, or talk your way out of this mess.

Vesicles on the axon end of the synapse release neurotransmitters. Neurotransmitters change the shape of receptors on the dendrite, opening a membrane that allows the signal to flow from one neuron to another. Neurohormones and neurotransmitters like epinephrine play a huge role in how we feel about life, the universe, and everything else. When your inner pharmacist doses you with dopamine, for example, you feel rewarded and satisfied. Endorphins block pain and generate pleasure rather like opiates. Oxytocin and vasopressin make you feel desired and trusting. Serotonin affects your feelings of safety and happiness. Hundreds of others have been identified but their roles are mostly vague, especially in combinations. As with everything in this field, we tread lightly. Just as we don't all respond to drugs in the same way, we don't all respond to neurotransmitters in the same way.

The conscious feeling of fear, or any feeling for that matter, comes *after* the initiation of your physical response—sweating, trembling, muscle tension. Your brain doesn't determine that you should be afraid and then generate the feeling of fear; it generates the physical response to fear and that physical response is fed back up to the thalamus and then to the amygdala, which generates the sensation of fear.

Within about 0.2 seconds of your saber-toothed encounter, your amygdala does two things. First, it engages your flight mechanism and you sprint the hell out of there. Second, it forwards the decision to your forebrain.

Your visual processors take an additional quarter of a second to refine the image of the saber-toothed tiger. Just after the image is ready for your Feynman to contemplate, your inner puppy's decision to flee arrives at your Feynman with a dose of hormones that produce a feeling of certainty. The confidence born of that certainty convinces your Feynman that it actually made the decision to flee so that it doesn't waste time second-guessing your inner puppy instead of getting the hell out of there.

But make no mistake about it: A preponderance of experimental evidence indicates that immediate decisions are made in half the time it takes the signal to propagate from your inner puppy to your inner Feynman. You simply cannot be conscious of decisions made in less than half a second. For some reason, probably to ease intellectual digestion of the progression of events and maintain a feeling of continuity, we have evolved the ability to automatically reorder sequences that occur in less than about three-quarters of a second. I can't speak for the genuine, though dead, Richard Feynman, and would never disparage his fine reputation, but our inner Feynmans, like spouses and corporate executives, seem to require the illusion of control.

Fortunately, since the saber-toothed tiger operates with similar wetware, your initial response and the cat's operate on the same timescale, so you have a chance to get away. But once that 0.2 seconds stretches into 0.5 seconds, if the cat hasn't caught up with you, your inner Feynman needs to come up with a plan.

Let's take another look at what has happened so far, this time with the continuous input of data in mind.

Say you meet the big cat at t = 0 seconds. The light reflected from the tiger excites the rods and cones in your eyes. Data from your rods and cones are transmitted up your optic nerve to your visual processors. Those processors get to work. The first crude rudimentary images—outlines, edges, and boundaries—are compared to images previously stored in your memory. Then your initial bodily reaction and that rudimentary association of the image arrive at your amygdala and, finally, at $t = 0.2$ seconds, you start running.

In the time interval from 0.2 to 0.4 seconds, the data input and processing cycle repeat. With more data, the image is almost ready for your inner Feynman to ponder. You are sweating, your heart is racing, you're scared shitless, and, yes, you're running like hell. Still more visual, sound, and scent data arrive in your respective processors. Your amygdala refines your physical and emotional responses.

So far, you're not even conscious that anything has happened!

Finally, at $t = 0.5$ seconds, that feeling of certainty, combined with unbridled fear, prevents you from wasting time pondering the situation. Instead, you start associating the only now emerging refined images, scents, sounds, and physical sensations with the context of where you are, what tools might be at your disposal, and how to deal with cats. That is, at $t = 0.5$ seconds, you initiate the process of putting the situation into context—even though you've been running for 0.3 seconds.

After almost a full second, your first conscious thought trickles in. By "thought," I mean that you experience the association of processed sensory data with memory and movement. This association is essentially a *prediction* of what will happen in the next half second or less. That thought goes to the thalamus where it is sent to the various sections of your brain.

Different processors feed information to each other and to your arms and legs. All subsequent data, including fresh sensory data and new, more abstract data created by your brain make their way back through the loop. Your frog reacts first, then your puppy, and long after they've been able to react, act again, and then again, your inner Feynman finally starts stroking its chin and pondering a plan.

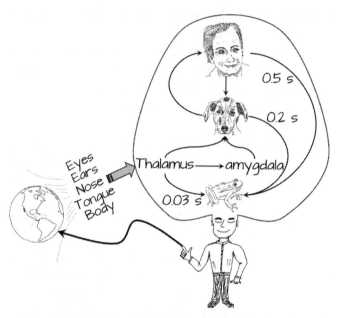

Figure 5: Your frog, puppy, and Feynman.

Your edge is that you can use tools. The saber-toothed tiger's edge is altogether too obvious. Sorry, my money's on the cat; your Feynman is too slow.

Okay, let's stop here.

What if, when you walked around that corner, you were instead confronted by a wizened old geezer sitting at a table with a chess set challenging you to a game, rather than a saber-toothed tiger?

As with the cat, your thalamus sends the data off for processing, but now, when your amygdala receives that data, it doesn't generate fear—unless you're like me and the thought of losing a game of wits to a venerable codger is too horrifying to consider. Instead of your inner puppy telling your inner frog to crank up its heart rate and run like hell, your amygdala directs your body to slow down and focus your eyes on the board, the geezer's face, and the time clock. Rather than forwarding an immediate sense of certainty to your forebrain Feynman, it offers mild uncertainty. Rather than a "get the hell out of here," your amygdala passes the data along with a shrug of its limbic shoulders.

The decision of whether or not to accept the geezer's challenge has many influences. With plenty of time to process the situation, your Feynman provides context and evaluation. But that evaluation and context are not cold and calculating because your inner puppy remains piqued, with tail wagging and ears perked. As your Feynman associates learned properties—how chess is played, experience in competition, how much daylight remains, the weather, etc.—it feeds predictions back to the thalamus regarding the possibilities of victory, defeat, and boredom. Those data go back through the same feedback loop for processing by your puppy's amygdala, which generates bodily responses to the potential glory of victory, agony of defeat, and tedium of boredom. These predictions weighted by your judgment of their probability generate an emotional response that affects your heart rate. Maybe you start chewing a fingernail, maybe you take a seat and move pawn to king-four, or maybe you check your watch and indicate that you need to be somewhere else.

In any case, the thought processes that generate your reactions result from a massive feedback/feed-forward system that integrates your environment, your body, and your brain. No decision is made without both emotional and physical responses and only those decisions that afford timescales of at least a few seconds include intellectual deliberation.

2.4.1 Reaction timescales

Reaction times are limited by the speed that signals propagate from neuron to neuron, sense to brain, frog to puppy to Feynman. Since the speed of a signal propagating along an axon is roughly 100 feet per second (70 mph or 110 km per hour, about a tenth of the speed of sound), decisions made by processors in close proximity occur faster than those requiring coordination of distant processors.

Action Potential	0.001 seconds
Reset synapse	0.005 seconds
Facial response	0.03 seconds
Perceive emotions	0.1 seconds
Inter-hemisphere signaling	0.18 seconds
Hit the brakes!	0.2 seconds
Awareness of an image	0.3 seconds
Conscious thought	0.5 seconds
Grow a synapse	20 minutes
Walk	13 months
Talk	18 months
Reproduce	14 years
Drive	16 years
Drink	21 years
Die	73 years

Figure 6: Timescales for different types of reactions.

Your inner frog operates in a few hundredths of a second, your puppy in less than a quarter of a second, and your Feynman in no less than half a second. But your Feynman trains your puppy and frog. For instance, when you make a silly mistake—type the wrong key, hit the clutch instead of the brake, or order a Coors Light instead of a beer—your anterior cingulate cortex raises its error flag in less than 0.07 seconds, which is frog speed. Your inner frog knows nothing about keyboards or cars, though even a frog can identify beer.

The timescale of conscious and unconscious processes shows that many of our decisions are made before we've had time to think about them.

2.4.2 Positive and negative feedback

Feedback turns out to be kind of a major theme in studying how the brain works, so we should probably give it a little time in the spotlight.

Think of feedback as feeding previously processed data back into the input of the processor. Your eyes collect a vision and your nose a scent, yielding a processed image of a cold, frothy beer. You respond with a watering mouth that reinforces the frothy image and you ponder the malt-hop balance. Because of the time scale, your frog spins through about fifteen reactions for every three from your puppy and one from your Feynman.

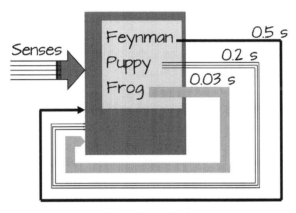

Figure 7: Feedback.

Feedback comes in two categories: positive and negative. Positive feedback reinforces and compounds its input and, left unchecked, leads to extreme behavior. Negative feedback suppresses extreme behavior. Positive feedback amplifies and negative feedback balances or stabilizes.

That loud, high-pitched, and annoying sound you hear when someone speaks into a poorly placed microphone is positive feedback. The speaker talks into the microphone. Her amplified voice comes out of the speakers behind her. The sound from the speakers hits the microphone and is amplified again, this secondary sound hits the microphone, is amplified and transmitted into a third version that hits the microphone, is amplified and transmitted, and so on; this happens over and over, getting louder and louder even after the person stops talking.

The easiest fix to audio feedback is to point the speakers away from the microphone.

As a snowball rolls down a mountain, more snow sticks to it, making it larger and larger until the snowball effect culminates in an avalanche. Positive feedback loops reinforce themselves and go ape when left unchecked.

On the flip side, negative feedback prevents systems from going crazy. Negative feedback is a balancing, rather than amplifying, impetus. Hot summer days are caused by bright sunshine. The longer the day, the hotter it gets. But then the sun sets and things cool off. The negative feedback of darkness pushes the temperature to a stable point between hot and cold extremes.

Hunger is negative feedback: You get hungry, you eat, you get less hungry, you stop eating. Beer is positive feedback up to a point. You drink, you feel better, you drink more, you feel still better, you drink still more, and you hurl. Then the next morning you feel sick. Addictions, including addictions to food and alcohol, occur when negative feedback breaks down; this allows the positive feedback of satiation and/or buzz to overwhelm the balance.

Our all-new oversimplification of a deludable left brain and a watchdog right brain gives us a window onto the delicate balance we need to get through life. Frank Ransom told me that he lived the happiest life ever lived, but he didn't say it was the easiest. He brushed off those kinds of questions. Maybe his delusions of happiness got him through the manure.

That critical balance teeters now and then for all of us. Addictions occur when, for many reasons, the right brain watchdog lets its guard down. People with addictive personalities frequently, though not universally, have reduced capacity in the right sides of their frontal lobes that reduces the negative feedback of destructive behavior.

2.5 THE REALITY INTERFACE

The funny thing about reality is that you can only get so close to it. Our senses compose an interface between our brains and the universe, a reality interface.

The axon cables that run from your nose to the center of your brain, from your eyes to the back of your brain, from your tongue to the center, and from your ears to your cochlea, right there already in your brain, and from that spiny, bendable, bone-wrapped cable that runs from your ass bone to your head bone and into your brain provide everything you get in here from out there. The in-here/out-there model sort of resembles Descartes's dualism but without requiring a metaphysical component.

Everything we experience and everything we are and ever will be are ultimately derived from sensory input. The genetic code that formed when your father's sperm penetrated your mother's egg started its random walk through naturally selected mutations a couple of billion years ago. The recipe that made you resulted from the responses of and decisions made by your ancestors—every one of them, from algae to ape—based on their sensory inputs. And now you create everything—the scent of an orchid, the touch of a lover, the sound of music, and the view of the stars—from electrical signals generated by your own sensory acquisition equipment.

I find it strange that there are no nerves in our brains. The thing is packed with neurons, axons, dendrites, myelin—all that stuff that nerves are made of—but we can't feel anything inside our brains. A surgeon can go in and poke around while you're wide awake, and you won't feel a thing. How weird would it be if we could feel our own thoughts? Contemplating your goal to become a guitar legend would tickle the space just behind your forehead; envisioning a bird in flight, soaring on thermal breezes above the sea, would make your occipital lobe itch. The medical industry could save a fortune in imaging devices.

"Well doc, it hurts when I picture her with that guy."

"Heartbreak is tough, son."

"Seriously, right here in the back of my head, a rip-roaring pain."

"Oh. Take an aspirin and write a poem."

2.5.1 The inescapably subjective nature of our realities

Here's a simple definition of reality: stuff interacting in space. That pretty much covers everything that happens, right? Even daydreaming is stuff, since it's made of neurons exchanging electrical energy stored in sodium, calcium, and potassium ions that move around in your head.

Objective reality would account for everything everywhere, but we don't have access to that. Even with equipment, we're not even close.

You only see three colors, two or even one if you're colorblind, a tiny fraction of the colors that stars radiate. So we build equipment to see light beyond the rainbow's spectrum, supervisual light like x-rays, and sub-visual light like radio waves. It's the same deal with sound: You can hear as low as 20 Hertz (Hz) and feel lower frequencies if they're loud enough—the steady beating of bass lines blasted from tricked-out cars—and maybe as high as 20,000 Hz, far from what dolphins and bats hear, 150,000 and 200,000 Hz respectively. One Hz is a cycle per second, about the rate of your heartbeat. Envision how a strummed guitar string oscillates back and forth. The number of oscillations per second is the frequency in Hz.

Since the universe doesn't *really* exist the way you experience it, there's a huge gap between absolute reality and your perceived, subjective reality.

What's more, since our senses are not identical, the raw data we each use to create our realities differ, and we each create different realities. Maybe I've been to louder concerts and lost a bit of hearing; perhaps your sense of smell wasn't trashed by smoking various substances in your well-spent youth; maybe you didn't suffer from migraine headaches that trained you to avert your eyes from bright lights.

The contexts of our perceived realities also differ because our experiences differ. Where you might hear pleasant, creative music,

I might wonder why someone would blow a horn when she could thrash a Stratocaster?

Our realities are continuous chains of perceptions. By perception, I mean the association of stimulus and thought. For reality to make sense, we need context. To create context, we associate our current perceptions with what we've experienced in the past and our expectations for the immediate future, and then we squeeze the present right into the gap in a way that makes sense. Since we have different experiences and expectations, what makes sense to you isn't likely to make sense to me. Listen carefully the next time you talk to someone. The two of you will talk about the same subjects, but if you listen closely, I bet you'll notice that you're not having exactly the same conversation, not quite talking about identical ideas and phenomena.

If you were plopped into whatever situation you now find yourself—at the same age and with the same physical body and brain but with no experience, no previous thoughts whatsoever, no language skills, no learned abilities—nothing would make sense. You'd be worse than lost; you couldn't even claim to exist! You couldn't claim anything.

Since our perceived realities are derived from thoroughly processed sensory input, all reality is virtual. Einstein nailed it when he said, "Reality is merely an illusion, albeit a very persistent one."

2.5.2 The realities of whales, dogs, and trees (and naked people)

To get an idea of how our differences affect our perceptions of reality, let's take a look at the perceived reality of an animal whose senses are tuned for a completely different environment.

Sperm whales are the largest predators on earth and have the largest brains of any animal, about six times the size of a human's. We share the same five senses but use them in different ways.

Whales have huge eyes but don't use them for the bulk of their visualizing. It's murky underwater. At the depths where sperm whales like to hunt, almost two miles deep, a mammalian eye isn't of much use. To see, whales, dolphins, and porpoises emit tightly directed sounds. When these sounds hit something, they echo back. From the timing of all the echoes, whales construct three-dimensional images including shape and location.

We see by looking around and gathering the ambient light reflected from things, but when a whale looks at something, it projects bursts of sound in specific, considered directions and then assembles images from the reflections.

The differences in visualization techniques result in big changes in perception. First, the length of time it takes from the emission of the sound to detection of the echo indicates the distance between a whale and an object. From less than about 15 feet (5 m), people use parallax—the variation between what they see in their left and right eyes—to gauge distance. At larger separations, we use scale combined with experience. If someone looks really small, you figure that they are proportionally farther away. Whales determine distance by the time interval between when they transmit their sonar sounds and when they hear the echoes; the farther away, the more accurate their measurements, the opposite of humans.

Whales "see" how fast something moves and whether it's coming toward or going away from them because the sound frequency shifts. If a fish swims toward a whale, then the reflected sound has a slightly higher pitch, just as the sound of a car approaching has a higher pitch than when it's departing—the Doppler effect. Since specific pigments don't alter the way that sound reflects from an object, whales don't see colors. Instead, they "see" how rigid something is. Since steel reflects sound with a sharp, high-frequency response and mud and kelp are more absorptive, whales "see" hardness, fragility, and malleability. They would never believe a big boulder-shaped piece of Styrofoam was actually granite.

Seeing by directing sound at things is like using a flashlight in the dark. In a well-lit room, you can look at me and I won't know you're looking unless I catch you. In a dark room, if you flash a light at me, I know you're looking. In whale society, everyone knows where everyone is looking all the time. Just as we can recognize each other's voices in a crowd, whales recognize each other's gaze. No peeking allowed! Plus, sonar can penetrate skin. If a female whale is pregnant, everyone knows. If someone has a tumor, it's the talk of the pod.

Adding perception of an object's distance of separation, speed, resilience, and a bit of ultrasound to the overall "vision" equation, and removing color, alters reality in far-reaching ways.

Black's Beach is the closest beach to the University of California, San Diego, where I went to college. North of the point, Black's unofficially welcomes naked people. South of the point, few people expose their undercarriages or mammary glands to sunlight and the view of others.

One sunny spring day during my sophomore year, I was reposed south of the point in baggy shorts while reading Heidegger's *Being and Time* when a particularly attractive naked woman and two similarly attractive naked men frolicked past. The woman pranced into the surf and grabbed a long seaweed vine. She spun it above her head and threw it in the manner of a lasso at one of the men. The other man took a piece of seaweed from the beach and threw it at the woman. The three of them continued this dance for several minutes, cavorting in and out of the ocean, wrapping themselves and each other in seaweed, running to and fro—all while the two men were clearly competing for the attention of the woman.

In the course of their cavorting, one of the men produced an erection and the other did not. My first thought was that the man jumping around the beach with a hard-on must be embarrassed—after all, the woman reacted by staring at his penis and laughing with both hands over her mouth. I turned back to my book, but then it occurred to me that, no, perhaps the man without the woody was more embarrassed.

Can you imagine walking into a bar where the patrons are acutely aware when your gaze sweeps past them? Where everyone can see through clothes and skin? Culture would be drastically altered.

If we had a bit of outer puppy just as we have plenty of inner puppy, that is, if we had tails, society would be quite different. Flirting would take a totally different turn. As it is, if the target of your flirtations has refined social skills, there's no way to know how receptive they are to your advance until you become increasingly obvious. But what if you could see their tail wag?

People key on vision; dogs key on scent. When someone leaves the room, their image goes with them, but their scent lingers. Imagine how fashion would change if, upon leaving a room, we left our shadow behind for a few minutes.

At another extreme, consider the reality of General Sherman, a 275-foot-tall (84 meters), 2,500-year-old giant sequoia in Sequoia National Park, California. If you look at the tree every day, you don't see much change. If you look at it a few times every year, you see it go through the cycle of winter, spring, summer, and autumn. A year to a tree is sort of like a day to a person. Spring is morning, summer day, autumn evening, and winter night. Trees don't have neurons, axons, dendrites, or any obvious processors that we can identify as brain-like, but they do have sensory detectors; they respond to sunlight, wind, and rain. They inhale carbon dioxide and exhale oxygen at a rate so slow that it's hard for a mammal to think of them as breathing. They reach out for nutrients and then wick them from the ground up to their canopies. They distribute water from the soil and leaves through artery-like channels in both trunk and twig.

A tree experiences a reality that differs from ours in almost every way. To say that a tree *experiences* anything might seem silly. You and I have very similar senses. Our perceived realities have much in common, but we differ around the edges and don't agree on everything. The reality of a tree, though, is as far beyond our grasp as absolute reality itself.

While I risk sounding unscientific, I'm unwilling to condemn a tree to an experience-free existence, at least until my own experience has transcended the pure subjectivity of my perceptions. As scientists, our greatest tool is knowing the limits of our understanding, both as fuel for curiosity and, as we'll see in certain terms by the time we get to chapter 9, as a way to dispel prejudice and open our minds to avenues of new research.

Here's an overused philosophical question: Is the red that you perceive the same as the red that I perceive? I suspect that our reds are nearly identical because the color detectors in our eyes are quite similar, and we process that information in very nearly identical regions of our brains.

I will never know if your red is the same as mine, but I do know that blue is a superior color.

2.6 THE POWER OF PERSPECTIVE

The realization that we have pretty much the same emotional processing equipment as animals contradicts assumptions people have made for thousands of years. We're driven by emotions like other animals—not just other primates, but dogs, cats, rats, whales, and birds too. Unlike most of the other animals, and maybe all of them, we have the ability to realize that sometimes our emotions might not be our best guides. Perhaps we could even measure our own enlightenment by how often we practice this ability.

A particularly amusing result of being animals capable of understanding that we're animals is that we also have the capability of denying that we're animals. We're about evenly split on the issue. Now, for me, if something eats like an animal, excretes like an animal, has sex like an animal, suckles from its mother, experiences fear, anger, affection, love, and hate like an animal, well, it just might be an animal.

Every step we take in expanding our worlds is born of simple electrical excitations, networks that reach across the 3-pound (1.5 kg) organs in our heads. The more associations we make, the further our minds can reach. One feedback loop germinates another and another, and so on, a feedback loop of feedback loops, expanding our realities with each increment until we're wide awake with consciousness.

We create our own realities from the simplest sensory input all the way to the most abstract constructs. From light and dark to danger and security to choosing what color earbuds to get for our smartphones, we create everything, and a big slice of our reality pie is baked so fast that we end up with just a sliver. Animals create their realities too, but people do it to a crazy extreme.

Combining the rational brilliance of our inner Feynmans with the irrational passion of our inner puppies has allowed us to set goals, to plan, to worry, and to evaluate. Our ability to associate ever higher levels of thought, from instinctual comprehension of fanged threats to concepts of the fundamental rules of how stars and atoms form, has led to our greatest achievements in art and science and everything in between.

We have been unleashed by our tacit understanding of our own limitations. Can't see through someone's skin to check a broken bone? Use x-rays. Want to transmute lead into gold? Learn chemistry and see why you can't.

We can use tools to get different perspectives, but the most powerful tool is our brains. Wondering about the ways of things? Tools from poetry to mathematics bring us closer to the answers. Our ever-widening creation of reality, spurred on by tools made of silicon, of horsehair, or by the Fender Corporation, along with tools built from thoughts written on scratch paper, spreads our lives across longer timescales and larger spaces.

The challenges we face demand new perspectives. If we could solve our problems with the same old perspectives, they wouldn't be challenges. By thinking about how other people, other animals, and other life-forms perceive a challenge, we can see it in a new light. Innovations emerge from new perspectives.

To get the perspective we need in order to ponder consciousness—how it comes about, what its limits are, and why it hurts so much when someone we love loses theirs—it's best to think like an alien.

3

LIFE & DEATH

PRETEND YOU ARE A SILICON-BASED LIFE-FORM from Andromeda, the galaxy that's a mere two-and-a-half-million light years from here. Life on your planet evolves in a completely different way than it does here. Earth's carbon-based life is just as foreign to you as your silicon-based life is to SETI, the Search for Extraterrestrial Intelligence over here on Earth.

One day, while you're lounging around eating rocks and drinking a frothy sand cocktail, you get a message from SEAL, the Search for Extra-Andromedan Life. The message says that intelligent life could form on the third planet from a modest star in the Milky Way. SEAL provides you with an in-depth analysis of Earth's chemical makeup and geology. Your job is to predict the forms of life that have evolved on Earth. Fortunately, you have a complete grasp of physics and chemistry.

"It's an impossible task," you tell the supreme commander.

The supreme commander, who isn't paying particular attention to you, says, "All righty then," and walks away.

You sigh and stare at your workstation, dust off your monitor, and realize that it's not an *impossible* task; it's an *improbable* task. So improbable that it might as well be impossible, but if I were intimidated by "might as well be," I wouldn't be talking to a made-up life-form in Andromeda.

The reason people search for carbon-based life in outer space isn't because they reject different forms of life; it's because we are a living proof-of-principle that carbon-based life exists. It's all we've got. You, on the other hand, in your ultra-advanced stone glory, aren't so prejudiced. You realize that your understanding of stone-ology (it would be biology, except for, you know, the silicon-ness of it all) might be completely useless in this search.

To accomplish the improbable task, you assemble a computer program that includes all of the atoms on Earth according to the geology and geography that SEAL recorded. Then you flip the switch and simulate the interactions of those atoms.

Since computers have been around, simulations have become the most effective way to understand complicated systems. Rather than trying to figure the whole thing out in a nice, tidy way, you assign every atom on the planet a position, direction, and speed. Then you advance time by a tiny fraction of a second, moving each atom according to the laws of physics. At the end of that time interval, you alter the directions, positions, and speeds of each atom according to what they encountered during that time. With the new positions, directions, and speeds, you advance time again, and so on. If (if!) your physics theories are close enough to the truth, the smaller the time interval, the more accurately your simulation reproduces reality, which is, after all, just stuff moving in space. The big advantage of simulating systems is that we can let the computer do all the work while we hang around in bars.

Since every measurement has uncertainty, including your geology and geography measurements, there are an infinite number of possible initial starting points. To account for the possible courses of evolution, you'll need to run about a gazillion separate simulations, but that's okay because you Flintstones in Andromeda have more computing power than you know what to do with.

After each of your gazillion simulations have worked through about four billion years, you check the results. Life never formed in some of the simulations, but it did in most. If you've ever lived in the tropics, you probably have a feel for how well suited this planet is for supporting life. A few of the simulations produced silicon-based life similar to what's in Andromeda, but most life came out quite differently. Because of Earth's composition, you got many different carbon-based, water-dependent biological life-forms.

When your supreme commander comes back the next day and asks for your predictions, you provide a list of 392,035,816,185 different possible types of life. Included in that list are seventy-eight versions that are similar to what really exists here on Earth, though none of the simulations reproduces exactly what we have here.

The supreme commander says, "Which one is it?"

And you provide a list of probabilities. Well down on that list is the 0.00000002 percent probability of human beings with trees, dogs, frogs, and birds. Even if it is the highest probability result on the list, it's not a very useful prediction.

Your boss is pissed off.

3.1 EMERGENCE

Emergent phenomena are those that seem to defy prediction. Starting with the chemical makeup of Earth four billion years ago, your existence could not be predicted, much less that you're sitting where you are reading this book. But here you are!

That *something* would emerge is certain. What that something might turn out to be is uncertain. No matter how endless the possibilities, the sum of all the probabilities has to be one (100 percent). You might say that the possibilities are infinite, but the probabilities are finite.

People can get as wound up about the meaning of emergence as they do about religion. Pick any old random emergent system, like consciousness. Can it be reduced to its constituent parts? Can you imagine one hundred billion inanimate objects with one thousand trillion interconnections collectively fussing over what to wear to the prom? It's especially hard to imagine when you're using one hundred billion neurons with one thousand trillion connections to do the imagining. But no matter how low the probability is of that phenomenon emerging, if it's possible and you've got the physics right, then when you simulate enough configurations of those constituents, eventually you will see that phenomenon emerge in your simulation.

But what if it is magic? Maybe some systems simply cannot be understood in terms of their constituents, cannot be understood *in principle*. I don't know about you stoners in Andromeda, but over here in the solar system, we are a long, long way from having a clue of what we can understand, much less what we can't. Until then, if you say that something like consciousness results from magic, I can always say, "When you have a better understanding of the system, you'll realize that it's just an emergent phenomenon that would arise in a sufficiently accurate simulation." This confirms Miles Dylan's belief that "all discussions of the supernatural eventually lead to either blind faith or smugness."

Stepping away from my smugness, which, after all, is just prejudice with an arrogant veneer, I find it difficult to deny that the emergence of life and awareness, love and humor, hives and families is anything short of a miracle. If a miracle can be understood, is it any less miraculous?

Thinking itself is just such a miracle. Neuroscience has some clues about how we think. The tool within our craniums does a lot of pattern-recognition, model-building, and predicting. Understanding as much as we can about how our thought tool works can help us think more effectively. The flip side is that when you understand a little about thought itself, you have to face what it means to no longer think.

The theme of feedback and feed-forward loops—the ability to process a continuing onslaught of incoming and already processed information—applies to how things live and die on Earth.

Life is built on death. We have to eat other organisms to survive. More than that, though, the components of life require vast amounts of dead organic material.

Life is inseparable from death, but that doesn't make dealing with it any easier.

3.2 BEING ALIVE AND AWAKE

Neuroscientists and cognitive psychologists like to separate thoughts into bottom-up and top-down processes. Bottom-up thoughts include the myriad unconscious processes involved in processing the continued onslaught of sensory data, including internal bodily data like aches and pains. At every instant, a huge number of bottom-up networks activate across your brain. Even when you're kicked back, not paying attention to anything, your default network lights up your brain with more activity than when you concentrate.

For the most part, we're aware of top-down processes and unaware of bottom-up processes.

Bottom-up processes reach across our brains and associate perceptions with experiences that have been stashed in memory. This association provides the background context that we need to assemble the ongoing stream of sensory information into predictions and expectations. Those predictions propel our most recent experiences into the future.

Top-down processes feel like a single thing, one consciousness, though everyone who talks to themselves knows that their self has more than one voice.

Rather than getting tangled up in the loaded term "subconscious," we will use the word "unconscious" for all processes that happen in our brains without us noticing; that is, we are aware of conscious thoughts and unaware of unconscious thoughts. But we have to be careful because the line between the conscious and the unconscious can change; you can lift otherwise unconscious thoughts into consciousness by thinking about them. Try it: you're looking at ink on a page (or lit pixels on a screen), right?

We have no working definition for the words consciousness or thought, yet we forge ahead, appropriately into a bar.

3.2.1 Your stupid, bottom-up, parallel, unconscious processors

You walk in and scan the beer taps. You want something hoppy but you also want something new. You zero in on a tap labeled IPA.

Let's stop here and take a look at what's going on.

Figure 8: A bar

The bar is packed with people including those on barstools sitting between you and the beer taps. You're aware of them but not paying attention. Still, if your mother is on one of those barstools, you'd recognize her. You might even be surprised to see her in a bar (not me, though, my mom likes bars).

Sensory data pour in from every direction: People talk and move around; TV monitors show three different baseball games, a soccer match from Brazil, and a cooking show. But as you zero in on that IPA tap, you're not paying attention to any of that.

Then someone says your name.

Even with all that ruckus, if someone says your name, you'll hear it. Your name has at most a few syllables, but even with a dozen people nattering away within ten stools of where you stand and with no conscious direction, you will dig that miniscule signal out of the noise. It's no trivial process, though it feels like one: Receive the sound, process it into a pattern, associate that pattern with a word, the word with your name and identity, associate that sound with a location, instruct your eyes to zero in on that location, process the several human faces into patterns, try to associate those faces and the timbre of that voice with memories, and bingo, you realize that it's the guy who lived upstairs from you five years ago. All that work occurs in an instant, unbidden, yet you still can't remember the guy's name. You wave and ponder the notion of going over and hanging out with him.

Farther down the bar, your mom will also pick your name out of the noise, even though she's nursing a scotch and soda and talking politics to the bartender who is praying that you'll order so she can ignore this crazy woman.

Have you eaten lately? Because a waiter carrying a steaming plate of chicken fajitas just passed behind you. You're not paying attention though, right? Well, if you're hungry, your inner puppy just barked and is about ready to dance for your supper. How did you dig the smell of fajitas out of the smells of generations of spilled beer, the tequila the guy to your left is about to knock back, and your own sweaty shirt?

In all that sensory noise, how can you hear your name and lust for those fajitas when your intent is to catch the bartender's attention and ask for a nice, hoppy ale?

The vast majority of our thoughts are unconscious ones.

Are you really only paying attention to the beer taps? Of course not. Your senses are firing up networks all over the place and trying to associate every input with every other input, as well as every memory you've ever recorded. Your head is a busy place.

A picture emerges of separate parts of your brain going about their business. At the lowest level, each sense has dedicated processors that reconstruct their own inputs. At each stage of reconstruction, the networks of neurons that perform the low-level reconstruction forward their results to the layers above. Since these low-level, bottom-up processors perform isolated rote tasks without a whole lot of attention to or from other processes, and since there are lots of them, I call them dumb parallel processors: parallel because they work alongside, but pretty much independent of, each other, and dumb because I don't respect them as much as I should.

Consider your mother. Your eyes catch light and transmit raw data along the million axons of your optic nerve. Since they're carrying electrical signals, thinking of them as wires isn't too far off the mark. One leg of information goes to your thalamus, part of your inner puppy; the rest goes to your primary visual cortex.

The first processing network discerns contrasts and boundaries and produces crude, cartoonish images from the huge set of light-dark intensity and colors transmitted from your retinas. Those crude images are fed to the next layer, as well as the layer above that (let's call them V2 and V3), and all the way up the visual-processing food chain. As V2 sets about filling in the details of the cartoonish image, V3 compares that crude V1 image to the vast store of images stashed away in your cranium.

Since you're looking at the beer taps, the only light your eyes are receiving from this woman is from the periphery. That light comes from saccades, the constant flitting about of your eyeballs. The illusion that you see an entire scene when you really only look at details one at a time serves as an outstanding example of the amount of processing between your experience and reality itself. You're not even looking in your mother's direction—at least not yet.

V3 provides whatever similar images it finds in your memory to V2. V2 uses your experience hanging around in bars to identify both what you're looking at and everything in your field of view that you're not paying attention to. Included in that morass of images is a female human. Meanwhile, higher up the food chain, processors offer the crude images from lower processors far and wide for association with other senses and memories of similar experiences.

At the same time that V1, the lowest processor on the totem pole, passes the crude images up the hierarchy, your audio processors perform a cursory analysis to distinguish sounds from the TVs, glasses clinking together, pointless chatter, rhetorical questions, laughter, sighs, and belches. An important detail to keep in mind is that you know you're in a bar. Stuff that you expect to see in a bar is likely to be ignored unless, as with the fajitas, your processors are on alert to elevate them for wider association.

When V2 finishes tidying up the image, it sends its results back down to V1, as well as farther up. Back at V1, the tidier image is used to more accurately and quickly process the still-incoming visual data. Your brain takes shortcuts at every opportunity, which is usually okay, because it also double-checks everything for consistency and context.

V3 combs through the results from V1 and V2 to identify the people around you to the extent that it can. If you're attracted to women and feeling a bit lusty, your higher-level visual processor will stash images and locations of women for further consideration—one of which will generate all-too-conscious embarrassment as soon as all the results arrive, in about another half second.

The processing performed in the visual cortices of your right and left brains differs, though there is redundancy. For the most part, your left brain focuses on your hunt for the ideal beer, and your right brain keeps a lookout for trouble, but they talk to each other. Your right brain wants to elevate some of the faces to threat level, and your left brain inhibits those efforts. Your left brain wants all resources tuned into that one tap, but the right brain overrides it when it sees another set of taps at the other end of the bar, one of which has both the letters "IPA" and the image of a floppy-eared dog.

But then, holy shit! Your bottom-up processors raise a flag that your top-down processors can't ignore. There's a woman to your right wearing your mother's perfume.

3.2.2 Your brilliant, top-down, serial, conscious thinkers

At the holy-shit instant, this huge network of unconscious thoughts boils this one association up to your forebrain, insula, and medial prefrontal cortex where it becomes a conscious thought, an experience.

Let's stop here for a second. I said that the unconscious thought boils up to consciousness. The boiling metaphor is so accurate that I'm tempted to say something stupid like "it literally boils up." This temptation comes from my suspicion that the transformation from unconscious to conscious follows the physics of percolation—one of the amazing things about physics is how often the mathematical description for one process can be leveraged to explain something that seems completely different.

Old coffeemakers used percolation to brew coffee. A tall pot filled about halfway with water sits over a flame. The flame heats the water to boiling and the boiling action pushes water up a tube. At the top of the tube, the water is deflected by the lid of the pot into a little basket holding coffee grinds. The hot water filters through the grinds, drips back into the pot, rejoins the rest of the water, boils back up, and so on, producing a rather thick, bitter pot of coffee. The lid of coffee percolators includes a clear glass tip so you can see the color of the brew as it percolates.

Here's the metaphor. Each drop of water in the pot is a thought. At any instant, the whole pot can be boiling, but only one drop of water at a time percolates up to the top and drips down through consciousness. Some of those drops stay in the basket of consciousness grinds, but most of them filter their way through and drip back down to the unconscious parallel processors.

The emergence of a thought into the consciousness grinds creates consciousness itself. We'll fill out this idea later, but first, you need to dump the half-processed image of your mother from your list of

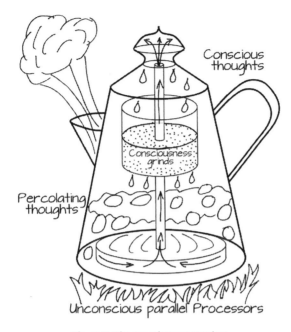

Figure 9: The percolator metaphor.

attractive women and curse your inner Freud. Then, if you're a good son or daughter, call the bartender over and buy your dear mother a drink. And, as long as you have the bartender's attention, get yourself a beer. You'll need it to wash down your Oedipus complex.

In this horrifying example, notice the trajectory of your conscious thoughts. You go into a bar, you ponder the perfect beer, you're surprised to see your mother, and you buy her a drink, surprising her just as much as she surprised you. Of all the processing in your brain, you were conscious of just a tiny fraction.

You were certainly aware that you bought your mom a drink. That was a top-down process; you directed it by choice. Whether or not that choice resulted from free will is a dicey question that we'll deflect until later.

Other than the obvious fact that you're not conscious of them, how do we know that our brains have processing centers that aren't part of our wide-awake existence? Scads of data back up the idea. Here are two examples: Blind sight is caused by injuries to V1, the bottom-level image processor. People with blind sight are not conscious of vision. You might think that they can't see, right? They claim to be blind, after all. But if you hold up an apple and ask them what it is and where it is, their inner puppies manage to convey the what and where. They can't see it, but they know where and what it is.

Here's another example: People who have brain injuries in the region where the inner Feynman processes sound into melodies, an ailment called agnosia, are incapable of detecting the melody itself, but they know, by virtue of their inner puppies, whether those melodies sound happy or sad.

The only way we can manage all the data that's constantly clobbering our senses is to have lots of processors going about their business without conscious attention.

3.3 WE ARE PATTERN-RECOGNIZERS AND MODEL-BUILDERS

As we go about our lives, our bottom-up parallel processors constantly look for patterns by comparing our current situation with previous experiences. Images are associated with memories of other images, as well as the constant incoming stream of sounds, scents, and so on. When a pattern is recognized, the situation is consistent with an expectation, such as "here I am in a bar," and a low-key sense of certainty is generated and fed forward.

Consistency with the incoming data is sufficient for recognition: consistency, not confirmation. Confirmation requires point-by-point comparison of the incoming data with the expectation; consistency is a much looser criterion. Consistency gives fast approximation; confirmation gives slow precision. If the consistent pattern turns out to be wrong, it can always be corrected, but if we took the laborious route to precise confirmation, we'd still be unclear on whether it was a kind little kitty or a saber-toothed tiger as the feline throat belched our final essence.

The process of pattern-recognition permeates the entire thought process. Our brains have evolved to optimize our ability to decipher patterns even when they are buried in noise.

Let's go back to the bar.

You're scoping out the taps. A dozen people are talking within a few meters of you, plus the sound from the TVs, and in that cacophony of noises, you pick out the sound of your former neighbor's voice saying your name. When the bartender turns to you and you ask for the IPA, she nods and pours.

Consider all those voices. Within our socially tuned brains, various voices sound quite different. But in objective reality, human voices are limited by the length and tension of vocal cords, just like the sounds of a guitar are limited by string thickness and tension from the tuning knobs. Since people follow the same essential blueprint, the size and tension of our vocal cords don't vary much. We can decipher two human voices even when we've never met the people—nothing to it—but to a rhinoceros, we all sound the same.

Bars are packed with scents too. While a dog could decipher the smell of week-old vomit, bleach, ancient cigarette smoke, the scents of each person, each drink, and every food on the menu, we can't even distinguish a fresh fart from well brandy. But the scent of your mother's perfume fits a well-established pattern in your brain, not just because you've smelled it all your life, but because you associate it with a host of feelings.

The cost of being highly tuned pattern-recognizers is that we're not always right, and sometimes we see patterns that aren't even there.

If you happen to be dancing and it starts to rain, then someday during a drought you dance again and it rains a second time, well, you might as well buy a lottery ticket.

Superstition is built on our ability to recognize patterns.

Composing a complex whole from a limited set of possible components is more efficient than composing it from a continuum of possible elements. We build colors from the three primitives that the cones in our eyes distinguish: blue, green, and red.

Just as Starla built an ever-more sophisticated experience of a rainbow from light/dark, then color, and so on, we build our catalog of experiences and memories by assembling combinations of perceptions, ideas, and memories from patterns that we already have stashed away.

3.3.1 First impressions

The first time you see something, your left prefrontal cortex reacts in less than 0.13 seconds. The next time you see it, provided that it's not threatening, you react in 0.4 to 1.0 seconds. In other words, your first impression demands your attention faster than you can hit the brakes. The second time you encounter it, it takes you from three to eight times longer to respond, if you even bother to notice it.

Consider your first love. As you picture that person, that defining moment of your sexuality, you unfold an archetype against which, like it or not, you measure every other attraction. Odds are that person has come to define your "type"—her flowing brown hair, wide forehead, gently curving jaw, delicious blue eyes, delicate lips, and tender smile, if only she would have danced with me when I asked. Ahem. It's just as well that those first experiences are fraught with imperfection; otherwise, how could anyone else measure up?

The same goes for your first hate, the bully in second grade who brought attention to your giant forehead, tiny body, and overall cartoon-character appearance. That bastard, with his black hair, pasty skin, constantly running nose, and snorting laughter left an impression, didn't he? The very thought of him still inspires the desire to strike back. You nearly want to search for him on a social network just so you can dress him down now that you're—whoa. Sorry about that.

Just as we build every color from combinations of the three primitives, when you first meet someone, you build models of them from your archetypes. By combining pieces of archetypes into a model for the new person, we provide a way to immediately judge them as friend or foe, fun or boring, smart or dumb, liberal or conservative, long before we have interacted with them at all.

If nature rewarded justice rather than reproductive proliferation, then maybe we'd weight impressions according to their frequency of occurrence in different situations, their density rather than their intensity. Instead, to survive the second impression, we overweight the first impression. Having survived two, that archetype/pattern becomes ingrained, though, to be sure, first impressions can be replaced by particularly intense later impressions.

3.3.2 Prejudice

We categorize patterns. Rather than store every variation of a circle, we know the pattern: For it is round. The rainbow of light our eyes can detect spans wavelengths from roughly 350 to 750 nanometers; one nanometer is a millionth of a millimeter. Rather than distinguish every wavelength of light from 620 to 660 nanometers, we put them in the same category and call it red. Until a specific need arises to distinguish between two shapes or shades, it is okay to let circles be round and red be red.

The tendency to categorize generates stereotypes. Since we recognize patterns so easily, we get lazy. Sometimes we accept the category, the form, instead of recognizing how things or even people depart from that form. It's easier to file things into existing cabinets than to build new ones, so sometimes we put our carts before our asses and willfully declare that the pattern comes before the distinction.

Stereotypes are examples of categories that turn out to be misleading far more often than they're accurate. Everyone stereotypes other people—but stereotyping is always lazy! The problem is that, at least for cave people, quick and dirty categorization provides a huge advantage in recognizing danger with little survival cost in accuracy. For you and me, trying to have civilization together, stereotypes based on gender, ethnic background, or income bracket put us at a disadvantage far more often than they protect us from danger. In pursuit of efficiency, Mother Nature made it easy for us to be bigots. Apparently she didn't foresee civilization.

3.4 HOW COME NOVELS WORK?

To understand the world and our place in it, such as we do, we combine the patterns we've come to recognize into models. Our mouths don't water at the sight of steak, chocolate, or beer; they water at our predictions based on past experiences. We don't interact with the real external world; we interact with our models of that world.

When you read a novel, you assemble the words on the page into your model of the world. You lie on a beach, open a book, start reading, and soon you're laughing and crying; your heart rate goes up, and you don't want to put the book down any more than you want to leave a party while engaged in conversation with a friend.

Stories excite within us the very circuits through which we interact with the world. Like any other experience, that interaction alters our models and changes our worldview. As you envision a setting, your visual processing centers activate in a way that is strikingly similar to how they would activate if you were actually there. In other words, novels are virtual reality. When a novelist does a good job portraying a character in a rose garden, you catch a hint of the scent; an act of fictitious injustice makes you feel outrage; a good sex scene perks you right up.

What gives? Novels are just ink on paper; how can they do this to us? It's because of resonance.

When you push a kid on a swing, the child goes higher with each push. But you have to push at the right times—at the resonant frequency of the swing—to produce that amplifying effect. Try pushing at random times and the kid will jiggle back and forth and glare at you, maybe start crying, and probably ask for another parent, maybe even be emotionally scarred for life.

We resonate with stories because our neurons mirror the experiences of the characters. Neuroscience has a little pile of evidence for special "mirror neurons" that activate when we watch someone perform an act just as they activate when we ourselves perform that act. The same thing happens with emotions and thoughts. When we see someone else experiencing joy, grief, humor, or even the "aha!"

instant of discovery, some of our joy, grief, and lightbulb neurons fire in response.

While there is evidence that we have special neurons whose specific job is mirroring, that evidence has not reached the preponderance level necessary to claim a discovery—at least to a jaded physicist. For us, within the pages of this book, it doesn't matter whether mirror neurons really exist because whatever we have in our brains is doing plenty of mirroring. The alternative to mirroring is called mentalizing. Mirroring or mentalizing, whichever mechanism turns out to be closer to the truth won't affect our conclusions, so let's just call it mirroring.

One suspects, wink-wink, that mirroring might have something to do with, nudge-nudge, the popularity of pornography. You know, maybe.

3.4.1 Theory of mind

Have you ever wondered if you thought it all up? Could the entire universe be a figment of your imagination? Maybe nothing exists beyond your thoughts. If so, I appreciate you thinking of me.

Solipsism is sort of half true. You exist only in this dream world of my imagination. I hope you don't find this offensive. Or, I should say, I hope my model of you doesn't find this offensive.

In its circularity, solipsism is an airtight, useless philosophy. People who experience solipsism lack many things, including a theory of mind.

Your theory of mind is simply your belief that I have thoughts, that my brain, encapsulated in this bony shell atop my animated corpse, experiences the world more or less the same way that you do. It should really be called your theory of other people's minds. Children develop their theories of mind by age three, about the time they start forming long-term memories; the two phenomena may or may not be related. Some studies indicate that our theories of mind emerge around eighteen months, about when we learn to talk.

Ultimately, having a theory of mind boils down to the legitimacy of a statement that we make all the time: "I know how you feel."

Consider that statement.

Our models of the world have to be similar enough for us to agree on pretty much all factual information. Red is red, after all. Maybe what you and I see differs, but we agree it's red.

But feelings?

It's as if we can read each other's minds. How often do you interrupt someone mid-sentence because you know what they're going to say? I get you; I know where you're going. Sometimes we misunderstand, but more often than not, we experience empathy that is all but indistinguishable from mind reading; mind reading that is the mirroring of emotions.

When we detect each other's perceptions, reactions, biases, and assumptions, as well as emotions—whether through body language, facial expression, or perspiration—we react to it, at least partially, as though we are sharing that experience. We express, we sweat, and we think. And we mimic each other. That reaction is fed back through the thalamus and on through the whole chain.

3.5 SENTIENCE AND CONSCIOUSNESS

Sentience means being aware and capable of acting on sensory input. Consciousness means worrying about being aware.

The continuing interplay of billions of processes feeding patterns up and down, forward and backward is at once the cause and experience of consciousness. Or at least, that's the best explanation that neuroscience has right now. The trick is not to think of all these simultaneous processes, some synchronous and some asynchronous, and how they emerge into something so unlike themselves, but to keep in mind the constant rush of new data that has to be processed even as the slightly earlier data are processed and the still-earlier data are processed. Consciousness does not exist independent of time's passage.

Perhaps the single most acute indication of consciousness is the realization that it is inextricably the experience of time passing, and that someday it will end.

3.5.1 Consciousness threshold

How much bottom-up thinking is required to generate top-down thinking?

When you boil water, you heat it until it reaches a critical temperature, the boiling point, at which time it becomes steam, a transition from one state to another. The universe is packed with phase transitions like water to steam, ice to water, quick to dead—shifts between states that have quite different properties.

Most neuroscientists believe that consciousness emerges when the accumulation of bottom-up processes surpasses a threshold of complexity. The idea is that there is a point where the interactions of bottom-up processes reach a complexity threshold—like a boiling point—and the simple electromechanical processes of interacting neurons make a transition—liquid turns to steam—and consciousness emerges.

Of course, no one knows for sure.

The three different levels of consciousness consist of sentience, primary consciousness, and higher-level consciousness, distinctions that follow the evolution of the brain from your inner frog to your inner puppy to your inner Feynman.

Sentience means being capable of processing and responding to sensory input. Frogs, lobsters, and fish are sentient. Even trees and plants respond to external conditions, albeit on different timescales, so let's put them into the sentient bin too.

Mammals, like dogs, apes, dolphins, deer, mice, and cows, as well as birds, especially the uncannily clever crows, ravens, and parrots, show every sign of having primary consciousness. All these animals create realities for themselves and perform some level of planning on a timescale of at least several seconds. But are they aware that they are aware? Do they have higher-level consciousness? Do they worry?

3.5.2 Consciousness spectrum

Instead of a threshold, maybe consciousness is a continuous property that varies in degree, like the continuous increase in temperature of water from cold (33°F, 1°C) to hot (211°F, 99°C), rather than the transition from liquid (at 212°F, 100°C) to steam (still at 212°F, 100°C).

Instead of big jumps from unconscious rocks to sentient plants to reactionary reptiles to primary conscious mammals to higher-level conscious people, let's entertain the possibility that consciousness ranges from the experience of plants like General Sherman that have no neurons and presumably nothing resembling consciousness, to people, with every creature appearing somewhere along that continuum.

Perhaps this consciousness spectrum is ordered by brain size—after all, complexity increases with the number of processors. More processors mean more neurons, and more neurons mean a bigger brain. Ordering by brain size puts people well to one side of the spectrum but below many animals including elephants, killer whales, and sperm whales, who have the largest brains of all.

The standard approach to gauging the intelligence of a species, going back to Aristotle, is to use the "encephalization quotient"—jargon for the ratio of brain weight to body weight. The idea is that a big animal needs a bigger brain to handle its big body, so the excess size doesn't mean that the big-brained, big-bodied animal would be smarter than a big-brained but smaller-bodied animal. Humans win the brain-weight-to-body-weight ratio competition.

Self-awareness indicates consciousness. If you recognize yourself as yourself, then you're probably aware of your awareness. Put a red mark on the nose of a baby and then put her in front of a mirror. Between six and twelve months old, she'll respond to her reflection as if it were another baby. From twelve to twenty months, she'll find the image a bit confusing and might reach out to touch the mark on the reflection's nose or avoid the reflection altogether. At right around twenty-four months, the baby sees herself, notices the mark, reaches up to her own nose, and wipes it off. Mature elephants, dolphins, orcas, and many birds also pass this so-called rouge test.

Dogs don't usually pass the rouge test. Vision is the primary sense for people, elephants, and birds, but dogs rely more heavily on scent. Of course, dogs recognize their reflections in the smell of their own pee, fur, and bedding. How many times have you seen a dog stop to sniff a fire hydrant? Like checking the sign-in sheet as you walk into a meeting, dogs like to know who has walked through the neighborhood and like to sign in themselves too.

My favorite way to approach the idea of a consciousness spectrum is to use information theory, but then I'm kind of a geek, so it figures that I'd like a mathematical approach. Information theory comes from thermodynamics, the physics of order and entropy. Neuroscientists Gerald Edelman, Giulino Tononi, and Kristof Koch calculate a quantity called integrated information to determine the level of organization of a whole and compare it to the sum of the organization of the parts—a quantitative way of answering whether or not a whole really is greater than the sum of its parts.

The idea of integrated information is that the difference between the organization of your neurons and the organization of what emerges from your neurons is the amount of consciousness you experience. Integrated information leads to a spectrum that allows for any organized group of inanimate objects, like neurons, to experience consciousness. So far, there is no unambiguous way to measure the organization of your brain or your mind, but they're working on it.

More likely than either a threshold effect or a continuous spectrum, consciousness probably emerges in different amounts in multiple steps, rather than either a smooth slope or a single giant leap. This moderate position follows the incremental complexity of brain evolution—brainstem to limbic system to neocortex—without neglecting that the whole system is rewired and re-optimized at each stage of that evolution for every critter.

The question then becomes: What states of awareness lie between sentience and consciousness and what might lie beyond?

I've conveniently overlooked the role of language in our ability to elucidate our thoughts not just to each other but to ourselves. Maybe the ability to formulate thoughts in a structured way gets us over the threshold to high-level consciousness. We'll return to this later.

3.6 FREE WILL

Can you choose what to do with the information that percolates into your consciousness?

Are you free to choose to toss this book aside? Maybe have a nice book burning? Wait! Don't do it! Please come back. Of course you can make that choice.

Or is that choice an illusion?

We saw in chapter 2 that lots of decisions are made by bottom-up processes before we become aware of them. Your inner Feynman had nothing to say about whether or not you ran away from the saber-toothed tiger. Piles of experimental evidence show that trivial decisions occur before you're conscious of them.

Does the evidence that we make decisions from the bottom-up rather than the conscious top-down indicate that our free will is an illusion? Many neuroscientists reject free will in favor of a deterministic view of choice. That is, instead of being free to will a decision, we seem to be driven by bottom-up processors to make decisions without the conscious will to alter them. Perhaps the illusion of choice is a mechanism for making sense of the world, just another association of disparate memories and instincts providing impetus to act.

The whole feed-forward/backward loopiness of emerging consciousness and hanging around in bars with your mom is chaotic. You kick a normal football and it goes through the goalposts. If you kick it a tiny bit differently, it will still go through the uprights. But if you kick a chaotic football just the tiniest, teeniest bit differently, it goes straight up or backward; it's chaotic and that means we can't predict where it will go.

Your brain is chaotic too.

Thirstiness boils up to consciousness, and you decide—whatever that means—to go to a bar, try a new beer, watch some TV, maybe exchange a few wisecracks with other humans. Your bottom-up initial conditions include things like where you place your feet, how you hold your head, and the trillions of your other miniscule attributes as you enter the bar. If your path happens to guide you past someone drinking a piña colada and your head is positioned such that you get a whiff of the coconut, it could change your mind. You're thirsty, after all, and you haven't had a piña colada in a while, so your top-down consciousness starts firing the possibilities down to your processors, including your taste buds, and you start jonesing for a fruity rum concoction. That desire percolates up and a mai tai sounds even better, and the best mai tais are a few blocks down the street at the tiki bar! You turn around, go to the tiki bar, start drinking rum, hit it off with the bartender, whom you eventually marry, and never realize that your mom was sucking down scotch and arguing politics at the bar you left the night of the world-changing mai tai.

We can all point to tiny events, miniscule changes in the conditions of our lives that led to large differences in where we are and how we got there. A while back, we ran into the deeply interconnected circular process of how we create a coherent, single reality from the constant stream of sensory input. The picture-in-a-picture-ness of that process consists of a large number of tiny effects, most of which have a tiny impact, but a few of which, like getting a waft of piña colada, have large consequences. It's called the butterfly effect—the idea that a butterfly flapping its wings in Fontana can cause a tornado in Tulsa.

Assume for the moment that you do not have free will.

The fact that your brain is a chaotic biochemical machine, and the fact that it is fundamentally impossible to measure the complete state of that biomechanical machine with perfect accuracy at any time—after all, nothing can be measured with perfect accuracy—means that it is impossible, not just improbable, but impossible, to predict your behavior.

Adding it all up, there is no way to *determine* whether or not you have free will; therefore, you are an indeterminate animal who either has free will or the precise equivalent.

And so is your dog.

3.7 THE ESSENTIAL WEIRDNESS OF DEATH

We've all lost friends and family to the inevitable end of their consciousnesses.

No matter how short or long the process, whether dead from some immediate cause that gave no warning or dead after a drawn-out struggle, the weirdest thing about death is the sheer on/off of it. How can someone switch from being a thinking thing to being a non-thinking thing?

The insanity that a thinking being could exist one minute and be meat the next, the essential weirdness of death, comes from the way we build our realities.

The person you knew was a model of the actual person you had in your brain. If wisdom is to know others and enlightenment is to know oneself, then wisdom and enlightenment are worth pursuing but are also goals that can never be obtained. We're too dynamic. The instant you attain enlightenment, you change. It's like trying to pick up a watermelon seed; as soon as you get a grip, it spurts away. Do you know someone, really know her?

Look at figure 10. The circles on the left of each pair represent your models of a person and those on the right represent who he really is—his character, opinions, abilities, faults, quirks, everything about him. In (a), you've just met. Your model of this guy is built from your expectations that is, from patterns that your bottom-up processors assemble from his physical appearance, his T-shirt, what he's drinking, whom he's with, what you may have heard about him from other people, and on and on. Those prejudices are fed forward and, just below your high-level consciousness, you assemble a model of what to expect from him. The overlap of the two closed curves measures your model's accuracy.

As you get to know each other (b), your model grows more accurate; some of your prejudices were right and some were wrong. Eventually, in (c), there's pretty good overlap between your model and the actual person. Good friends know how each other responds to politics, religion, music, and beer; they know how and when they can rely on each other.

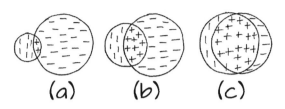

Figure 10: A graphic version of the process of coming to know someone: (a) just met, (b) getting to know each other, (c) an old friend.

Bring your best friend to mind right now. Picture her. Pretty easy, isn't it? Now ask her if she's read this book. You probably don't know for sure but pretend that she says yes. Now ask her opinion. You have a pretty good idea of what she would say, don't you? You can even gauge what she liked and didn't like and why she read it in the first place. At this stage of your interior dialogue, you start a little internal banter, exchange inside jokes, or argue with each other.

She's not there, but the model of her is still in your head. That disconnect between your internal awareness of this person and the external reality that she's not there is weird enough when the person you're thinking of is alive. It goes off the rails when you think of someone who's dead.

When someone close to you dies, even a dear pet, it is literally incomprehensible that this person is dead, gone, demised. Yes, *literally* incomprehensible because the model of this person in your mind did not die. The model didn't even change; it stopped changing. And that's the disconnect that brings the painful dissonance.

You think of the dead person the same way that you did when she was alive, right up until that jolt of reality comes back and you remember that your friend is gone. If you're religious, your faith might provide an attachment to that model, a heaven-sort-of-thing where you can imagine your friend as you did when she was alive. Whether or not it's true, that religious attachment is yet another pattern, a model you construct in your brain.

When someone dies, their experience of time passing ends, but your experience of them doesn't.

3.8 GOOD, FAST, OR CHEAP: PICK TWO

We are model-building, pattern-recognizing predictors—which makes us lazy bigots. It's as though Mother Nature said, "You can be good, fast, or cheap—pick two," and natural selection said, "We'll take fast and cheap." In biological terms, cheap means efficient.

You learned the sound of your mother's voice before you left her womb. You had to learn most patterns, but you came out already able to recognize nipples. Booting up a brain takes years because you need a trove of patterns in order to think. You have to break a few neurons to get your first few patterns. In the next chapter, we'll figure out how babies' brains adapt to the initial onslaught of reality.

That we can be aware of our prejudices and correct them means that prejudice is a form of laziness. I mean prejudice in every form, not just bigotry, but "idea prejudice." Every thought that we discard because it doesn't immediately match a pattern that we're comfortable with could have led to something great. We could have been contenders! Suppression of ideas is the antithesis of creativity, and idea prejudice is suppression, suppression of ourselves.

Mirroring helps us develop our theories of other people's minds. Knowing that other people think and relating to how they think fits patterns of others to our pattern of ourselves and, as we'll see, forms the basis for the value of everything created, engineered, and available for sale at a retailer near you.

Feedback seems to be the key to how all this stuff works. The brain does more than create reality; it makes us actors on the stage by controlling our bodies—those extended pieces of our reality interface where we reach out and change reality itself.

If we're all actors, are some of us more talented than others? What are we born with, and what can we change? Do we lean more toward nature or nurture?

To investigate the tangled web of talent and skill, we turn to a man of considerable talents—a real person this time.

4

TALENT & SKILL

ON AN AUTUMN DAY IN 1962 NEAR THE NORTHERN border of South Sudan in the town of Turalei, a woman named Okwok gave birth to a remarkable boy. Like most boys of the Dinka tribe, he spent his childhood tending the family cattle. One day, legend has it, as the boy guided cattle among patches of grass across the lightly treed plains, a lion attacked. The boy leapt to action, killing the lion with a wooden spear.

In his forties, the Dinka tribesman became a political activist who helped his homeland recover from civil war. He promoted peace and reconciliation, especially in Darfur. He considered education the key to peace and prosperity and built a school in his hometown.

He was a special guy, right? He didn't have a royal lineage, but was treated like a Diinka Duke when he visited Sudanese refugee camps. He never practiced politics and he wasn't a member of any religious clergy, but in the 1990s, American congressional representatives welcomed him to discuss problems that he believed would emerge from Islamic fundamentalism and, in particular, Osama bin Laden.

What made him special was neither a knack for diplomacy, a flair for oratory, nor success in business or academia.

No, Manute Bol stood 7-foot-7 (2.3 m). Being of this stature, Manute Bol had an enormous advantage over others in the court of basketball. But Manute's greater talent came as a defender. Defense in basketball generally involves the defender attempting to obstruct the path of the ball as it flies from the shooter's hands toward the hoop. Manute's outstretched arms spanned 8.5 feet (2.6 m), providing an immense range for blocking shots. And so it was that Manute Bol set a National Basketball Association record for blocked shots in his first season and became one of the league's most imposing defenders.

4.1 TALENT

To discuss talent and skill we need to be precise because this feedback loop is one tight knot. Talent is what you bring to the game before you start playing. Skill is what you acquire through education, training, and practice, whether you have any talent or not. Talent without skill will rarely ascend someone to the top of their field, but talented people start with an advantage over the untalented. It is in this sense that Manute Bol's height served as basketball talent. That he used this talent to develop into a great statesman might demonstrate an even greater talent, but there's no observable or measurable demarcation between a physical predisposition and a desire, so we can't say for sure—that's the knot!

Certain physical traits, if valued by society, give people an advantage that facilitates the person's ability to develop a skill: Elizabeth Taylor had violet eyes and the genetic "disorder" distichiasis, which provided her double rows of eyelashes to set off her eyes. Now, if oddly colored eyes with extensive framing were not deemed valuable in society, she might not have survived in Hollywood and she might not have developed her talents into acting skills.

4.1.1 Whence talent?

Kip Keino started winning Olympic gold medals in long distance races in 1968, six years after his first international competition. If Keino had been a pure talent phenomenon, that is, if his abilities were based on sheer talent devoid of skill, he'd have won his first race. Instead, like all great athletes, musicians, painters, physicists, brick layers, brewers, etc., he improved with training.

The conditions where he grew up encouraged running. His success drew a crowd of coaches and trainers to the region and lo and behold, the environment was ripe for finding talent.

The first few Major League Baseball greats from the Dominican Republic, Ozzie Virgil, Julian Javier, and the Alou brothers—Felipe, Matty, and Jesus—had the same effect. Radios took to the air, kids took to the field, scouts took to the bleachers, and an oasis of talent and skill was produced.

Yes, those "talent" oases were *produced* by a confluence of events just as much as they were *discovered* by scouts, and there's no way to tell how much of the oasis is talent and how much is skill.

Like an epic Monty Python skit, we see hordes of treasure seekers hunting for sand on a beach. Hands shading their eyes, these intrepid talent forty-niners search the horizon for sand, glorious *sand*, and all the riches that come with it. Marching for months along the coast, they search, and then, finally, one of them looks down and sees that his feet are buried in the treasure of silicon dioxide. Rather than looking at their own feet, the others rush to that one discovery, that sand Sutter's Mill. Instead of realizing that the whole beach is covered in sand, that the whole planet is teeming with talented humans, the talent scouts push and shove their way to the *discovery*.

Should humanity's lemming-like behavior come as a surprise?

Remember the scene in *Life of Brian* where Brian tries to dispel the crowd by telling them that they're all different, all individuals? And then one guy says, "I'm not."

People! You don't have to go to Kenya to find a great marathoner! You don't have to go to Romania to find a great gymnast! You don't have to go to the Caribbean to find the next Willie Mays! You don't have to follow the deer off a cliff to get a nice steak! The circular feedback loop of scouting for talent is a macroscopic example of the disproportionate impact of first impressions from chapter 2 and the perils of stereotyping that we discussed in chapter 3.

4.1.2 Skill

Manute Bol's height provided a formidable advantage, but there have been other 7-foot-7 basketball players, and none of them were as adept at shot-blocking as Manute, though many were better shooters. Paris Hilton's pedigree sets her apart from the crowd, but most children born wealthy don't achieve celebrity despite trying.

The concepts of talent and skill are knotted together. Many contemporary books have attempted to prove that talent is an illusion, but that's absurd. Variations in physical makeup provide different advantages and disadvantages. You can't practice yourself into Brad Pitt's cheekbones, Liz Taylor's eyes, or Frank Sinatra's voice.

I suspect that the popularity of denying the value of intrinsic talent stems from a cultural desire for society to reward merit rather than lineage. We want to admire people who strive, sweat, and struggle for success, rather than those who succeed by purely genetic advantages—otherwise, how the hell am I going to get anywhere? Wait, it gets tricky here too, because you could have the right genes, but if you aren't in the right place doing the right thing at the right time, your genes could sleep through your potential.

4.2 LIKE RINGIN' A BELL

Consider a country boy named Johnny who is interested in playing the guitar. Each day after school, Johnny puts a chord chart and his guitar in a gunny sack and carries it to some trees near a railroad track where he practices. As Johnny struggles to synchronize his strumming right hand with the shifting fingers of his left hand, neurons from his eyes, ears, and motor cortex fire signals across his brain seeking patterns. He begins with a conscious, top-down awareness of just how badly he plays—which is why he practices by the railroad tracks.

4.2.1 The wetware

I've been pretty cavalier about throwing around concepts like motor cortices firing signals through neurons to build associations into patterns. It's time to get our hands dirty.

You create every aspect of your universe through the interaction of eighty to one hundred billion neurons. Each neuron has an average of ten thousand synapse connections; so, at the receiving end, the dendritic tree consists of an average of ten thousand branches. A hundred billion neurons each with an average of ten thousand connections yields a million billion unique connections and the potential for a stupefying large number of possible combinations of circuits.

So far, neuroscientists have documented thousands of different types of neurons. The distinctions have to do with their shapes, response times, and whether they excite or inhibit other neurons. About 80 percent of your inner Feynman neurons are the elite, highly connected pyramidal ones that connect far and wide across your brain.

When Johnny sits in the shade of an evergreen tree between the railroad tracks and a bayou with his guitar on his knee, a chord chart on his lap, and strums, neurons from his senses convert sounds, sights, scents, tastes, and sensations into electrical signals. Engineers call things that convert sensory data into electrical signals, or vice versa, transducers—microphones, speakers, televisions, electric thermometers—the world is rife with transducers, and so are you.

When Johnny looks at his guitar, light reflected from the strings enters his eyes and knocks around electrons in the rods and cones of his retina. For a fraction of a second, the chemical structure of that rod and/or cone changes. These front-end chemical changes propagate to another layer of neurons, still within the eye, that sends them along the optic nerve to Johnny's brain. The same sort of thing happens in your nose when a molecule hits your olfactory glands or taste buds on your tongue: Chemical change at the front end of a nerve propagates up an axon to the first layer of processing and then to your brain.

When Johnny strums his guitar to the rhythm of passing trains, the strings vibrate, whacking air molecules. Those air molecules collide with neighboring air molecules that bounce into more air molecules until this compression-decompression wave enters your ear and hits your eardrum like, well, a drum. The sound waves continue on the other side of the eardrum up a spiral-shaped cochlea. Sounds wiggle little hairs at different points within the cochlea. Those wiggling hairs are the transducer ends of auditory neurons. The wiggling knocks electrons around, which changes the chemical structure of the axons and creates electrical signals that excite another layer of neurons and so on, propagating up the auditory nerve and into the brain for processing.

Here's the weird thing: Once the signals enter our brains, they all look the same.

At the front end, sensory inputs look totally different—fingers, ears, eyes, nose, and tongue—but once the front end nerves transduce the worldly data into bioelectrical signals traveling up axons, they look the same. Seriously, if you were to climb into Johnny's brain and examine a bunch of axons from his eyes and ears under a microscope, you couldn't tell which was which. If you plugged those axons into an electrician's equipment like an oscilloscope or spectrum analyzer, you wouldn't be able to tell which signals came from the chord he's strumming or the train he's watching.

So how come the experience of looking at something is so distinct from the experience of hearing something? Why don't we hear tastes and feel smells?

People with a rare condition called synesthesia experience sights as tastes, sounds as colors, and so on. Synesthesia is crosstalk among the senses. The most common symptoms are more amusing than confusing, like associating numbers with colors.

4.2.2. The signal

Our sensory transducers produce electric signals that propagate through circuits that compose the networks that create our thoughts. The signal itself is a spike of electrical energy that propagates down axons to synapse connections. By spike, I mean a brief, localized surge of electrical energy. These action potential spikes are nothing like the currents traveling along wires in your electrical gadgets. Currents in your body are carried by salts dissolved in the gooey fluid contained in neuron cells, not at all like tidy copper wires.

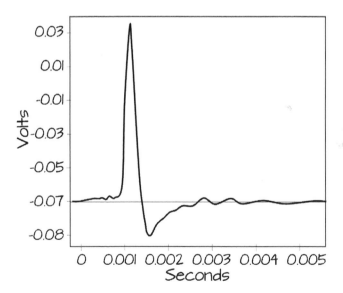

Figure 11: The spike of energy transmitted by neurons to other neurons, called an action potential.

Everything that happens in your head consists of patterns of action potential spikes dancing among neurons. Those neurons that participate in a given thought compose a neural circuit.

At the synapse connection between separate neurons, the spike's electrical energy releases neurotransmitters—stuff like serotonin, oxytocin, dopamine, and what have you—that cross the synapse into the receptors on the dendrite of the other neuron and are converted back into a spike that travels down the dendrite to the cell body of the receiving neuron.

Consider a single neuron. As thoughts course through your brain, that neuron receives and combines signals from thousands of others. If the total of all the signal spikes it receives surpasses a specific threshold, then that neuron either sends out new signals or stops sending out old signals. If the total is below the threshold, it continues whatever it was already doing. Neurons can be classified as either excitatory or inhibitory. Excitatory neurons, as you might have guessed, try to excite other neurons to act, and inhibitory neurons try to inhibit them.

The old right-brain-is-creative/left-brain-is-analytical dichotomy came from the observation that the left hemisphere sends more inhibitory signals to the right hemisphere than vice versa, reducing its capacity to act. For Johnny to become a great musical artist, many of those inhibitory neurons need to acquire higher thresholds so that they don't cramp his creativity.

We need to slow down here or we risk missing the magic. Somewhere, somehow, within the neuron cell, action thresholds are set so that each neuron knows the best way to respond to the signal it receives.

The fingers of Johnny's left hand are controlled by neurons in his motor cortex. Those neuron thresholds must be tuned so that they move his fingers across the frets just right. Otherwise, Johnny's guitar will sound like Ransom's, and passersby will never say, "Oh my, that country boy can play."

The mechanism for this magic, which is also the reason I call it magic, is not well understood. Computational neuroscientists model how neurons fiddle their thresholds to get the right result. That fiddling, I think, is the magic: how a single cell working in a team of billions alters its response to input.

And the thresholds aren't fixed. As Johnny learns to play, those thresholds change—learning at a molecular level.

4.2.3 The transition from playing notes to playing music

The first time Johnny plucks a string, neurons from the excited parts of his brain—visual, audio, motor control, as well as the higher-level processors that will become note-reading, symbol-decoding, and song-recognizing centers—fire signals. Since those signals don't correspond to a recognizable pattern, the lit-up, confused axons start making random connections with other neurons.

Biological growth doesn't happen immediately; the axons grow more like a plant. On hot sunny days, morning glory vines grow fast enough that you can see progress over the course of hours, but you can't see minute-to-minute growth. Signals flowing in Johnny's axons excite the process and, as he practices, his axons grow and make synapse connections to more neurons. As the neuron thresholds adjust, his skill improves.

The rule for synapse generation is "those neurons that fire together, wire together," known as Hebbian learning. Since Johnny's concentration focuses on the audio-processing wetware, that's where axons grow and new synapses form. The size of his brain actually increases in the regions he uses to make music. Analyses of musicians' brains have shown an extra 30 percent more wetware in the audio-processing centers.

Within the neighborhood of the active axons, the synapses make random connections. Well, whether or not they're actually random isn't completely known, but other systems in nature use this random "Monte Carlo" technique for finding the best configurations. Trying random configurations often turns out to be a more efficient way to optimize certain systems in uncertain territory than following a methodical map.

As Johnny practices, his conscious top-down process tunes neuron thresholds to recognize the musical patterns that link finger-string positions and sounds. It amounts to teaching the unconscious bottom-up processors to recognize those patterns in an instant. At that point, the process becomes automatic, and Johnny makes the transition from playing notes to playing music. Instead of thinking about where to put his fingers, Johnny thinks of the sounds he wants to make, and the bottom-up processes direct his fingers to the right frets and strings in a way that feels automatic.

Though Johnny never learned to read or write very well, his experience of the transition from playing notes to playing music is much like the transition you experienced when you went from combining letters into words to reading stories.

4.3 TALENT OR SKILL?

Practice creates skill and develops craft.

Audio patterns in Johnny's brain translate directly into visual and tactile patterns complete with finger positioning, strumming, and rhythm. Does talent play a role at all?

In learning to read, we follow a sequence like this: start with the alphabet, associate sounds with letters, sound out combinations of letters, recognize the word, associate meaning with the word, and move on to the next word. The first time you ever read a sentence, you probably forgot the first word by the time you worked through the second. Then you had to go back and do it again. It's a top-down, serial process.

I remember going through flash cards with my mom and coming upon "embarrass." I sounded it out: em, bare, ass. I said, "em-bare-ass," my older sister laughed, and my mother smiled and asked me to try again, but I didn't recognize em-bare-ass as a word. Eventually, she had to say the word for me to get it. The instant she said the word, it all came together and the multiple entendres cracked me up. I never missed that word again.

Yet hnre you aze, reqding thms whwle pavigraph witnont souvding out amy of tve words.

You are a talented reader because you have all the wetware in the right place to assemble the neural circuits necessary for reading. We don't think of this as a talent, of course, because almost everyone can do it.

Most of us also have the necessary wetware to play music. But someone like Johnny, Jimi, Joan, Nancy, Eddie, Eric, Joni, Gretchen, Jimmy, Joe, Bonnie, or Kaki—they have something extra. Is that extra a physical thing? Most of them have long fingers capable of reaching across four frets to play difficult chords—the same sort of talent Manute had—but some of them make their little fingers go a long way.

Great musicians, people we think of as talented, have the ability to distinguish and identify tones that most of us don't have. Is that a talent or a skill?

4.3.1 Neural pruning and synesthesia

Once Johnny's ability to play guitar becomes as easy as ringing a bell, something weird happens: Synapses start disappearing. By making large numbers of random connections, the probability of making the right connection is quite high. If you throw enough mud at a wall, some of it is bound to stick, right? But the probability of making the wrong connections is higher, so it leaves a mess.

Once people start coming from miles around to hear Johnny play, the neurons that don't make music stop firing. Synapses that don't fire fade away.

This idea of "neural pruning" or "neural Darwinism" gets really weird.

We seem to be born with acute synesthesia. Infants have two to three times more synapse connections than three-year-olds or adults, a huge mess of connections between the senses in a state of massive confusion. With no other experience to weigh against it, the confusion doesn't freak out our infant selves. Instead, we set about investigating the world and differentiating sensory inputs, and, just as Johnny's brain trims away the connections that didn't help him play, our brains prune away the axons and synapses that experience inter-sense crosstalk. Maybe the day you were born, you saw sounds, heard tastes, felt scents, and so on. Maybe the simple experience of being in the world cuts those lying connections, leaving your senses with axons finely tuned to reconstruct reality.

Learning things makes the brain a bit larger, but most of that size is pruned away as expertise is achieved. Biological systems abhor waste, and cutting out unused wetware leaves a leaner, more efficient machine.

4.3.2 Brain size

Manute Bol had long legs and arms; Eric Clapton has long fingers; Albert Einstein had a large brain. We can probably agree that Einstein had talent, but did the size of his brain have anything to do with it?

Birds have really small, lightweight heads that carry around some of the smartest brains in the animal kingdom. Ravens perform simple arithmetic and show greater evidence of self-awareness than dogs.

No study has produced a correlation between genius and brain size. While Einstein had an extra large brain with some peculiar abnormalities, there have been plenty of pinheaded geniuses too.

In Einstein's parietal cortex, along the sides of his brain just behind his ears, two creases merged into abnormally large patches where most people have folds. We use this region to comprehend positions in space and the timing of events; it also plays a role when we do mathematics. Did the decades Einstein spent concentrating on the relationship between space and time cause this difference? Or was he born with a brain uniquely suited for conceiving relativity?

On the one hand, I'm tempted to argue that this region of his brain shouldn't be extra large, because once he formulated special and general relativity, the extra wetware should have been pruned away. On the other hand, maybe it reflects how he struggled for thirty years trying to unite gravity and quantum theory.

By pruning the unnecessary connections to improve efficiency,

I wonder if Mister Know-It-All, you know, that guy who knows *everything,* has the smallest brain of any human. After he's acquired all knowledge and the ability to perform every possible task, all superfluous connections would be clipped away, leaving a tiny but perfect brain. You and I, on the other hand, have big brains because we're still sorting things out.

4.3.3 Perfect pitch: talent or skill?

Johnny's perfect pitch enables him to play beautiful music. His ability to distinguish differences between notes that sound the same to most people allows him to compose and play the special melodies that draw people from miles around.

Is perfect pitch a talent or a skill?

The answer is a resounding maybe.

As Johnny practiced, canoodling with the tuning knobs, bearing down and concentrating to tune that E string just so, he deciphered ever-smaller variations between notes. After repeating the process thousands of times, he got better at it.

We decipher pitch with snail-like pieces of wetware called cochlea in our inner ears. If we unroll a cochlea, it looks like a pair of parallel tubes about 1.4 inches (3.5 cm) long. The tubes are filled with sound-conducting fluid, and the cochlea is lined with tiny cilia hairs that wiggle when sound comes in.

Just as different colors of light excite cones according to the mix of red, green, and blue, we distinguish different sound frequencies, from bass to treble, about 20 Hz to 20,000 Hz, by which cilia wiggle. The cilia are the far ends of axons, sound transducers that convert vibrations into action potentials. As sound travels up the cochlea, lower frequencies continue up the tubes and higher frequencies die out. When cilia way up your cochlea wiggle, you hear a low note; if only the cilia at the opening wiggle, you hear a high note.

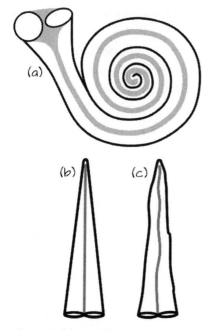

By spending hours trying to distinguish different notes, Johnny directs attention to the sound processors that acquire data from the cilia. That conscious attention causes more synapses to form, and he improves, that is, he improves his note-identifying *skill*.

But that skill is limited by the structure of his cochlea. Since the feedback loop between synapse formation and practice generates the wetware end of his sense of pitch, it's hard to identify where the skill ends and the talent begins, and vice versa. However, if his cochlea has imperfect geometry, if sections of it are swollen or constricted,

Figure 12: (a) A cochlea, your bass-treble detector, (b) a perfect unrolled cochlea, (c) an imperfect unrolled cochlea.

then Johnny's ability to distinguish tones from the cilia near the bad spots would be forever limited, regardless of how much he practiced.

4.4 NATURE & NURTURE

Clark Kent writes an investigative blog for *The Daily Planet*, but now and then he comes upon nefarious individuals who plot against the continued harmony, such as it is, of life on Earth. At such times, Clark steps into a Starbucks, takes out his cell phone and, while talking loud enough to annoy everyone, removes his glasses and transforms into Superman, tights and all.

But back on his native planet Krypton, he doesn't have these superpowers. No, Clark's talents can only be expressed under the light of a yellow sun like ours. Under the red sun of Krypton, Clark has no remarkable talents other than a journalist's ability to crank out two thousand words a day.

Did Clark's super talent result from nature or nurture? Both; nature and nurture don't compete, they collaborate.

If a single concept has emerged from our discussion so far, it's the way that feedback loops feed-forward loops, and feed-sideways loops with multiple inputs and outputs process their inputs in such a way that the outputs, which usually double as inputs, become an insufferably complex knot—much like this sentence.

If we ask the question: Is the brain more of a blank slate that can be nurtured to do great things and corrupted to do rotten things, or is it a predefined set of abilities, biases, and talents, we'll miss the point.

The nature *versus* nurture question points us in the wrong direction.

Remember Gregor Mendel, the friar who invented genetics by studying beans? Like the development of every science, his discovery of dominant and recessive genes turned out to be the outer layer of a big ignorance onion, a first-order observation, more like detecting light from behind closed eyelids than distinguishing colors in the rainbow.

Characteristics resulting from pure, inflexible genetic hardwiring turn out to be less common than epigenetic characteristics. Environmental factors flip epigenetic switches to activate or shut off genetic traits, potential talents, inadequacies, features, or bugs. Clark Kent's super talents only work if he lives on a planet with a yellow star; but the interplay of nature and nurture hardly ever has such a simple trigger. Your talents emerge from how your nature is nurtured—where you hang out, whom you hang out with, what you eat/smoke/drink/snort and, of course, whom you choose to have sex with—which for a lot of us is better described as whomever is willing to have sex with you.

On the other hand, if your parents are twentieth-generation red-haired Celts, you're not coming out with freckle-free ebony skin no matter how much Guinness your mother drinks while she's pregnant or how much subsequent sunlight exposure you get. You might turn out to be blonde, brunette, curly- or straight-haired, but you are going to have pale skin. On the other hand, or really on both hands, I could probably learn to play the guitar if I put in some effort.

The environmental switches that crank up your talents come in every color. People with diseases or those who spend a lot of time injured, sick, or in pain are at an obvious disadvantage to those with more robust constitutions. It might be tempting to blame genetics for these impairments and call it lack of talent, but the complexity of environmental interactions renders such a blame game a waste of time. Clean water and air, nutrition and immunization, parental encouragement and access to quality instruction, and on down the long list of easy-to-identify levers push us toward the nurture side of the ledger, but without the nature side already in place, the switches and levers have no effect.

You're born with instincts and the ability to develop algorithmic recipes. It's tempting to argue that nature provides the instincts and nurture the sophistication, but without nature's wetware in place, none of the sophistication can develop. Think of instinct as preprogrammed processors and sophistication as the ability to configure new processors. Both are tools embodied by networks of neurons; both require nature.

You weren't born talking, but you did come out primed to learn languages. Nature provides us with a set of processors tuned for speaking, listening, and interpreting sounds into words, but it doesn't provide a single word. Words are like the ingredients of the language recipe, parameters of the language algorithm, the nurture component.

When nature produces someone without the gray matter pretuned to learn language, the process of learning a language is likely to become that person's single lifelong goal. Without the nature, this guy is screwed, but check you out, a little nature and you're gossiping by the time you're three.

The nature-nurture question is not "Does nature or nurture play a greater role in determining a person's talents?" The question is "Does the environment in which a person is nurtured make the most of the genetic nature of that person?" Like democracy or a long-lasting marriage, the key to success isn't which party contributes more, it's how they interact.

4.5 PRODIGIES

The brain's electrical and chemical equilibrium is maintained by a delicate balance of inhibitory and excitatory action potentials. Someone born without that delicate equilibrium will behave atypically and see the world differently. Difference can provide a competitive edge, diminished capacity, or both. Seeing the world differently is a key to innovation and discovery. Manute Bol was atypical in height. I consider myself atypical, though not in height—I'm exactly the normal height for a male human being on Earth. I'm certain that you too are atypical in many ways—you rascal.

Studies of savant phenomena are just beginning to peel the outer skin off the onion. The first-order observation was "Wow! These kids can really count/play/memorize." But as we dig a little deeper, the miracles start to make sense.

Variations from typical behavior, like those that put people on the autistic or dyslexic spectrums, can engender abilities that dazzle us. But if that person's genius appears in only a tiny corner of the wide space of human behavior, and she's not so adept at the simpler tasks of life, that is, if she's adept at one thing and incapable of doing anything else, she's called an idiot savant. The seemingly contradictory qualities fascinate observers. On the surface, they look like miracles.

Society confines our behaviors far more rigidly than we notice. Our colleague from Andromeda probably wouldn't notice the difference between sitting and standing on a chair, but a waitress would.

If you're incapable of conforming to society's expectations except for a few acceptable behaviors, you're likely to excel at those behaviors. Did the Rain Man count so quickly because he had super wetware or because he couldn't do anything else without getting into trouble? Careful analyses of savant behaviors like fast calculation and early musical or artistic talent indicate that the answer might be less miraculous and more Carnegie Hall-ish.

Randy is a problem child. His weak grasp of language doesn't prevent him from incessant high-volume babbling. He screams and fights at any perceived injustice. His parents' explanations for why these behaviors aren't acceptable have no impact. He simply doesn't have the inhibitory circuitry to discriminate between courteous and discourteous, tidy and messy, interesting and boring, etc.

Randy doesn't fit into society, so he spends a lot of time sitting in the corner. Soon, he discovers that it's safe there, that looking out the window isn't so bad compared to being hollered at for variations in his behavior that he can't understand.

One day he counts the leaves on the tree outside the window. He tells his mother that the tree outside his window has 17,740 leaves on it. She says, "Oh, honey, you can't count that high, you can barely talk." Which sends Randy into a frenzy, so back to the corner he goes. When his time is up, he tells her that there are 133 leaves on the ground below the tree. This time, he says it softly, and she starts to wonder if it could be true. She goes out and counts them herself.

Soon, Randy is a counting prodigy.

The positive feedback loop looks like this: Get in trouble à sit in the corner à count stuff à announce amazing fact à be rewarded with praise or be left alone, which is reward enough for many people with autism à get in trouble à sit in the corner . . . continue the loop hundreds of times until it reduces to count stuff à count stuff.

Is Randy talented, or has he perfected a skill?

Savant phenomena occur in 10 to 30 percent of people with autism. Savants possess intense focus, enhanced sensory function, prodigious memory, and/or a large capacity for practice. The talents that emerge are concentrated in areas that include musical performance, drawing, painting, sculpting, and mathematics limited to arithmetic and geometry.

Some children with severe autism demonstrate astounding artistic abilities that defy the practice-skill model. The talent/skill of idiot savants also tends to peak immediately, reach a point of proficiency, and stay there without notable improvement.

Remember, neurons can inhibit as well as excite. By reducing some inhibitory effects, through injury or deformation of parts of the scrupulous left brain, certain abilities are unleashed. Some people who suffer strokes that damage their language-processing centers discover remarkable talents for sketching and painting. Perhaps they had this talent all along, but it was suppressed by their reliance and focus on language as a means of communication. Just as a blind person develops greater reliance on hearing and touch, maybe when one processing center shuts down, it stops inhibiting others and they open up. Learning Braille, for example, is far more difficult for the sighted than the blind.

Johnny showed how dynamic the brain is, throwing out new synapses, stretching axons all over the place in pursuit of pitch, harmony, and tunes. The current, tentative interpretation shared by many neuroscientists is that when certain processors are suppressed— by injury or defect—the brain goes into overdrive rewiring the suppressed regions of the brain to perform different tasks, even as unsuppressed regions step up their game.

Allan Snyder, director of the Centre for the Mind at the University of Sydney, has a different approach that fits the concept of myriad, mostly independent, bottom-up processors boiling important thoughts up to a monolithic top-down consciousness. Maybe idiot savants have lower boiling temperatures in the areas where they're talented. Maybe we all have bottom-up calculators, but due to Randy the leaf-counter's unique brain, his numbers boil up to consciousness and ours don't.

Snyder believes that savant talent can be induced by applying mild electromagnetic signals that suppress certain left hemisphere regions. His test subjects exhibit enhanced creativity that he interprets as evidence that shutting down certain pattern detectors allows other brain regions to boil up different ideas, ideas that the suppressed parts of the brain would otherwise inhibit.

In other words, when we're presented with a task or problem—

drawing a bird, solving a differential equation, inventing a new cock-tail—our brains scan solutions that have worked in similar situations in the past. Along with that scanning, our brains also suppress angles on the problem that, for whatever reason, we're prejudiced against.

The mathematician's brain is all "Get outa here poetry; this thing is chaotic!" The poet is all "Gimme a break; the number of syllables doesn't matter." Then, when the more rigid, more prejudiced brain signals are suppressed, the mathematician's inner poet comes up with a new trick. Maybe that trick works, maybe it doesn't, but either way, it alters the mathematician's perspective on the problem. Maybe the poet's inner mathematician provides a geometric view of the sonnet as a whole—a simplex sonnet—and the poet creates a new super haiku.

People with dyslexia have trouble decoding words. Symptoms include transposing characters, drawing mirror images of letters, and severe difficulty in learning to read. Dyslexics make up significantly higher student populations at art schools than at universities. Is the wetware that's used for interpreting written words in non-dyslexics dedicated to more artistic visual processing in dyslexic brains? Or are people with dyslexia driven to art because of their difficulty with written symbols? The answer to both questions is, of course, yes. The feedback/feed-forward nature of firing and wiring together means that the two answers are their own causes.

4.5.1 Child prodigies

Serena and Venus Williams, Mozart, and Tiger Woods were all offspring of people who immersed their children in a craft. Not every child born of parents who try to cram them into a talent corner emerges as a gifted genius.

Todd Marinovich was born to play quarterback. His father was an NFL coach who began teaching his son the nuances of the position as soon as little Todd could stand. Todd was a star quarterback in high school, starter for the University of Southern California, and, after his sophomore (second) year, a first-round draft choice for the Los Angeles Raiders. Despite the training and a desire to please his father, Todd didn't have the passion to dedicate his waking hours to improving. He never excelled at the sport's highest level. Todd preferred skating around Southern California beaches.

Being the child of a parent with passion for a field can have a huge effect on that child, but if the child never acquires the passion, none of the early signs of talent will benefit from the positive practice feedback required for the skill-talent loop to form.

When I was eight years old, my family went to the Oakland Coliseum Arena for some sort of exhibition. We came upon a golf club company exhibit that included a putting green. I knocked the ball in from thirty feet on the first try. A dozen men surrounded me in awe. They had me try again, and again, and again. And the damn ball never even got close to the hole. I was a grain of sand but not the sand they wanted me to be. It's just as well though; I don't look good in plaid pants.

4.5.2 Adult prodigies

Michael Jordan didn't make his high school varsity team until he was a junior. Albert Einstein got a job at the patent office instead of a faculty gig at a university. Jerry Rice wasn't offered a scholarship to a Division I college.

Adult prodigies are far more interesting and encouraging than child prodigies because they demonstrate that you and I still have a chance!

At 6-foot-6 (1.98 m), Michael Jordan had garden-variety physical endowments by basketball standards. At age fifteen, in his sophomore year of high school, he and his buddy tried out for basketball. He was denied, but his friend made the team. His Airness took it personally and went on a practicing tirade that allowed his talent to emerge.

Similarly, Jerry Rice was never the fastest man on the field, but the fastest man hardly ever caught him, unless the fastest guy waited around until all the other players had gone home and caught up with Jerry still out on the practice field.

Vincent van Gogh took up painting at the age of twenty-seven. He led a troubled life, always clinging to and fighting with his brother on whom he was dependent for both moral and financial support. He worshipped his friend Paul Gauguin, and the two of them shared a tempestuous relationship.

In other words, van Gogh had the ideal temperament for an artist!

He cranked out over two thousand works of art in ten years and then died, probably by committing suicide. Van Gogh serves as an excellent example of talent and skill. He tried every approach to oil painting, watercolors, and sketching that he could find. He worked hours that would make a twenty-something engineer at a high-tech startup seem like part-time help. Van Gogh took whatever talent he had and plied it with skill and an open mind and produced post-impressionist art of a quality that had never been seen before. His broad brush strokes with excessive paint accumulation produced images on canvas that appear to be three-dimensional because they literally poke out from the canvas.

4.6 SKALENT FUEL

The talent-skill feedback loop is tied as tight as any we'll see. I think that the spectrum from Manute Bol to Muggsy Bogues demonstrates how impossible it is to unfold one from the other, but there is a single driving force that unites them: passion.

Muggsy Bogues got shot in the arm when he was five years old. As a boy, he watched one man beat another to death with a baseball bat. At twelve, his father was imprisoned for robbery and drugs. And, at 5-foot-3 (1.6 m) tall—4 inches (10 cm) shorter than the global average height for a male human and 16 inches (41 cm) shorter than the average NBA player—Muggsy Bogues worked his way from the mean streets of Baltimore to professional basketball, the twelfth man chosen in the 1987 draft.

How the hell did a little dude like Muggsy play basketball at its highest level for fifteen years? Of course, he wasn't a prolific shot blocker like Manute Bol, though he did block thirty-nine shots during his career. He could jump 44 inches (112 cm), so he would have been able to dunk the ball if his hands were big enough to hold it.

Muggsy used every tool he had and practiced and practiced. We could lean back in our chairs and ruminate on Muggsy's incredibly talented dexterity and agility—he was one of the fastest players of his era, a prolific ball stealer, and an ace passer—but we'd be kidding ourselves. Practice is how the hell a little dude like Muggsy made it to the highest level of professional basketball.

Motivation comes in every stripe; for Muggsy, basketball was an island of safety in a world of brutality. Some kids get all the breaks. Maybe it helped that he grew up with three buddies who also ended up playing pro basketball—or did it? Which weighs more in determining success? Having three tall friends to practice with could help, but having three superstar basketball players in the same talent pool dramatically reduces the odds of a little guy ever getting time on the court. Unless, of course, that level of difficulty encouraged him to raise his game to levels that no one could ever have guessed possible.

Johnny's mother told him that someday he would be the leader of a band that people would come from miles around to hear. Having his mother believe in him made it easier for him to believe in himself.

Remember Starla's rainbow? Talent and skill don't form a spectrum with talent at one end and skill at the other and combinations of the two forming different colors between them. As skill is acquired, talent is revealed. As talent is revealed, skill is acquired. One doesn't come without the other.

Yogi Berra said, "Baseball is 90 percent mental and the other half is physical." If Yogi were keeping score, he'd say that this chapter barely touches half the question! How does intellectual talent differ from physical talents like being tall or having double eyelashes?

We need to investigate how we learn new things, especially really abstract things that would never help Butch take down a hippo. More than that, we need some idea of *how* we know whether or not we know something.

Nurturing talent requires plenty of passion, but it needs something else too. Our first hint of this missing ingredient comes from the story of Vanessa Mommylove and her son Vinnie.

5

INTELLIGENCE & INTUITION

HIGH-POWERED ATTORNEY VANESSA MOMMYLOVE faces an exhausting day of depositions, client meetings, and a jury trial after lunch followed by a meeting of partners. As she drops her four-year-old son Vinnie at Kiddie Care, we can forgive her distraction.

She walks Vinnie through the rainbow-arch entrance and into a classroom abuzz with children in various states of anxiety and glee. She kneels down, face-to-face with little Vinnie, and takes in his big brown eyes. Each day, Vinnie acquires greater responsibility for himself, and Vanessa feels the heart-wrenching mix of pride in his growth and yearning for time to slow down. This morning Vinnie buttoned up his violet-checked shirt all by himself—but he didn't quite line up the buttons. Vanessa checks her watch and makes a decision that she feels good about. The deposition can wait a few minutes for her to button her son's shirt properly.

She unbuttons the shirt and aligns each panel. "See how they line up, Vinnie?" she says. Vinnie looks straight down and his adorable pudgy cheeks contrast with his slightly furrowed brow as he concentrates on the shirt-buttoning process. She says, "I'll hold it while you button." And Vinnie attaches the buttons in the proper order. There are five buttons, and it takes every second of a minute for him to attach each one. She checks her watch several times but does her best to convey patience.

Around them, Kiddie Care maintains its state of limited chaos. Vanessa can feel the kindhearted gazes of other parents and preschool teachers, but none of that compares to the feeling of time slipping away—both the immediacy of being late to work and the looming bittersweet nostalgia for her son making the transition from toddler to boy to man.

As Vinnie attaches the top button, all the way up under his chin, his eyelashes turn up and Vanessa swims in those brown eyes again. Vinnie's cheeks puff out as he grins and holds his arms out as wide as he can, proud of himself and certain of the approving hug he's about to receive.

Vanessa takes him up in her arms, squeezes him tight, and says, just as she does every workday morning, "I love you so much; I could just eat you up!"

And he responds the same way that he has since he learned to talk: "Don't eat me mommy!"

She sets him down. He turns his head and pushes his cheek against her lips, and she pretends to bite him.

Their daily ritual complete, Vinnie launches into the fray of children, toy cars, balls, dolls, and stuffed animals.

Vanessa rises, smooths her suit and turns toward the door. She stops at the rainbow arch and looks back. Vinnie has climbed on a beanbag chair and is pushing a plastic dump truck into another child's toy tiger. The cluster of children moves this way and that, and Vinnie's violet-checked shirt, black hair, and sweet cheeks move with them, an island of affection on a continent of youth.

Now ten minutes late, Vanessa rushes to work.

Her day provides no respite, no chance to ponder her mortality, no opportunity to reflect, just the constant rush of busy interaction, argument, and a brutal afternoon headache. As evening approaches, she rushes back to Kiddie Care intent on getting there before six o'clock, at which time late fines accumulate. The fines are nothing compared to the guilt of seeing Vinnie there alone.

But traffic is light today, and she pulls into the parking lot at 5:30 p.m., peak pickup time.

She walks under the rainbow arch into the high-pitched cacophony of children playing and scans the melee for Vinnie.

A child in a violet-checked shirt runs up to her. He has black hair, huge brown eyes, and when he gets to her, he holds out his arms and turns his head to the side—precisely the ritual that Vanessa shares with her son.

But this isn't Vinnie. Oh yes, this child looks exactly like Vinnie, wears the very clothes she left him in nine hours ago, and portrays the motions of her son, but Vanessa *knows* this is not her son.

The child waits several seconds, as though he expects Vanessa to kneel down and pretend to bite his cheek. Instead, Vanessa scans the crowd for Vinnie. She figures that he must have swapped clothes with this tiny imposter, so she examines each child's face. None of them look like Vinnie. The child at her feet wraps his arms around her legs, and she tries to shake him off.

Shards of panic stab Vanessa's heart.

The child at her feet starts to wail, "Mommy, bite my cheek!"

Vanessa peels the boy's arms away from her and takes his hand. She walks the boy, who is now sobbing, to a teacher and asks, "Where is Vinnie, and why is this child wearing my son's clothes?"

"What?" the teacher replies. "Is this some kind of sick joke?"

"Where is my son?"

And the child screams, "Mommy, it's me!"

Vanessa looks at the teacher and then the child. She turns away and tries to concentrate. You see, Vanessa is a woman of extraordinary intelligence and self-discipline. She's got that feeling of alarms going off in her head not just because she can't find Vinnie, but because she knows that she's overlooking something. Combing through her undergraduate studies, she finds it. In a lecture she attended a decade ago, her psychology professor described Capgras syndrome.

Capgras syndrome is a rare neurological disorder caused when part of the inner puppy is separated from the inner Feynman. You see, when Vanessa looks at Vinnie, she doesn't get that rush of emotion she expects upon seeing her son. She doesn't want to bite his cheek or hug him tight. He's cute, but try as she might, the disconnect between her feelings and her intellect runs so deep that she is incapable of perceiving him as her son.

Vanessa takes a breath, reviews her day, and recalls that headache after lunch. It laid her out for an hour, complete with loss of breath and a shallow pulse. She started to feel better and made it through the day, but now she realizes that she must have had a stroke.

Once Vanessa's intellect overcomes her intuition, she understands that this crying child who looks identical to her son is indeed Vinnie. She kneels down and holds her arms out as she would for Vinnie. He launches into them, and she carries him through the rainbow arch. By the time they reach the parking lot, Vanessa finds a substitute for her own affection. She has made the conscious decision to treat Vinnie as she would any child who has been separated from his parents. She shakes her head at the thought because Vinnie has, most certainly, been separated from her.

5.1 WE CAN'T SEPARATE INTELLECT AND EMOTION

Vanessa expected to recognize her son at a glance. She freaked out when her ability to immediately identify him failed. She had to make a deliberate effort, a Herculean effort. Few people could hold back their panic and concentrate enough to come to a well-reasoned conclusion, but Vanessa is a woman of tremendous intellect.

Just as we enjoy the delusion that we can observe culture, politics, science, and even art with cool objectivity, we like to think that our intellectual inner Feynmans can make decisions without consulting our emotional inner puppies. We're equally full of shit in every case.

We expect to know some things without thinking. We learn to trust our gut reactions. How many times have you been out walking around and gotten a feeling of impending doom? When you make a major purchase, your gut has a big say, doesn't it? Some people intuit trouble with astounding accuracy. Others, like me, have stupid guts. I'm deeply impressed by people whose intuition gets it right, but I'm never surprised when they get it wrong.

My prejudice is that we're better off thinking things through, at least when we have the time to do so. There's a big hole in that logic, though. My prejudice has led me into the trap of thinking that intelligence and intuition are different things.

Intuition boils up with that feeling of understanding, of knowing you're right even when you're not. We get the same feeling when we deliberately think our way through to the answer. Vanessa remembered the lecture on Capgras syndrome, the pieces came together, she identified the pattern, and got the feeling of knowing. With no emotional attachment to Capgras syndrome, the feeling of knowing wasn't so inhibited. She couldn't identify her son because her Vinnie pattern was built on affection, and the stroke distorted it beyond recognition.

To learn, to know, to believe, all these experiences rest on feelings. If you're not *certain*, you'll never "get it," and getting it is sort of what it's all about, so even our inner Feynmans rely on their guts.

The question is: How did our guts get so damn smart?

5.2 LEARNING

Since the brain is a raw, physical thing, it stands to reason that brains come with different types and levels of talents, just as legs, hands, fingers, faces, and eyelashes do.

Intellectual talent is dicey for lots of reasons. Around the end of the eighteenth century, a physiologist named Joseph Gall developed phrenology. Phrenology proposed that the skull is like any other body cavity and that the brain that fills it is composed of separate organs that tend to separate tasks. Just as a competent eighteenth-century physician could diagnose the performance of organs by examining eighteenth-century bellies, Gall analyzed the shape and size of people's skulls to determine their mental capacities and even their criminal potential.

Measuring the bumps and size of someone's skull to judge their capacity to create art, practice medicine, or invent stuff doesn't work nearly as well as measuring someone's height and weight to guess how they might perform on a basketball court.

Most art forms combine the physical and intellectual. Creating physical objects, like paintings, sculptures, cabinets, and making music require elements of agility and manual dexterity, as well as the gray matter required to create. Mathematics, on the other hand, I think, is as close as we can get to a case where physical prowess hardly plays a role at all.

The venerable IQ test attempts to combine everything we think of as intellectual talent into a single number. We can probably agree that intelligence includes the ability to learn and understand, reason and communicate, innovate and create. Measuring a complicated, multidimensional, multifaceted, and not particularly well-defined entity with a single yardstick is sort of like measuring a football field by the height of the grass. You learn something important but risk the delusion that you know the whole story.

The best-known predictor of future success is not a high IQ; it's the ability to forgo immediate gratification, that is to say, self-discipline kicks IQ's ass. If you're trawling for future Nobel laureates, doctors, judges, and presidents, assemble your candidates and offer them a deal: You get one cookie right now, or you can wait ten minutes and get two. The kids who can wait will dominate the greedy little bastards.

Should we think of self-discipline as talent or skill? Your answer might depend on your experience reasoning with three-year-olds.

5.2.1 Recipes and algorithms

If you peel off your inner Feynman, that is, your neocortex, you get a thin, gray, wrinkly shell that looks pretty much the same across its surface. It has six layers: a mat of axons at the bottom and tightly packed neurons of different types in the other layers. Layers two, three, and five have mostly pyramid-shaped neurons, layer four has star-shaped neurons, and the outer layer has differently shaped neurons concentrated in different regions, like the slow-reacting neurons behind your forehead. It's one big network with ample connectivity, kind of a mess.

Neuroscientists assign names to the cortex's folds and ridges to identify the regions that are genetically tuned for specific processes. While different processing centers perform different tasks, they aren't truly independent of each other, and it's not known how or even if their physical structures differ. It's possible that the entire neocortex consists of identical, repeating structures. In any case, each processor has to learn how to do its job, whether that learning occurs over the course of natural selection from generation to generation—like our instinctual abilities to see, laugh, and yearn—or whether that learning consists of education or training—like algebra, plumbing, and sculpting.

To get to the heart of how we learn stuff, think of a recipe: a list of ingredients combined with instructions on how and when to combine and cook them. A recipe is an algorithm for cooking a particular dish. If you flip the pages of a cookbook in a language you can't read, the recipe for lasagna looks the same as the recipe for cake. If you can read the language, you'll see that the ingredients differ, but the recipe format and steps are similar, that is, the structure is the same but not the details. If you were born to cook, then you learn that structure early, and as you gain experience, you learn which ingredients and which mixing and cooking techniques work for each dish; you start with an algorithm and tune the parameters.

We have a talent for recognizing people because we come equipped with algorithms for facial recognition. We come with the recipes but have to learn the ingredients for everyone we recognize.

Alligators don't recognize their own children. Seriously, momma alligator drops her kids off at gator daycare in the morning on her way to the swamp. After a long day lounging in the sun, eating squirrels, kittens, and fish, she goes back to pick up her children. Entering the daycare wetland, she can't tell her kids from anyone else's; she's happy to eat any of them.

How can you instantly distinguish your children in a huge crowd? I mean, it's one thing to recognize your beer from all the others sitting on the bar, but children all look the same.

On your way to work, you drop your brilliant four-year-old daughter Bril at Kiddie Care on your way to the cubicle swamp. You spend the day floating between meetings, drinking coffee, spreading rumors, sandbagging your boss, creating and presenting astounding but underappreciated works of sheer genius and then, on your way home, you stop at Kiddie Care to pick up Bril. You walk in and see a horde of children between the ages of two and five. Which one is Bril?

You scan the horde. Bril's voice, hair color, face, height, body shape, all the details/parameters/ingredients come together and, despite the constantly moving swarm of children, you pick her out of the crowd with ease because she's yours.

Unimpressed? Me too. But consider this: At four, Bril looks nothing like she did two years ago. Since she wears different clothes each day, she barely looks the same today as yesterday. Unlike the alligator mommy, you constantly tune the parameters for identifying your child.

It gets worse—if you're a parent of a child over age eleven, you're already aware of this. Comprehending your child's character requires massive, dynamic pattern association. Their appearance is a tiny fraction of who they are. Their emotional and intellectual states require far greater processing. The constant proclamations of adolescents that parents don't understand them arise from the irritating fact that they're right, and that parents are busy. The patterns of a child's state of mind in a parent's brain tend to lag reality. We have a tendency to parent a child who is months or years younger than the actual child, until some crisis forces us to update our wetware. It's exhausting, yet somehow we recommend it to others.

Our neural networks perform like algorithmic recipes that recognize and associate patterns in a very general sense. Instinctual actions come with preset parameters, while others require learning. In an ever-growing tree of abstraction, our wetware algorithms recognize patterns and create other algorithms to recognize more patterns.

In neuroscience jargon, the spectrum from instinctual to learnable, from concrete to abstract, ranges from low to high plasticity.

5.2.2 Plasticity

Your inner frog fears snakes. Your inner puppy hates vacuum cleaners. Your inner Feynman is confused by credit default swaps.

Natural selection develops ever-more sophisticated wetware to handle more sophisticated situations by reusing equipment from previous developments. Frog neurons aren't so different from Feynman neurons, but once people started talking—to be more specific, once we started complaining—physical evolution was too slow to accommodate our spiraling demands for better entertainment options. Cultural evolution ramped up to speed. Natural selection didn't provide specific circuits for the advanced calculus that Feynman used to formulate quantum electrodynamics. No, the great mathematicians that preceded him repurposed the symbolic processors in their brains to invent new ways to think, and Feynman learned from them.

Your ability to coerce your own brain into doing what you want is called plasticity. Bendable plastic can be remolded for different purposes.

Each layer of sophistication uses earlier layers. Craving sex and craving a solution to quantum gravity don't use the same wetware, but in the sense that they are both appetites, they're more similar than they are different.

5.2.3 Education

I've drawn a cartoon of the top-down process of education. The teacher presents patterns to students. The students consciously ponder the patterns. I mean patterns in the broadest sense of things that we recognize: facts, processes, ideas, every type of concept. The new concepts go to the tip of the students' hierarchical thinking structures.

Figure 13: Ransom's model of education.

The teacher coerces the student to integrate the new pattern into her store of pattern forms through readings, drilling exercises, essays, laboratory activities—all of which fit under the heading of practice and experience. As the teacher packs those patterns ever deeper into the student's thinking structure, the student begins to associate patterns with other patterns, new and old, without having to deliberate over every detail. From up here at a high level, the process resembles what Johnny does down by the railroad tracks. Just as Johnny made the transition from playing notes to playing music, at some point, the student starts to get it. Having mastered a lesson, the student can then apply that skill to the next lesson.

Bill is studying neuroscience. He's lived among humans all his life and has picked up some psychology, philosophy, and history—a stash of established patterns—along the way. When a new topic comes up, his bottom-up processors try to match it to a pattern they already recognize. If they find a good fit, he moves on. But if he doesn't get it, then his mostly right-brain internal bullshit detector generates a feeling of confusion. As he puzzles over the confusing concept, he pulls up established patterns and uses his conscious top-down processors to modify them, adapting them until he thinks he has a new pattern that solves the puzzle.

He evaluates the new pattern by feeding it back to his bullshit-detecting watchdog. His bottom-up processors compare it far and wide to even more preexisting patterns for similarities, the toeholds of understanding. Having evolved to favor speed and efficiency over accuracy, Bill constantly predicts the final outcome, always reaching for the "I get it" blast of satisfaction. Good students keep concentrating, keep delaying that gratification.

When he finally comes up with a pattern that doesn't contradict the parameters of the puzzle, he proclaims, "I get it," and triumphantly heads off to a frat party to celebrate.

5.2.4 Memory

We build our models of reality on a foundation of memory. Without a continuously developing log of experience to provide us with context, we have nothing.

Since the ability to remember is common to all mammals, it figures that our inner puppies would handle memory formation. Two organ-like processors, the hippocampus and the amygdala, are involved; the hippocampus files away explicit memories, stuff like people, places, objects, and equations, while the amygdala arranges unconscious motor skills and immediate perceptions. The two play some handball when it comes to memories with heavy emotional content. Remember, the amygdala houses your fight, flight, freeze, or mate wetware, so it needs quick access to information for immediate life-saving decisions. The hippocampus and amygdala also judge what's worth storing and what's not. Your hippocampus can take up to three years to record a permanent memory.

Memories aren't stashed away like books in a case or files on a disk. Evidence is piling up that they're recorded as engrams—associations distributed across many parts of the brain. Engrams are usually described as holographic. Holograms are like photographs except that, instead of recording the color and brightness of light reflected from an object, they record the diffraction patterns of the light reflected from the object. Don't you hate descriptions of concepts in terms of more complex concepts? Let's work through it.

When Johnny learns a G chord, he associates a host of separate patterns. He associates the chord with his visual cortex, so he knows which strings are involved; his motor cortex, so he knows how to put his fingers on those strings; his sound processors, so he knows how it sounds; and his symbol processors, so he knows how it looks on sheet music. The association of all those processors forms a web of axon-dendrite connections spanning across his brain ready to be fired up at any instant. Or, if you think of your brain as a map, then a memory is like directions to your favorite pub. The map exists all the time, but the specific path from where you are now to your local bar only lights up when you're ready for a pint.

Whether it's playing guitar, learning to read, or less book-learning stuff like how to swagger on Mean Street, strut on Telegraph Avenue, or stride through an airport, when patterns are tamped down to lower and lower processors in our thinking hierarchy, they become automatic. Instead of carefully placing each finger here and there, sounding out letters, or watching your step, you can play awesome heavy metal, read great literature, and strut through neighborhoods on a whim.

One could say that developing understanding to this low, automatic level is equivalent to training intuition. One could say that, and we will, but not until later in this chapter.

5.2.5 Answer resolution

Say you're sitting on a power line over a wide-open prairie. Looking down, you see something in the grass move. Since it's so far away, you know something is moving, but you can't see what. You turn to the eagle perched next to you and ask, "What's going on down there?"

The eagle says, "There are seven baby mice in the process of being weaned. I'm waiting for their mother to come back, and then I'm going to eat her. Would you like me to score you one of the babies?"

You look back down. All you can see is a shadow in the grass and some irregular movement. "Seven baby mice?" you ask.

"Right, seven," the eagle says. "See how big my pupils are?"

You look into the eagle's eyes, and you notice that they're all pupil.

The eagle says, "With those puny pupils of yours, it's amazing you can resolve two houses on a block. But with my eagle eyes, I can resolve objects separated by the width of a blade of grass from one hundred feet, or would thirty meters make more sense to you?"

Resolution is the ability to distinguish between two things that are close together. The idea comes from optics. Lord Rayleigh, the nineteenth-century British physicist who demonstrated why the sky is blue, showed that the ability to resolve two close objects depends on the size of the pupil, or the aperture; the bigger your aperture, the finer your resolution.

Our thought process of pattern-recognition-categorization-prediction is limited by the number of patterns we have stashed away. The more patterns we've acquired, the larger the apertures of our brains, the greater the resolution of our thoughts, the more accurate our predictions, and the less prone we are to suffer from mistakes made by idea prejudice.

That is, education improves our answer resolution. Education in any subject—the vast piles of books consumed by students of the liberal arts, the never-ending homework problems solved by students of science and technology, and in any form, the raw experience of life on the streets, in the mountains, or at sea—ultimately consists of exposure to different patterns.

A musician can resolve two tones that might sound the same to you and me. Painters resolve colors, historians resolve epochs, politicians resolve, well, never mind.

The uber-genius who knows everything has perfect resolution: a unique category for every phenomenon, however abstract. At the opposite end, the unter-dolt piles everything into one or two categories and misses every nuance, every distinguishing characteristic. You and I are somewhere on that spectrum. We have our prejudices, but the more we learn, the greater our exposure to education and experience in their broadest senses, the finer our answer resolution grows and the less our prejudices interfere with our appreciation of the world. Well, we can hope so.

5.3 THINKING WITH YOUR GUTS

One of my top-five favorite books (and movies, for that matter) is Nick Hornby's *High Fidelity*. Like most of Hornby's books, it's about a self-absorbed man-boy in search of love and satisfaction (gee, I wonder why I enjoy his work so much). Toward the end, the man-boy says, "I've been thinking with my guts since I was fourteen years old, and frankly speaking, between you and me, I have come to the conclusion that my guts have shit for brains."

Our guts make a lot of decisions for us, some more obvious than others, some well within their purview, but others, well, sometimes we need to think things through. Listening to your gut while investing in the stock market can destroy your fortune. World leaders who listen to their guts instead of evaluating complex diplomatic situations cause calamities, tragedies, depressions, and recessions, though they still have a knack for getting reelected.

Brandi loves to surf, and a typhoon hit Baja last week bringing perfect waves today. Carrying her tri-skeg (a surfboard with three little fins on the bottom—bitchin') down to the beach, she has a feeling of excitement. That excitement comes from associating the size and shape of the waves—smooth cylinders that fold sequentially from north to south—with the exhilarating combination of physical mastery, tenuous control, and unbridled acceleration along with the risk of taking shitless face-grinds in the sand—gnarly.

Brandi spends all day in the surf and does a melon for lunch (she eats an entire watermelon—brutal).

As the sun sets into the ocean, she peels off her wetsuit, feels a pleasant tightness in her muscles, and heads home. Walking along Cliff Drive, she sees a Burger Dive and seemingly out of nowhere, she needs french fries. Brandi surfed all day and she sweated a lot. Her watermelon lunch provided energy and fluid, but not salt, and now her inner frog demands it. As the thought boils up, Brandi's inner puppy refines her inner frog's request into a desire for french fries. The pleasure Brandi anticipates in potatoes boiled in fat and bathed in salt is easy to relate to. Deer, bears, everybody likes a lick of salt now and then.

Brandi's desire for salt followed a one-way path from her gut to her appetite. Salt didn't even come to mind; the association of salt was sufficient to spur the simplest intuition.

Those occasions when an answer simply appears out of the blue, when we see something and know the answer, even when the question hasn't been asked, are like Brandi's craving for salt. Many unconscious processes pass along the intuited answer to an unasked question.

Two feelings are key to our ability to understand: the dissonance you feel when you don't get it and the consonance you feel when you do. Dilemmas generate the dissonance of doubt, as in "Where did I put my beer?" Solutions bring the consonance of certainty, like a fine meal devoured when you're hungry, as in "Gosh Bill, that turkey and stuffing and—oh my God, the bread pudding—sure were consonant!"

Intuition comes from bottom-up processors boiling up an answer into consciousness without being aware of either the question or the process used to derive the answer. The unconscious thought processes that generate intuition are just a step below consciousness. Our metaphorical pot of water heats up; the water's really hot, about to boil; and the answer comes up without any accompanying conscious deliberation.

5.3.1 The feeling of knowing

How come you enjoy solving complex, abstract problems? What drives you to invent Internet karaoke? Money? Did Monet paint all those lily pads so he could get laid?

When your supply is depleted, salt brings simple physical satisfaction in the form of a neurotransmitter cocktail that makes you feel satiated. The specific ingredients of these cocktails have not been resolved. Salt satiation probably includes GABA (gamma amino butyric acid), serotonin, and endorphins. Surfing, or whatever launches you down your tube, serves an exhilaration cocktail that includes dopamine, epinephrine, and endorphins, but why paint lily pads? Why invent, discover, or create? What's the buzz?

If Butch the caveman won't get laid unless he thinks of a way to cart the hippopotamus home for dinner, then he's going to derive some serious satisfaction when he invents the wheel and a wagon to go with it. Accomplishments trigger the production of neurotransmitters and hormones that make you feel good. Understanding does the same thing. Our internal pharmacist delivers the feeling, just as it generates post-coital bliss and satiation.

The sensations of light and dark, hot and cold, smelly and fragrant, loud and quiet go directly from our senses to our thoughts. One step further up in processing, exhaustion, hunger, fear, and desire result from the associating instinctual patterns and that sensory input. Another step up, and boredom, happiness, sadness, and contentment come from the synthesis of separate patterns, ultimately from our senses, but a couple of steps higher in processing.

The feeling of conviction, of knowing, is like an abstract sensation. We feel it; there is no unringing the bell. It's not directly related to sensory input; it requires processing. It's specific like hunger, but it involves synthesis and association, like happiness and other forms of satisfaction.

The weird thing about the feeling of knowing is the way it pops up. Seemingly out of the aether, we realize that the pieces of a puzzle fit together. Sure, we have to get all the pieces, we have to throw them around and try different things to see how they fit together, but without that essence of understanding, we'd never know we were finished.

The feedback/feed-forward loops involved in how you interact with the world and how it interacts with you are replicated over and over again, and not just in individuals. You affect my brain, which affects my body, which affects my brain, which affects your body (and I apologize for that, it was incidental contact), which affects my bank account, which affects . . . through group dynamics at organizational levels, over and over again.

The structure of these layers of similarity is called a "fractal." Why mathematics and every other field like to invent jargon will be covered in a later section, though perhaps only by inference. To avoid burdening you with jargon, I prefer the term "self-similar" to fractal. Self-similar systems look nearly the same at every scale, that is, they look nearly the same whether you see the whole thing or just a slice.

The self-similar structure of the brain replicates feelings at ever-higher levels of abstraction. The feeling of a problem, the dissonance of trouble, the feeling of knowing, and the consonance of understanding emerge from similar structures to those that encouraged Brandi to crave french fries for their salty satisfaction.

We share the need for salt with other animals. We do not share the need for money with them. And so it is that my dog is totally cool with overdrafts, while they make me nervous.

5.3.2 Priming

After dropping off her surfboard and showering, Brandi walks into town to get a beer. A mile away, Randy does the same thing. On the way, they each have to cross a busy street. Brandi approaches the crosswalk. The first car, a tricked-out Honda Civic, pauses immediately and the driver smiles and waves her across; Brandi smiles back and strides into the street. Other cars follow suit.

Across town, Randy comes to a crosswalk. A staid Acura approaches from a block away, with plenty of time to yield the right-of-way. Randy steps into the street. Rather than stopping, the Acura veers around Randy at a speed well over the posted limit. The car following the Acura, which has just been cut off, doesn't notice Randy until the last instant and, instead of trying to stop at the crosswalk, honks and blows past him. Randy now stands in the middle of a four-lane street. Traffic from the other direction stops and waits for him. Randy takes his time crossing. In response to Randy's slow passing, the driver of one of the waiting cars offers him an unfriendly gesture involving a middle finger.

Brandi and Randy get to the tavern at the same time. They sit at opposite ends of the bar, and each one motions to the bartender. Whom do you think I'll serve first?

Brandi's in a better mood. You can see it on her face. She's happy. She'll be pleasant to serve and probably tip better. Randy's brow is furrowed; he looks disgruntled and is tapping on the bar, already impatient with me. I'm heading in Brandi's direction, even though it's obvious that Randy needs my help more than she does.

Priming is a form of the placebo effect. If you believe something good will happen, you are far more likely to interpret whatever does happen as good than bad. Sure, it's all in your head, but if I've convinced you of anything by this point, it's that, yes, it *is* all in your head.

For example, if you assemble a thousand people with migraine headaches, give a presentation that goes into explicit details of how a new medicine conclusively solves the migraine problem and then provide them with empty capsules, about 20 percent will experience relief—not fake relief, genuine relief.

The placebo effect has been so well demonstrated that scientists who perform tests on people and other animals have spent enormous effort refining methods to understand how it works and how to remove it from scientific results. The double-blind technique assures that the people who perform experiments don't know whether they have administered a test drug or a placebo so that they can't prime test subjects.

A more familiar example of priming is forcing yourself to smile when you're in a bad mood. Eventually, your mood will soften. Take a deep breath and count your blessings, that sort of annoying crap.

Priming biases your gut-decision circuitry.

We've been using the percolation metaphor for the confluence of bottom-up parallel processes and unified top-down consciousness because I suspect that it might be an actual percolation phenomenon. Let me switch metaphors for a minute.

If bottom-up, unconscious, parallel processes form ripples on the surface of a pond, then priming is like a steady wind blowing in a specific direction. Since winds cause currents, the priming wind pushes the ripples in a specific direction—happy or sad, high or low, bitter or sweet. Rather than a set of symmetric, circular ripples from each processor interfering and combining into unbiased solutions, the ripples are blown in the direction of the bias wind. They still interfere and combine, but not in an unbiased way.

Familiarity doesn't breed contempt so much as it reduces suspicion. Familiar situations reduce our vigilance compared to foreign situations, whether or not they're more dangerous. The probability of being mugged in Geneva, Switzerland, is far lower than it is wherever you are now (unless you're in Geneva or some place safer than Geneva, if such a place exists), but you're less vigilant here, where you live, than you would be there.

Con artists capitalize on priming. You're a far easier mark when the con includes generating a mirror response that puts you in the predicament of a supposed victim or if it relaxes you into a good mood with friendly people who express their appreciation for your talents and good looks than if you're surrounded by people who set off alarms or doubt your genius.

If an optimistic wind blows, you'll experience the power of positive thought. You'll be primed to recognize opportunity. Your priming connects you to people around you. The car that stopped for Brandi gave her a positive feeling that she brought to the bartender. Frank Ransom learned about priming early, so he laughed in crowds and wept alone.

We're primed by everything we encounter to some degree. The people you hang out with, the weather, the music, and the traffic prime your mood, ambition, politics, and religion.

5.4 PRIMING YOUR GUTS

Our guts are less likely to have shit for brains when our brains have been packed with a wide variety of patterns and good answer resolution. Learned intelligence and study feed our ability to understand, but understanding of all types comes in intuitive bursts. Vanessa relied on intuition's instant understanding to recognize her constantly changing son and freaked out when it failed her. We rely on intuition to provide the seamless instant-to-instant recognition of answers to all the questions we face that are answered so quickly that the questions never seem posed, like Brandi's need for salt.

We rely on these same processes to assemble pieces of puzzles that are too complex, too numerous, and too difficult for us to assemble consciously. By focusing on a problem, large or small, we prime our bottom-up processors to provide the insights we need. As I type, words feel as though they bubble up spontaneously, but without my desire to communicate with you, these words wouldn't surface.

The extent to which pure talent, like Manute Bol's height, affects the accuracy of gut reactions is wide open. Muggsy Bogues practiced his way to the top, but practice will never make him taller. Even though I'm seriously overeducated and have spent time on Mean Street, Telegraph Ave., and in airports, compared to many people with less answer resolution, my guts still have shit for brains. Maybe I just don't trust my guts enough. Maybe the degree to which our guts boil up accurate answers to unasked questions depends as much on some sort of intellectual talent as on how they're primed.

If you convince yourself you can make it, you have a far better chance. The coach who asks her team how they'll react to defeat is less likely to win than the coach who asks them to plan their victory celebration. I've never been much of a rah-rah guy, loners rarely are, but there's no denying the home-field advantage, as long as a team is well prepared.

Our malleable, elastic, plastic brains are the kings of reuse, recycle, and repurpose. Understanding starts with simple things, the same things that other mammals take for granted. Then we construct scaffolds on top of them. A grunt becomes a word, words become symbols, some symbols become logic, other symbols become symbolic impressions, and so on up the abstraction scaffold.

The issue, then, is how to prime our ability to think, figure, and analyze in a way that both complements and takes advantage of our intuition so that we can reach farther, climb that scaffold, and see things in ways they've never been seen before. When we face a challenge, whether it's deeply personal, some dumb thing at work, a huge problem affecting billions of other people, or just trying to help a kid get through a tough day, the answer comes from the creative process.

We create things constantly. We're good at it. No matter how much experience you have, your past is a legacy of creativity. You've encountered problems and created solutions. We get good at something and reuse our solutions as much as we can, but sometimes we dig in so deep, we inhibit our ability to see as far and wide.

Now, please indulge me in a metaphor about the power of analysis and its relationship to creativity.

6

ANALYSIS & CREATIVITY

HIGH ATOP A MOUNTAIN, THE TEMPERATURE FELL. Mist condensed into rain that turned into snow that accumulated on the mountain peak in the shade of short winter days. For five months, it snowed, not every day, but most days, building up a deep icy base. The planet continued on its way around the sun, the days grew longer, the shadows gave way, and the snow and ice began to thaw.

The melt began with a trickle. An infant stream of water tumbled down the mountain; the trickle wove its way, pooling against stones until it reached around them or the rocks surrendered to its pressure. As the sun shone down, the trickle grew into a rivulet, a brook, and then a creek. When the water found cliffs, it dove over their edges, fell to earth, and dug in.

Then the days got shorter again, the shadows returned, the temperature dropped, and the mist turned to rain and then snow. The cycle continued, and each year, each lap of the planet around the sun, each oscillation of warming and cooling brought another flow to the trickle, the brook, the creek, and it grew into a river. As the river poured down the mountain, it converted valleys into lakes until they too overflowed their boundaries in first a trickle and then a torrent. The river worked its way ever downward, following the siren song of gravity to its salty sea home.

The work of the river dissolved soil and rock, spread nutrients and minerals, and left behind sandy shores as it fed the engine of life, the oceans.

The river flowed mighty in late spring and serene in autumn. The periodic nature of the seasons, each lap of the planet about its star, each accumulation and melt, dug the river ever deeper until what had started as a trickle altered the landscape into a canyon.

The planet pushed back against the river, pushed this way and that. The continental plates converged here, diverged there, pushed up ridges that formed dams and diverted the river's path, granting it greater structure, drawing it into snaking turns.

Now, with the mature river flowing through an adult canyon, the destiny of each new drop of melted snow is determined. In the days of that first trickle, any new drop might have taken a different turn upon meeting a pebble or root. Those first drops could have tried any direction to get to the sea, but these drops nowadays know only one way. From the river, no new drop can see past the next turn, much less beyond the canyon walls. But it doesn't matter; they know where they're going and how to get there.

6.1 THE CANYON FLOOR AND THE MOUNTAIN PEAK

Like tributaries merging into a river, analysis combines closely associated concepts. The analysis river carves the land into a canyon of mastered terrain and can sweep away any challenge in its way.

To create, you have to climb out of the river, up the canyon walls to the top of the mountain. From up there, you can look across the horizon and connect totally different concepts into completely new solutions. What a rush!

When you analyze a puzzle, you have to be conscious of many different pieces. We're pretty good at focusing on a few things at once, turning them inside and out, mixing them together, shaking and stirring, but we can only be aware of so many at one time. So what do we do when a challenge comes with too many pieces to fit into our conscious Feynmans at the same time? Well, we use tools. That's what this chapter is really about: tools.

When a puzzle comes along that has inconceivable parts, either because there are too many of them or because they are literally not conceivable, we combine analytical tools with the buried, prolific tools of creativity.

Having just worked through intelligence and intuition, it's tempting to take the bait that intelligence goes with analysis and intuition with creativity. There are similarities, but neither is straight enough to draw such simple parallels. Creativity often feels as though it blossoms out of nowhere and, just as intuition emerges from learned intelligence, creativity flows from the hard work of analysis.

The inspiration that guides creativity isn't a thing; it's more like a setting, let's say, the temperature of a room. If anything resembles a muse, it's the concept of priming. The angel flies in, sets the thermostat to the perfect temperature, and combines your bottom-up parallel processors and top-down consciousness into a single coherent instrument of creativity, a tool made of tools.

6.2 TOOLS FOR THOUGHT

We trashed the myth of analysis and creativity as separate left- and right-brain processes in the first chapter. The left brain would chase its tail forever without the right brain contributing context, resolution, and judgment to the results. The right brain can detect relationships between disparate pieces of a puzzle, but it won't put them together. The methodic, almost-plodding nature of analysis complements creativity's knack for associating widely separated concepts. When the two get together, they integrate and differentiate ideas into new concepts—fulfilling creativity's promise.

True creativity and effective analysis require both hands on deck.

Even so, no matter what we do or who we are, we're limited by our brains' circuitry. Plasticity allows us to adapt our circuits for a huge variety of tasks. For example, when we combine the circuits in our language centers that we use to handle the rules of grammar with our ability to position things in space, voila, we get algebra and geometry.

We're a long way from understanding the limits of plasticity. It's possible that when we adapt separate processing centers to new tasks, our new abilities limit our old ones. Maybe my algebra fluency detracts from my ability to grammar.

6.2.1 The binding problem

You're walking to work on a Monday morning, stuck in the crowd, wishing people would get out of your way, and something catches your eye: a rosebush. The words "stop and smell the roses" come to mind. You surface from the inner turbulence of Monday-morning moodiness and summon up enough perspective to stop and smell a rose, just to satisfy your inner Buddha.

Okay, hold it. A lot just happened. As you were walking, your forebrain pre-stressed about all the crap you have to deal with when you get to work. Since you were thinking about your boss, something that she's been whining about boiled to the surface, some stupid thing about the seven habits of whatever: "sharpening your mental saw." That idea excited your business cliché processors. They hunted around and found thousands of associations. Had you not passed a well-pruned rosebush at that instant, maybe some other cliché would have reached your consciousness, maybe not. But like a gardener in a bingo parlor, your pleasant bout of Monday morning anxiety was interrupted by this thought: "Roses. Bingo! Better stop and sniff them."

All a single neuron can do is fire action potentials down an axon or acquire them from other neurons. The number of spikes transmitted depends on your transmitting neuron's enthusiasm. How the hell do complex associations "come to mind"? How does your wetware keep clichés, roses, appointments, and all the rest integrated, yet separate and within your grasp? And how do you pull it all together when you need it?

The answer begins with this: "Well, there are about one hundred billion neurons, and each averages ten thousand synapses, so there are at least a gazillion possible associations," which is science bullshit for "It's complicated, but there are so many active parts that it manages to happen, though if it didn't happen, I could explain that too," hence the problem.

You stop at the rosebush and take in the beauty of the pink blossoms. You reach for one flower.

Okay, hold it right there. Notice how you've already associated the color with the shape, texture, and anticipation of the scent? That's binding. It's not the color, shape, or texture that brings the scent to mind; it's the association. If the petals were brown, you'd get a different scent; if they were yellow, you'd get the same scent.

You touch the stem carefully to avoid the thorns.

The pattern of "rose-ness" brings together sights, scents, and anticipation of tactile pleasure and displeasure, all activated by a higher-order concept of successful business practices that triggered the "stop and smell the roses" cliché.

As you pluck the rose, you lean forward and inhale the pleasing scent.

More binding; all those concepts come together and your entire being knows what to do. Then, as you walk away, you start humming Poison's "Every Rose Has Its Thorn" and think that your boss may be a thorn, but the paychecks are on time, there's a nice coffeemaker, and after a few boring meetings, you'll get a chance to dig into a project that challenges and appeals to you. Now your inner Buddha blasts a message to your hippocampus: "See? Aren't you glad you stopped to appreciate a little part of the universe? You feel better now, don't you? And why? Because of me. That's right, I scored. Stash that away." Hopefully, the voice of your narcissistic Buddha remains below your conscious boiling point.

Six days later, you decide to plant a rose garden and can't remember why.

Binding is gnarly.

6.2.2 Reduction of the inconceivable

Reductionism gets a bad rap because it seems kind of stupid. Why would you take a big, complicated, interrelated system and break it into pieces instead of trying to appreciate the whole thing at once? Because we're kind of stupid.

To keep more than one concept handy, we have to pay attention. The word "pay" indicates that it costs something. Attention puts intent, interest, motive, and instinct to work. Since you can only focus on a given kernel of thought for about half a second, and since you can only perform a single operation at a time, when you try to make sense out of complicated situations, you should cut yourself some slack.

To understand something complicated, we have to break it down and reduce it to its constituents. Then, if we can make sense of the pieces, we have a fighting chance of understanding the whole.

Let's build something inconceivable from something simple.

Stick out a finger, any finger. Okay, even that one, I'm not offended.

That one finger is one dimension; now stick out your thumb. The space between your finger and thumb, but not above or below, just between, defines two spatial dimensions, a surface. With that finger and your thumb sticking out, curl your other fingers against your palm. They're in the third spatial dimension. Forward-backward, side-to-side, up-down: three-dimensions.

You can draw any one-dimensional object. You're like the Renoir of one-dimensional art. Me too; check out my one-dimensional drawing (figure 14). One spatial dimension is a line. It doesn't have to be a straight line, but it can't have any width or thickness, just length.

Drawing or thinking in one dimension is so easy that it's hardly worth the bother.

I try it again in two dimensions (figure 15), advancing an entire order of complexity. While my one-dimensional art is flawless, my two-dimensional art is, well, flawed. Still, even when masters paint, they do so one brushstroke at a time. We conceive great works in all their multidimensional greatness, but when we put them together, whether the act is physical or conceptual, we do so one piece at a time.

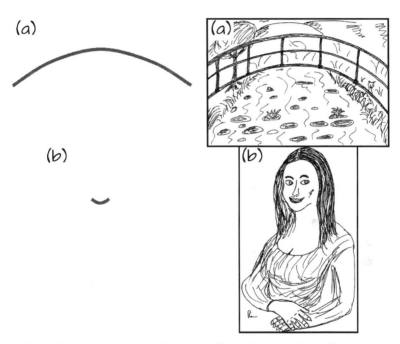

Figure 14: Ransom's one-dimensional
drawing of (a) a bridge over a pond with
lily pads (Monet has nothing on me in one
dimension), (b) the Moanin' Liza.

Figure 15: Ransom's two-dimensional
drawing of (a) a bridge over a pond with
lily pads (Monet has something on me in
two dimensions), (b) the Moanin' Liza.

I can draw a few things in three dimensions. Physicist training includes lots of calculations involving spinning tops (figure 16). Sure, it's difficult to portray three spatial dimensions on two-dimensional paper, but it's harder to sculpt something out of three-dimensional rock—even though it's done one chip at a time.

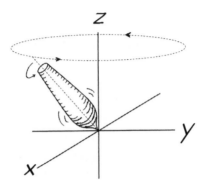

Figure 16: A spinning top in three dimensions, including a coordinate system, because I'm the kind of guy who includes coordinate systems.

The point of this silliness is to convey that the inconceivable can be conceived, and that reduction helps. While it is merely difficult to advance from one dimension to two dimensions to three dimensions, it is impossible to visualize something in four dimensions. Yes, I defy you.

The coordinate system that I couldn't resist including in my three-dimensional drawing shows a line in one dimension, two perpendicular lines in two dimensions, and three perpendicular lines in three dimensions; so a fourth spatial dimension requires a new line perpendicular to the three axes. Since we live in a three-dimensional world, there's nowhere to put that fourth perpendicular line; we've used up all the perpendicularity available.

Say you're out on a sunny day, walking around town and looking fine. You see your shadow on the sidewalk. Your three-dimensional self casts a two-dimensional shadow. You could reconstruct your three-dimensional shape by twirling around and looking at your shadow from many different angles. Similarly, we can imagine how a four-dimensional object would cast a three-dimensional shadow, but

I can't visualize a four-dimensional shape by looking at a bunch of three-dimensional shadows, and neither can you.

We hit a dead end. Four spatial dimensions are, literally, out of our scope.

Try to think of nothing; not empty space, nothing. Nothing is a not-place where there are zero dimensions, nowhere to stick out any fingers or imagine lines; nothing, not even space or time. Call me when you sort that out.

It's simple enough to write down "nothing" or "four dimensions" and talk about them, but when it comes down to trying to picture them or develop a feel for them, it's just too hard. We don't have the wetware required to process that kind of information.

On the other hand, it's barely more difficult to do mathematics in four dimensions or five dimensions, or even infinite dimensions, than it is in three dimensions.

Reducing systems to their simplest components makes it possible to figure them out—how they work, where they fit, what they do— even if we can't wrap our brains around the whole concept. The magic happens when we start out totally clueless, reduce the system to components, build it back up, and walk away understanding the whole thing.

Humans come equipped to learn a vast array of skills; the further those skills are from what cave people required for survival, the more difficult they are to acquire. We need tools.

6.2.3 Words

Language began with thoughts dying to be articulated. Words emerged as sounds, and then the sounds were mapped into symbols and writing was born. Apparently sounds weren't in such a hurry to be transcribed, since writing came at least a few hundred millennia later.

Languages have structure. Some are well ordered and others are quite messy. The structures vary across cultures. All spoken languages use inflection and pitch for emphasis. Tonal languages, including many African and Asian languages, like Mandarin Chinese, implement grammatical rules through use of pitch. Different languages use different combinations of rules and tones for syntax. At one end of the spectrum, if you're willing to think of software programming languages as languages, like Python or C, tone has no role at all. Sicilian-style Italian sits closer to the middle; it has grammatical rules, but hand gestures and inflections alter meanings.

In every case, nouns, verbs, adjectives, etc. combine to provide a structure, but perfectly good sentences can be composed that have no meaning. I composed the following sentence using a random number generator and a dictionary with the requirement that it follow the English structure: noun-verb-adjective-noun.

"Hypocrisy chokes boding trailblazers."

There are two reasons that you can dig meaning out of this sentence: First, you're a pattern-detector and, if you look hard enough, you'll find patterns whether they exist or not. Second, you're a metaphor-forager, a meta-forager.

Consider what that sentence means.

Done? Okay, my turn. Trailblazers don't follow the paths of others; they carve their own paths. A boding trailblazer must be one who is closing in on something. But a hypocritical trailblazer claims to carve his own path while actually striding in the well-worn steps of others. And so it is that hypocrisy trips up the boding genius of a would-be trailblazer. In other words, my pattern-detectors found this meaning in the random sentence: Arrogant people betray their own hypocrisy as soon as they believe in their own omniscience. I bet you didn't get the same pattern that I did.

Words and grammar are handled by separate processors. Words are assembled in Broca's area, in front of and about 4 inches (9–10 cm) from your left ear. Wernicke's area, behind and above your left ear, applies grammatical syntax. Meaning doesn't require the help of grammatical rules, but they help. You can see the value of syntax in this classic example of comma importance: "Let's eat grandma!" versus "Let's eat, grandma!" Still, if we were sitting around the table, and I neglected to pause at the comma, I doubt you'd stick a fork in grandma.

The way we convey meaning to others models how we convey it to ourselves. Language provides a tool for thinking that transcends rudimentary association and takes us to ever-higher levels of thought, from associating senses to associating thoughts to abstraction of thoughts and so on, until you end up with a philosophical crisis.

You abstract things all the time by removing an idea from the situation in which it arose, removing its context. Abstraction is a left-brain process. The right brain hangs onto the context and monitors it for consistency, but it is also perfectly happy to find a new context; and so, abstraction allows us to apply one concept to different situations.

The ability to abstract an idea transforms the beast, and language abstracts reality into words.

6.2.4 Mental tools—the power of scratch paper

Once you have the characters on the page, punctuation is bound to follow. You can picture it, right? There's one in every group: the bozo who demands rules, who must impose order, who desires authority in the form of periods, commas, and question marks. His name was Full Colon, but it was his daughter, Semi O'Colon, who did all the work.

If we were to insist on absolute syntax consistency and use the rules of that syntax to manipulate word-like things, we'd invent mathematics.

Just as letters are abstract symbols for sounds, numbers are abstract symbols for quantities. An interesting thing about numbers: Every culture with a written alphabet transcribes the first three numbers in a way that indicates their value. One is a single mark, two is a pair of horizontal lines connected by a line as though I'm too lazy to lift my pen after drawing the first line, and three is three horizontal lines, again with the laziness, but four—what the hell is that? Similarly for the Romans: I, II, III, IV. Once you have numbers, you might as well rule them by laws.

We're people; we need tools to accomplish things. The further we advance, the less our tools look like hammers and screwdrivers and the more they look like, well, nothing. Software is essentially nothing: symbols typed into a computer that are converted into voltage levels and currents by the voltages and currents resulting from other symbols previously provided to a computer. It's bits and bytes, switches and gates, all the way down.

Mathematics provides a set of rules and many different ways to manipulate symbols. Arithmetic is at the core, but the list of operations goes on and on. Numbers are one level of abstraction. The operations are an abstraction of grammar, so it's an abstraction of an abstraction.

Mathematics allows us to begin with a set of statements, that is, assumptions, and then combine, reorder, permute, hammer, and screw those statements into something new. The new thing rests on the assumptions you started with. When you get good at math, it's like making sausage: You start with some ingredients (for math, the ingredients are assumptions), you turn the mathematical crank, and out come predictions built purely on those ingredients/assumptions. If your assumptions are valid, then the predictions must be accurate too. Far more fun, though, is the opposite case (the corollary, if you will). If you test your prediction and it's wrong, then at least one of the things you started with, your ingredients, must also be wrong.

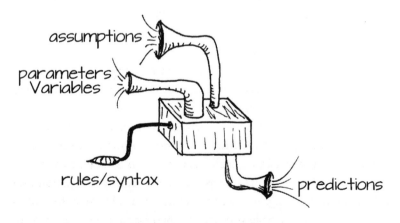

Figure 17: The mathematical crank.

The reason that most scientific and technological advances of the last 150 years have sprouted from mathematical or computational analysis is that these tools relieve the human brain of the impossible task of holding many different facts, concepts, and assumptions in consciousness at the same time. Math provides step-by-step methods that allow us to work with one thing at a time—which we're really good at—while making certain that nothing in the conversation is overlooked or forgotten.

Okay, I can hear you saying, "Whoa, dude. Math is hard for most people because you have to keep all those operations and rules in your brain at once."

And I'm all: "Sure, but once you catch the vibe of symbolic manipulation, you don't have to be conscious of that part of the process, just like Johnny can play music without thinking about notes, and you can talk without thinking about grammar." Assembling a complicated system by concentrating on one piece at a time might not be the only way that people can understand huge, messy, impossible-to-holistically (whole-istically, gestalt-istically) comprehend systems like climate, fluid flow, how stars work, the Big Bang, or tax forms, but it has the best record of all the other techniques.

We got nothing without scratch paper, baby. Scratch paper.

6.3 LATERAL THOUGHT

Let's start this section with an example at the crossing point of analysis and creativity. We'll then follow the scent and try to figure out what enables great creations.

In trying to understand how something works or where it's going or what will happen to it (it can be an atom, a brain, an economy, a piece of oak floating in a glass of scotch, but probably not a tawdry love affair), scientists and mathematicians assemble relationships between the pieces of the system and then try to determine the underlying principles that govern how the pieces fit together. The process amounts to writing down the relationships between components in mathematical sentences called differential equations—sentences in the sense that the symbols are abstractions for words and the relationships are abstractions of grammar. Erwin Schrödinger used this sort of analysis to create quantum mechanics.

Okay, maybe you've never heard of differential equations, maybe you were told that there wouldn't be any math in this class, but I have an all-important point to make, and DEs are a perfect example (yeah, like everyone else, mathematicians like to use acronyms to make sure no one else knows what they're talking about, as though "differential equation" would give it away).

Solving a differential equation amounts to finding the common theme, the trajectory of the system, a single predictive description of how the system it describes behaves through time and space. The problem with differential equations is that they're notoriously difficult to solve; there is no step-by-step method. Only a few simple classes can be solved by turning the crank, so most of these analyses reach a point that demands pure, raw creativity.

I bet you've been in a class where an instructor performed an example. You follow the example, but it still doesn't help with the more relevant question: "How did you know to do that?"

Professor Pedagogue says, "You just have to keep trying different things—sometimes you have to pull a rabbit out of your hat—until you find something that works."

In this context, trying something is sort of like trying different ingredients in a recipe. If it tastes good, it works. If it solves the differential equation, it works, and how you found the solution doesn't matter. Practice teaches you what things go together, where to look for the rabbit in your hat.

But what if you have a recipe that simply doesn't work? This is the situation at the edge of scientific discovery: a known situation without a description. General relativity and quantum mechanics have sat at this point for almost a century. Both theories rest on vast legacies of confirmation, but when you bring the two together, they don't work. By "don't work," I literally mean that putting Einstein's modification of Newton's theory of gravity into quantum mechanics doesn't add up; you get absurd predictions.

Trying different things means letting more ideas boil up. As new ideas surface, your top-down consciousness sends instructions to your parallel processors telling them what to look for. Trying different things calls on your right brain to look far and wide, to figuratively see something that's not right in front of you, where your left brain is focused, trying different contexts, different scenarios, and taking pieces from way over there and trying them over here—combining lateral thoughts.

Where do we find the missing piece?

Where does the magic bullet of an idea—the coherent concept that unites a bunch of facts, the missing piece to a plot, the riff that joins the melody and lyrics, the rhythm that conveys the right feeling to a poem, the perfect metaphor to illustrate lateral thought—come from?

Sometimes we find what we're looking for where we look for it, that is, through analysis, that concerted, focused, figurative banging of one's head against a pile of thoughts hoping to find the missing piece of the puzzle. The problem with analysis by head-banging is that feeding data into the same set of nearby circuits usually leads to the same or similar results over and over again. Genuine insight usually occurs when we turn away from a problem, take a shower, walk through a forest, or even sit at a bar.

Just as the river carves a canyon to find its way to the sea, we search for new ideas along the paths, tributaries, brooks, and creeks where we found old ideas. But what started out as a trickle has formed a rut, an efficient rut, to be sure, but when we get set in our ways, we have to scale the canyon walls to look across the horizon for a better way, a new idea.

When you walk away from a problem and do something else, the details and data unbind from your consciousness, but they don't go away. Your bottom-up parallel processors remain tuned in to the task and keep plugging away without interference from your top-down autocrat. The context-seekers in your right brain propose increasingly different, weirder, wider contexts, anything to string the pieces together as the less sophisticated, less certain, less critical, lower-paid unconscious processors in both hemispheres bring a broad range of associations to bear. You cast a wider neural net that accesses patterns far from the narrow focus of conscious analysis, off the by-now thoroughly beaten path.

The left and right hemispheres of the brain are connected by nearly two hundred million axons called the corpus callosum, a dense plate of white matter at the junction of the two hemispheres. Bands of axon threads lead from elite pyramidal neurons in every part of one hemisphere through this packed intersection and then, after crossing the divide, fan out to join every part of the other hemisphere. The corpus callosum is the ultimate associative network, the burners of your bottom-up boilers.

As processors churn away in both your left and right brain, they feed germs of ideas, little idea-lets, across the divide, assembling details into associations, and then, when your bottom-up fools stumble upon one or two candidates for the missing piece, the unifying concept, the ideal metaphor that brings everything together, you drop the soap and say those two most satisfying nonsensical syllables: "Aha!"

6.3.1 Synesthesia

Our brains create our worlds through the interplay of a bunch of processors that learn to associate sensory input with expected patterns. These processing structures span the spectrum from off-the-rack, preloaded instinctual formulas, like distinguishing the smell of a rose from the smell of garbage, to algorithms we build from scratch by adapting existing structures, like learning calculus. Wash-and-wear processes, like your ability to learn languages, lie somewhere between the instinctual and cooked-from-scratch extremes.

The neural circuitry that identifies the labels of fine craft ale has to have connections to the visual data processors in the back of your head. Sure, axons from the label-identifiers could connect to your visual processors no matter how far away they lie, but efficiency prefers to have related tools near each other.

Do different people come with different recipes that already have ingredients—pre-parameterized algorithms? Should we expect everyone to emerge from the womb with identical instincts? Of course not! We're all different (except for Norm).

Synesthesia came up in chapter 4; it's the disorder indicated by crosstalk between the senses. Synesthetics perceive numbers as colors, sounds as tastes, shapes as scents, and so on. Its hypothesized cause is incomplete neural pruning. That is, as babies' brains gain experience deciphering different senses, they prune away excess connections that don't help define the exterior world. Adult synesthetics retain some of that cross-wiring throughout their lives.

Might a brain with cross-wiring have an advantage at pulling rabbits out of hats?

A disproportionate number of successful artists, writers, and musicians are synesthetics. Could that crosstalk enable their brains to connect separate concepts and come up with more punch lines, more metaphors? Or are synesthetics at a disadvantage in fields that are heavier on analysis, and it's this disadvantage that drives them to art, literature, and music? Or does learning the skills of artists, writers, and musicians promote the growth of synesthetic axons?

Does synesthetic cross-wiring encourage brains to come up with not more but better lateral, right-field ideas? Since value is subjective, we need to be careful with the word "better." In science, better ought to mean more accurate; in engineering, greater functionality; but in the arts, better means that more people like it and/or that it pleases critics, or most importantly, that you like it.

I haven't seen any data indicating that synesthetics tend to be great mathematicians or software hacks, but I suspect that the relative population of synesthetics among scientists, engineers, and techies is consistent with the general population. Here's why: Suppose that synesthetics do have an advantage at relating concepts with processing centers that are literally close together. Being close together in the brain makes concepts easier to relate to for everyone. The easier they are to relate to, the more empathy they will generate.

When science types need to pull a rabbit out of their figurative hats, the value of that rabbit in accomplishing the given task has little to do with empathy. It needs to be novel in the sense that if it isn't novel, someone has already tried it, but it doesn't need to tie things together in a subjectively pleasing way. It just needs to work. And whether or not it works can be verified without asking critics.

6.3.2 Neural resonance, coherence, and flow

Resonance is the physical manifestation of the feeling you get when things match perfectly. Remember Butch, the caveman who has a hell of an arm? If he throws a rock with just the right speed at just the right angle so that it goes into orbit (a nice, steady orbit that does laps around Earth forever, the way that the Moon does laps around Earth and Earth does laps around the Sun), then Butch's rock is in resonance with Earth. That kind of fine-tuning—pushing a kid on a swing, you and me singing the same note—is timing resonance. Separate neural circuits that combine into creative thoughts exhibit a sort of resonance, a synchronous domino effect of relationship identification.

Let's go back to the binding problem. When something comes to mind, you assemble it in your working memory. We're capable of holding from four to ten separate thoughts in working memory at once, which is why I have whiteboards in every room of my house and always carry a notebook.

Your ability to bind separate thoughts—ideas, perceptions, sensory inputs, whatever—into coherent concepts requires coordinated timing of the circuits that do your binding. Holding thoughts in working memory and folding them over each other to create something new also requires coherence.

Coherence measures how much the separate pieces of a whole are related, how in tune they are in the general sense, not just the melodic sense.

Think of waves crashing on a beach. Perfectly coherent ocean waves would be perfectly regular mound-trough sequences of water rolling perfectly parallel into a perfectly straight beach. The waves would crash on the beach in monotonous regularity forever. Waves can only behave with such utter monotony if they are somehow related. Coherent groups of ocean waves are related by the wind that blew them into existence.

Changes in the wind and irregularities in the shape of the beach break the relationships between the waves and limit their coherence. The coherence time of a system is how long you can expect a set of related phenomena to last before losing their interrelationships, their synchrony.

With the idea of coherence right in your forebrain, dare I say coherently bound to the concept of resonance, picture a set of neurons transmitting action potentials to other neurons. Some neurons don't respond because the sum of action spikes they receive isn't high enough to engage them, but others respond by firing their own action potentials along to other neurons.

The binding problem boils down to coherence among all those action potentials; the stronger the binding, the longer the coherence time. The more in tune the resonance, the more dominos fall, the greater the degree to which the pattern that triggered them excites more patterns.

The "zone" is another type of resonance, the state of being in tune with whatever you're doing. Your internal breezes die down; the coherence time of your thoughts stretches out; you find it easier to assemble greater numbers of concepts and act on them with little effort.

The state of being in the zone is called "flow" by a psychology professor named Mihaly Csikszentmihalyi (yeah, it's a mouthful; just try "cheek-sent-me-high-ee"). Here are more descriptions of flow: intense engagement; involvement in the task at hand that's so intense that the rest of the world sort of falls away; balancing challenge and skill to the limit of your ability; the feeling that you're about to burst out laughing or crying, but aren't sure which. Picture your comfort zone as a chair; when you experience flow, you're at the edge of that metaphorical seat. Right on the edge doing something you're good at and that challenges you to the limit of your ability, just barely within that limit.

Flow is a resonant coherent state.

6.3.3 Language as spatial resonance

All the time spent practicing by the railroad tracks makes Johnny lonely, so he leaves his guitar under the tree and moseys into town. He walks into a bar where he's played often enough that the bartenders recognize him. He asks for an IPA and chats with the bartender. Then he sees someone walk in.

Having woken to the sight of a rainbow, Starla spent the day in a burst of creative joy, so inspired that she composed a dozen poems. The first one, about rainbows of course, came out so fast that she rode it into another and another, until a few minutes ago when she went for a walk and decided to pop in to her local bar for a quick pint. She sits on a barstool next to a man about her age.

Johnny and Starla have never met.

Starla admires his artsy appearance, his purple paisley shirt, his long curly hair, and his worn boots. She even notices his long fingers and the precise way that he lifts his mug and tucks his hair behind his ears. He uses his fingers like precision instruments.

When Starla sits down next to him, Johnny's blown away. She's beautiful in a way that locks into his preferences, not Hollywood or New York City beautiful, but capable, practical beautiful. The word "present" comes to mind, as though her mere presence is beautiful. She looks at him, and he pushes his hair back but can't think of anything to say.

She sighs.

He feels that he has to speak or risk losing this opportunity forever.

"So, umm, how's it goin'?" he says and immediately kicks himself internally. *Only losers ask how it's going!*

"Oh, not much," she says.

Mercy, he thinks to himself, *she's not even listening to me.*

Then she laughs and her laughter truly sounds like a ringing bell.

"I'm sorry," she says, "I meant that it's going wonderfully! How are you?"

He says, "Fine." And then there's a pause. He asks if she lives nearby, and she gives a vaguely positive answer. Then there's another pause. He feels her interest slipping away, but he can't think of anything to say. If only he had his guitar, he could let it do his talking.

Starla smiles inside. Could this day get any better? The man is smitten to the extent that he can barely talk. She lets him babble through a few more pointless pleasantries, and then she rescues him: "You have beautiful hands," she says. "Are you an artist?"

Johnny rubs his thumb across the calluses on the fingertips of his left hand. "I play guitar."

Starla says, "I write poetry."

"Have you ever set your poems to music?"

"No, every time I think of a melody, it turns out to be something Chuck Berry already played."

They laugh together and, now on common ground, they find their zone; someday, they'll make beautiful music together, or some other cliché. I apologize for that.

The combination of speaking and meaning that is language provides a simple example of spatial resonance.

When Starla speaks, a huge network lights up in her brain. The thought she's trying to convey forms behind her forehead in her frontal cortex. Circuits connecting the germ of the thought to the memories on which that thought is built light up like streetlights at sundown.

She wants to tell Johnny about her special morning. She envisions rainbows and circles and how it felt to write her poems. Her visual cortex pulls up rainbow images; her parietal cortex, the region toward the center and along the top of her brain, positions them in space. Her words form in Broca's area, just behind her left temple, and she assembles the words into proper sentences in Wernicke's area, halfway up the side of her head above her left ear. The sequence connects to her motor cortex, which coordinates the muscles from her chest to her throat, and she blows through the inner guitar strings of her vocal cords. As she hears herself speak, another circuit lights up, connecting her ears, and she listens, interprets, and associates her words with his response.

The point of mapping Starla's end of the conversation is to show how many separate brain regions have to work in concert, that is, how many circuits must resonate in a coherent fashion, before she has any chance of mating with Johnny.

6.3.4 Releasing your inner savant

In chapter 4, we talked about Allan Snyder's work enhancing the creativity of test subjects. By suppressing the inhibitory properties of neurons from certain regions of the left brain, creativity seems to be enhanced.

It makes sense in the context of lateral thought.

When analyzing a problem, really digging in and trying to determine the underlying connections to a jumble of details, our bottom-up parallel processors compete for attention. Those processors that have experienced the greatest success in the past naturally have an advantage. They're louder and capable of suppressing historically less-successful regions, but past performance is no guarantee of future results, especially when you're working on something that you've never done before.

We've seen how our neural circuits are disproportionately affected by first impressions. The first snowmelt plots the path of the river that later forms a canyon. When you do something that's never been done, you have to chart your own course. You have to try new and different things.

Miles Dylan once said, "The thing that makes complex systems impossible to understand is their complexity."

The novelty quotient of creativity requires that we entertain the wildest ideas we can come up with. Like medieval kings struggling to solve a drought, we need fools in our courts who can suggest ideas like importing beavers to build dams.

Creativity requires insight, and insights are produced when our background, bottom-up processors propose solutions we had not previously considered. By reducing our inclinations to suppress information from certain sources, we enable our own geniuses.

4.1 CREATIVITY

Susan Greenfield, a neuroscience professor at Oxford, insists that for something to be considered creative, it must be meaningful. It has to shift our perspective and provide a way to "see one thing in terms of something else."

Great paintings, music, and literature all make us see the world differently. Here's an old joke among novelists: Our job is to keep you awake at night and make you cry. The tears and laughter come when you see the world through the eyes of the artist.

Creativity happens when you reach into your hat and pull out a rabbit, but before you can get a rabbit, you have to pull out a lot of lint. Try stuff. When it doesn't work, try something else. Accepting, even anticipating and celebrating failure might be a key to creativity, but failure can be expensive. Along with resilience to failure, add these to your keys-to-creativity list: the freedom to try things, curiosity, confidence, exposure to as many ideas as possible, and of course, the knotted rope of talent, skill, and passion.

To apply a concept from one field to another requires lateral thought. To encourage ourselves to think laterally, we have to allow thoughts unrelated to the task at hand to float up. By silencing our tendency to anticipate and predict what comes next, we can push back prejudices, dice up categories, and open ourselves to new patterns. It helps to find the balance between engagement and anxiety, to get in the zone, stretch out, and slip into the puzzle. When ideas start bubbling to the surface, there will be periods of coherent resonance, and the best ideas will spread action-potential webs across your brain, front to back, left to right across your corpus callosum, and top to bottom from Feynman to frog.

When you play on a swing, you intuit its resonant frequency; you feel the harmony. I may sound like a new-age crystal salesman, but when you find resonance, you know it. When awesome ideas surface, they come up loud and clear—even when they're wrong.

6.4.1 People use tools to analyze and create

We take our tools and build things with them. That's about it.

The tools Michelangelo used to carve *David* from a block of marble look different than Professor Pedagogue's tools for solving differential equations. To a silicon-based life-form from Andromeda, a poet's tools look more like a mathematician's than a sculptor's. But in every case, the creator has a huge chest of tools and, as with everything else we do, the tools start out as sticks and rocks, grow more refined, like hammers and chisels, and then become abstract, like symbolism and software. We each assemble our tools and put them to work on one form of scratch paper or another—canvas, keyboard, marble, and, as we'll soon see, beer.

Shortly after we become experts with our tools, we discover their limits. Johnny's guitar doesn't limit him, but his mastery of it does. Every new riff extends his abilities, and he digs his canyon of expertise ever deeper and more complex. Our tools become extensions of ourselves. Seriously, many experiments support the idea that Johnny's guitar will become almost as much a part of him as his hands. You know this, though, because you have your own expertise. For me, even after thirty years playing with my guitar, it's a foreign object, but my pens, keyboard, and beer mug are extensions of who I am.

We find comfort zones within our own expertise, but eventually a challenge or a desire will pull us out of our comfort zones, out of the canyons where we are experts. Then we have to climb.

Picture yourself climbing up out of the canyon. From your river rut, your challenge looks like an impossible climb; at some point along the way, frustration accumulates; you're far from the comfort of your river, and then you finally realize that you've got a chance. You see the peak; sure, there's a glacier in the way, but the wind feels like raw potential. When you get to the top of the mountain, back to the place where that metaphorical snow first accumulated, where you first set out to become who you are, you feel brand new. With the wind in your hair and the sun on your face, you can see for miles (kilometers).

That's when Butch sees a disc-shaped rock and wonders if a rolling stone might be of use in transporting his dead hippo. That's when Johnny grows weary of the G-A-D progression and maybe takes a stab at jazz. That's when Vanessa looks at the child dressed in Vinnie's clothes and doubts her own intuition. And when Tony Magee buys a homebrew kit and adds more hops than the recipe dictates—we'll get to Tony in a minute.

It's not just that being in the zone and experiencing flow are not quite comfortable—they can't be both comfortable and thrilling. If they were, your bottom-up processors wouldn't launch you into action. To think laterally, you have to stand on a metaphorical mountain and take your old tools to a new valley. I know, the metaphor is sort of collapsing here, but I think I can pump it back up.

The novelty of Johnny's jazz creation may or may not have value. Butch's hippo-transporting wheeled wagon seems like a sure thing, but what if he's violated a cultural taboo requiring that food never be touched by round things? What if Starla's rainbow theory offends the Irish or violates a more well-established scientific principle?

We don't determine value by ourselves. If nobody likes Tony's homicidally hoppy ale, no tribe will show up at his brewery.

7

ALONE & TOGETHER

TONY MAGEE IS A STORYTELLER.

He had a high school teacher who conveyed the possible: Everything you do is easier than it looks once you get to work. Stories are told one sentence at a time; music is played one note at a time; and yeast eats sugar and shits alcohol one molecule at a time.

Tony thinks we're all artists, and he has an understanding of how we can find our places in the world: "If you're a musician, you're listening to Beethoven, Brahms, Frank Zappa, the finest composers who've ever existed on planet Earth. You're not comparing yourself to anything that's even realistic, and so your aspirations are limitless."

Then you start creating and "you try to put it out there, put it in a way that's honest, not the way people think you should or the way you think people expect it to happen. And you find your own voice."

In the early 1990s, desktop publishing put a dent in his printing-and-design business. As an iconoclastic, workaholic perfectionist, the lull threatened to drive him nuts. Fortunately, his brother gave him a home-brewing kit, and he set to work. "It didn't seem like a good idea to anyone around me, including my wife, but now she runs the plant, so I think I won her over."

His first beer, an early version of Lagunitas Dogtown Pale Ale, tasted like kerosene and broccoli—I know this because it says so on the label of the current Dogtown Pale. Laughing at his less successful brews and drinking and sharing the more successful ones, he found solace and buzz, the satisfactions and camaraderie of creativity.

"I didn't realize this at first, but I approached brewing like music. It's all the same thing; there are themes in the ingredients, how you present them. It spreads across your palette, and you get the next set of themes as it hits different taste buds and you swallow it and you get the hop aromas in your nasal cavities. It's like a little piece of music. That's what music is, a story. A story told in a language without words, and that's the thing that makes music so transcendent." Tony cites Frank Zappa a lot, and Zappa pointed out the continuity of creativity: Every note and lyric, every hop, malt, yeast, and drop of water, every label and beer mat, every brewer, bottler, distributor, and beer drinker are part of the symphony.

As with music, Tony has to know his audience. If he's the creator, then you and I are the beholders. "A tribe gets built around stories, commonly held stories that everybody agrees on. I don't think we're in the beer business; we're in the tribe-building business." An early label of Lagunitas Dogtown Pale Ale said, "No dogs were harmed in the brewing process." PETA got a kick out of it and served the Dogtown Pale at their annual fundraiser. Inside jokes, shared interests, and appreciation for the absurd all play their parts in the Lagunitas tribe, and all you have to do to join is pry the cap off.

Early on, Lagunitas grew too quickly. They had to buy a new bottler—a conveyer system that guides bottles one by one to a beer faucet that fills them, attaches bottle caps, and places them into boxes. The cost of it left them broke. Tony couldn't make payroll, so he held an all-hands meeting. Rather than laying down the law, as a conventional CEO might, Tony presented a variety of mixed metaphors so confusing that no one seems to remember what he said beyond "I can't pay you, so if you don't come to work tomorrow, I'll understand." The next day, about two-thirds of his crew showed up, some of them doing bad Tony Magee imitations and laughing at his unintelligible speech. In that moment, Tony realized that his company was just a community built of camaraderie and affection.

Tony takes success lightly. "Beer lovers are driving our bus, and we do respect the bus driver!"

Through most of human history, ale has brought people together and reinforced laughter and joy, courage and anger, bluster and sorrow. It's part of our story: "Beer speaks, meople pumble."

7.1 I WAS A LONER UNTIL I WROTE THIS CHAPTER

Back in chapter 1, I said that we're never alone even though we can't seem to come together. Alone-together is a feedback loop just like life-death, talent-skill, analysis-creativity, and all the rest, but this chapter might make you feel unsettled. You might get pissed off at me. I'm with you. When I wrote this chapter, it kept me up at night because it dismantled some of my more affectionately held opinions.

When we expand our own minds to include others, it's kind of like adding more layers of frogs, puppies, and Feynmans. The value of the things we create, beer for example, comes from what other people think. And people affect each other in different ways. There's the effect of people making choices, but there's also the echo-chamber effect of people mirroring each other, convincing themselves that they should choose something because their friends like it.

The value of your creations determines your wealth. By wealth, I mean the whole keg, not just your bank balance but wealth in a higher sense too. Much like how we boosted the concept of prejudice from simple bigotry to laziness of thought, we're going to bring wealth and value from their materialistic roots to the bigger question of what matters. Being wealthy has little to do with money, except that, without any money, it's hard to be wealthy.

The way that we all get together and determine what does and doesn't have value involves communication. The way we communicate with others kind of dictates how we communicate within ourselves. By ourselves, I mean all the people inside our heads: the child, the professional, the parent, the lover, the sibling, all of ourselves.

As we investigate how we fit together, we'll have to make sense of different types of communication, including smiles, laughter, and humor.

Seriously, it's going to get weird. But don't blame me; how we find, define, discover, and create our identities bugs me. I've enjoyed being a loner up to this point, but while writing this chapter, I was forced to give it up.

7.2 ARE WE A HIVE?

From the tomb of the womb to the womb of the tomb, we emerge into the world alone, and we leave it alone. Or do we?

We emerge with our ancestors' genomic legacy. We go through our lives with the reflections of other people constantly in our minds, and when the light goes out, well, was that light lit by a lifetime of interactions?

Are we really individuals, or are we so integrated into our tribes that what we think of as distinguishing characteristics are really fragments that we've picked up along the way from our people, our pets, and the wildlife—both human and beast—we encounter along the way?

Unfortunately for those of us, like me, who cherish the notion that we're loners in control of our own destinies out here on the metaphorical range herding our figurative cattle, the concept of individualism collapses at the first glance; okay, maybe the second glance.

7.2.1 The death of my inner rugged individualist

Remember solipsism? We talked about it in the context of the theory of mind back in chapter 3. Solipsism is the impossible-to-disprove "it's all a dream" philosophy.

What if your brain emerged into being without any contact with the physical universe? No sensory input, just a brain sitting around, existing with a nicely oxygenated blood supply. With no input, your entire reality would have to come from inside, truly a dream world of pure fantasy, except for one huge problem: In this brain, time doesn't pass.

Having never experienced interaction with an outside world, you've never seen anything, so you don't know what images are; your ears never heard a sound, so you have no sonic patterns either, and no scents, tastes, or sensations. Nada.

Consider that: no thoughts. Now try it.

Back in chapter 4, we talked about how babies are born with two to three times more synapse connections than three-year-olds and how their brains prune the connections that don't help them understand their surroundings. If there's no world, then it's likely that the pruning process would just keep going until the only synapses left are those required for the barest existence. You'd prune away everything but part of your inner frog.

In a brain that never interacts with the world, there are no associations, no perceptions, no ideas; it's just a hunk of meat, plugged in, but with the lights turned off.

Lobo is a rugged individual. Raised by wolves, she has never interacted with another person. Unlike a solipsist, Lobo interacts with the world, acquires patterns, and learns what to expect like every other person, except for a few glaring deficiencies.

Our brains require observation of other people right out of the gate, before they prune away the synapses that associate sounds with language. People who have spent their first decade or so isolated from others—raised by wolves or kept in a cell by a twisted bastard—spend the rest of their lives trying to learn to speak without much success. If she never hangs out with people, Lobo has no access to the conceptual tools she needs to think problems through, to develop a narrative of her life, or to assemble absurd but firmly held opinions.

A horse can run within hours of birth. A baby can't even drive until he's been loitering for the better part of two decades!

Humans continue developing after leaving the womb for far longer than other animals. The standard reasoning is that, if we waited the whole fourteen to eighteen months instead of just nine, our heads would be too big to get out of the hole. That might be it, but joining the pack early provides a huge extra advantage. Coming out prematurely as a courtesy to our dear mothers qualifies as an adaptation; natural selection killed off the mothers of the kids that lollygagged in the womb, and kids born with dead mothers don't fare very well.

Coming out early is also an *exaptation.*

Although it's easy to trace an adaptation to how it helps us deal with reality, exaptations also help us, but in a coincidental, lucky, and less obvious way. Natural selection forced fat-headed humans out early, but it came with another huge benefit: The exaptation allowed infants to finish developing their brains in the company of laughing, whining, and sweet-talking people.

Sure, we have our secrets. Science fiction author Kim Stanley Robinson famously delineated the secret lives of excretion, sexual fantasy, secret hopes, terror of death, experience of shame, inner pain and turmoil, and the dreams we never share. Existence can be lonely, but the existence of loneliness points to our interdependence, not to our solitariness. To say that we live solitary lives misses the point, the great big point of how and from where we assemble this concept of self.

It pains me to admit that we really are in this together.

7.2.2 Extending the consciousness feedback loop to others

Sorry, Prometheus, the greatest invention was not fire; too bad, Michelin Man, it wasn't the wheel; due apologies, Newton, not calculus either. When you're sitting in a café listening to teenagers flirting and gossiping, it can be hard to believe that language has any value at all.

Along with "thinking outside the box," the business cliché I hate most is "don't reinvent the wheel." Before the advent of language, pretty much everything had to be learned through direct experience; every wheel had to be reinvented for every wagon.

When children do stupid things, grandparents, usually in-laws, like to say, "The only way a kid learns not to make stupid decisions is to make stupid decisions." There's a ring of truth to it, but for the most part, people can learn from each other.

While our senses give us a reality interface, language gives us an interface between each other's brains. Sharing experience alters the timescale of evolution.

250,000 years ago or so, your 12,500th great-grandmother couldn't think beyond the next season. Thirty thousand years ago, your 1,500th great-grandfather could conceive of almost a century. As a product of the twenty-first century, your world extends over two thousand years. You're aware of the Roman Empire and have acquired the knowledge of hundreds of generations of other people. Not only do you travel a distance equivalent to halfway around the Earth every year (12,500 miles (20,000 km)), but you can watch live video feeds from Mars. Consider the body of knowledge learned in twelve years of education. By the time you were seventeen, you had acquired the intellectual tools achieved over three hundred thousand years.

How long would it take natural selection to produce people who could measure the lifetime of the universe? Probably the lifetime of the universe.

7.2.3 Imitation and simulation

You're standing on a corner in Winslow, Arizona, watching Randi Magoo walk down the street with her earbuds in, tunes cranked, typing text messages to her BFFs. She comes to a busy intersection and steps in front of a flatbed Ford. You suck in your breath, tighten your sphincter, get a blast of norepinephrine, and then, as the truck careens around her, you sigh in relief at her good fortune.

Since Randi's oblivious to the near miss, still typing LOL, your experience of the collision was more vivid than hers. As she stepped in front of the truck, you probably reacted. You might have jumped to the side, but not as far or with as much haste as you would have if it had really been you about to take a bumper on the chin.

Now approaching the opposite curb, Randi's still oblivious. Cars swerve around her. A Prius rear-ends a Charger. She trips on the curb and falls. Her knee, wrist, and cell phone hit the concrete at the same time. Sure, you feel some schadenfreude when the phone breaks, but you've tripped before and know how it feels. There you go mirroring again, now firing up your anterior cingulate cortex, that is, your pain center. You empathize with Randi's pain, and your heart races, but you don't feel that pain. The feedback loop between your muscles and your knees (but not your cell phone) notified your motor cortex and your pain center through inhibitory signals that you didn't actually participate in Randi's blunder.

Your emotional response to another person's trauma comes from your mirrored, simulated experience of that trauma. Mirroring in your motor cortex generates an immediate physical response to another person's facial expressions. While it takes 0.2 seconds to jump out of the way of a truck, your face reacts to other people's faces almost ten times faster. When your partner smiles at you, it takes about 0.03 second for your lip muscles to reply—not a full-fledged smile, but an immediate too-fast-to-control response.

A real smile is very difficult to fake. You can't just flash the pearly whites and be done with it. Fake smiles use different muscles than real ones. Look at pictures you've posed for. Your initial grin might be sincere (after all, posing situations are usually jovial), but the longer you hold that smile, the faker it looks. When you are behind the camera, hit the shutter as soon as you focus, before your subjects settle into a pose.

The thing is, we don't just smile with our lips. Real smiles take over your entire face, especially your forehead and eyes.

But why do we smile at all? The thinking on smiles is outer-layer-of-the-onion science. The idea is that half a million years ago, if you and I approached each other at a book signing, we'd bare our canines in a default don't-mess-with-me threat. Then I'd see your copy of my book, and you'd recognize me from the photo on the dust jacket, and our lips would wiggle a bit and the implied threat would transform into an explicit greeting. As eons passed, your mammalian snarl transformed into your winning smile.

Immediate, involuntary commiseration with each other ties us tighter into our teams, our tribes, our schools, our people.

We don't react the same way to rivals. Our responses to people we don't know, like, and/or trust, aren't so automatic. Flash a smile at a stranger so that they won't feel threatened and they'll probably leave you alone—that's a fake smile. The behavior geeks call it a social smile.

Our automatic reactions to allies and friends create positive feedback loops that reinforce our feelings. The more you like someone, the more you respond to them, the more they respond to you, the more you respond to them…and the more you like them. Unfortunately, a lack of automatic response to people you don't know is also a positive loop: The less you respond, the less they respond…, and the less they like you.

7.2.4 Well, are we?

A hive, I mean. As groups, bees and termites act like intelligent creatures. With less than a million neurons each, they're individually stupid, but throw a few thousand together and they hunt and gather food, engineer and build extensive structures, and they even know how to raise royalty.

What makes kings and queens exceptional is how other people treat them. Prince Georgie will be unique, not because there's anything special about him, but because the other people in the tribe have decided that he's special; it's the same with bees. You take any old working-bee larva, feed it a special diet, treat it with extra respect—bow, curtsy, overlook protruding noses and bad hair—and you get an autocrat, I mean a bee-crat, a queen.

Genuine hives become more intelligent than their parts. How

much did your inner frog improve by adding an inner puppy? And how much did your inner puppy benefit from a layer of Feynman? By adding language, we get a pathway to another entire brain of processing power, albeit a pathway that's slower and less efficient than direct axon-synapse-dendrite connections.

Imagine being a soldier on D-Day, one bee in a hive of 160,000 working in concert to a common end with absolute dedication. Maybe when you got drafted or signed up, your dedication wasn't so absolute, but once you hit the beach, it was move forward or die.

Command chains from prime ministers and presidents to generals, captains, sergeants, and corporals coordinated each other and all of the worker bees. No element functioned perfectly— 2,500 men died that day—but the swarm carried on.

Supreme Commander Dwight D. Eisenhower had an impressive title, but he also faced one of history's great challenges: navigating the egos of politicians and military officers. Word has it that British Prime Minister Winston Churchill had a rather large measure of self-confidence and an equally generous capacity for self-righteousness, yet Eisenhower convinced Churchill to give him complete authority over the Royal Air Force—a heroic accomplishment. After all, the outnumbered, under-armed RAF had won the Battle of Britain three years before. Why would Churchill give that level of control to a latecomer to the theatre? Because he understood the necessity of a coherent soldier hive.

Now, with you and me, that woman over there, and that guy in the hoodie, the feedback loop expands. But I've left out a crucial piece. We agreed to use the frog-puppy-Feynman model of the brain only if we remembered that it has to be re-optimized at each step of development. In Figure 18, I combined the already oversimplified model into a larger feedback system because I don't know how to draw the re-optimized connections between each person on the team, connections that include not just language but every other type of communication.

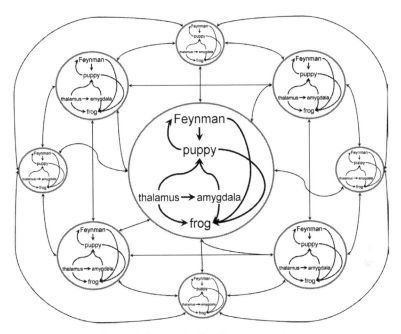

Figure 18: Communication flow among a team.

While natural selection re-optimizes the connections in each draft of the brain, as members of a team, we're responsible for re-optimizing our interconnections. Having participated on teams, we know that the connections need a lot of optimizing. Sometimes, the band comes together and plays as a single, perfect unit. Sometimes, we see the lightbulbs go on in the windows of each other's eyes, and we're able to convey the crucial next step, the key line of code, the ideal integrated circuit, the right blend of hops and malt without exchanging a word.

Teams mesh; people come together, but not the way bees do. When people behave like cogs in a machine following simple, specific rules, the way that individual neurons and bees behave, their talents are lost. Accomplishment, heroism, and magnificence materialize from people working together, recognizing the purpose of the whole while integrating their personal intents into roles dedicated to pursuit of that greater good.

So, is a corporation a hive? Is it somehow conscious? Could a group of people collaborating on an endeavor become so networked (dare I say Internetworked?) that genuine consciousness emerges?

Consider what that would feel like. You're in your cubicle doing your thing, a cog in the machine contributing to a mission along with a bunch of other cogs and, whoa, up boils an overall awareness. Each cog participates in that awareness, but would they be aware of that meta-awareness? It's a stretch to imagine that each of your neurons is "aware" of you. Is it a stretch to think that an individual bee is aware of the hive's awareness, assuming that awareness exists?

Neurons can combine into a conscious being, but can transistors?

At the risk of jumping off the science bandwagon into the deep end of the philosophical pool and suffocating in a sea of mixed metaphors, let me answer with a firm maybe.

Crowd-sourcing is remarkably effective. If you put a gazillion candies in a giant jar and then ask one hundred people how many candies are in there, the average of those one hundred guesses will be spot-on; that is, the distribution of guesses will be centered around the actual value, though any single guess is likely to be way off. Is this a step toward hive intelligence? Probably not. If instead of asking individuals, we assemble those one hundred people into a committee and assign them the task of estimating the number of candies, the committee's estimate will be almost as inaccurate as any single guess. As long as people guess *independently*, their average guesses will be pretty good, far more accurate than a *correlated* estimate.

Many studies show that people work best alone, but combining their efforts yields the best results. Brainstorming is most effective when everyone writes down their ideas without talking to each other. The best software is written by individuals composing their own components; the success of the Manhattan Project may have emerged from the component-wise secrecy of development.

Maybe we have hive-like properties. Maybe we interact in a way that groups people together in conditions just right for cultural revolutions. Maybe the individuals themselves don't matter at all, just the confluence, the critical thought mass.

But are we really a hive? Why are you asking me? We should ask a thousand people, not let them talk to each other, and average their answers.

7.3 VALUE

When you go shopping, the objects for sale come with price tags.

Prices are set by a cultural expression of value, the giant feedback loop that is an economy. The value of something is the combination of the supply of that thing, the demand for it, the supply of the stuff that the thing is made of, and the demand for that stuff, and so on down the spiral.

The word "demand" might be a capsule for never-ending neuroses. For example, people have decided that gold has intrinsic value. Gold has some useful features: It's a great conductor of both heat and electricity, and it doesn't tarnish. These properties make it terrific for use in technology. Gold cables, contacts, and circuits are all superior to copper or aluminum. But we've also decided that gold has value because it's shiny, yellow, and rare!

Shiny and yellow and rare!

The entire amount of gold mined on Earth fits into about a twenty-five meter cube. Any dude with that amount of bling is independently wealthy—as long as everyone else agrees that gold has value. So much for independence.

Figure 19: Scale drawing of the entire volume of gold so far mined.

I think money serves as the perfect example of the fragility of culture's foundation. If I suggested that we print small sheets of paper and cast little discs of cheap metal, and then tell people that they're valuable, do you think people would spend their entire working lives trying to obtain this currency, this cash?

7.3.1 The creator and the beholder

To say that beauty is in the eye of the beholder is to say that value is subjective.

We have different values, you and me, but if you're hungry, happy, or sad, I know how you feel. Empathy between the creator and the beholder creates the common ground that leads to value. Instead of calling them mirror neurons, maybe we should call them money neurons.

Picture the *Mona Lisa*; when you think of this painting, a network of associations lights up in your brain. Some of the nodes in that web bring to mind how critics, curators, other artists, and appraisers value this small portrait. Since it's as much an icon as it is a painting, you might find it difficult to separate your personal estimate of its value from your appreciation for artists and critics.

When you look at the painting, your bottom-up processors acquire information about shapes, colors, textures—all the details—and as pieces of that data boil up, you respond physically. Your inner frog and puppy respond to a woman looking back at you across centuries. She's smiling, but it's a wry, knowing smile as though she's onto you. She alters your heart rate, and you perspire under her gaze. Maybe you feel a bit threatened, maybe you're blown away by the vision, maybe you see something in her too, perhaps a hint of guilt; maybe you wonder what she's hiding.

Brilliant creators have the ability to provoke you.

When you look at the Mona Lisa, you and Leonardo da Vinci share feelings. You catch what he meant. You empathize, or you don't.

If an Andromedan shows you a thing and this thing is so foreign, so extraterrestrial, that you have no idea what it means, represents, or does, and if the Andromedan has no way of communicating with you, then the thing has no value. On the other hand, when you pop open a Lagunitas India Pale Ale, pour it into a clear glass, inhale the homicidal hoppiness, and take the golden liquid into your gullet, you're sharing something with Tony Magee. His beer does his talking, but your reaction determines its value.

7.3.2 Engagement and novelty

Engagement is the first step in the creator-beholder feedback loop. For a creator to get the attention of a beholder, she has to balance expectation and novelty. The beholder must recognize, read, or feel the intent of the creator and, whether she likes the work or not, it must at once conform to and violate her expectations. If it only conforms, then the bell won't go off in the beholder's head, and she'll yawn right past it. If it only violates expectations, then the bell will go off, but too loudly, and the beholder will run away.

For meaning to boil into consciousness, there must be novelty— but not too much of it!

A pirate walks into a bar with a ship's steering wheel stuck to the front of his pants. The bartender asks, "Hey, doesn't that hurt?"

The pirate growls, "Arrrgh, it's drivin' me nuts."

Humor balances punch lines on the fulcrum between absurd and tragic.

Willi the comedian takes the stage and tells a story, a garden variety story that could happen to anyone. You mirror a simulation of the story in your head. Your brain recognizes the story's pattern and predicts what will happen next. But then something happens that you don't expect. This surprise raises conscious flags: Pay attention, something's not quite right! And your bottom-up processors scramble around offering up choices of alternative contexts to integrate the story into your expectations. You stop for an instant, and then one or more of those alternatives boils up to consciousness. If more than one alternative percolates up and at least one of them is absurd, you laugh. The more absurd (which is to say, the less it jibes with your expectations), the harder you laugh. If two or more of the alternatives are either absurd or insignificant, you keep laughing.

The tenser the buildup, and the greater the deflation of the built-up expectation, the funnier the joke is. A joke can end in tragedy and still be funny if that tragedy is highly unlikely, but if the absurdity remains a gruesome possibility, only the demented will laugh. If just one alternative pops up and you don't find it absurd or if it closes the story on a sad note, you don't laugh. If no alternatives pop up, you don't get it.

The absurdity of the punch line is the novelty that gives a joke value. Novelty is the difference that makes people take notice. By tying two separate concepts together, value has a fighting chance to erupt, but if the novelty is too much of a stretch, all novelty and no expectation, all shock and no empathy, well, if you have to explain a joke, no one laughs.

The art of humor is the inconsistency of the punch line. How did the comedian introduce novelty? She starts with a story, observation, or situation, and then reaches around her brain—whether the process is conscious or not—hunting for remote associations, absurd, out-of-left-field alternatives to the mundane expectation. Or maybe she starts with the punch line, some ridiculous statement, and searches for a mundane context in which to place that perfect line.

That remote association is lateral thought. The story walks along in a conventional direction, but the punch line forces you into a lateral direction, the conventional notion that only fits if you turn it upside down.

Laughter is more valuable than gold, at least in the sense that every culture values it. It's a positive feedback loop: first you smile, then your smile smiles, then your smiling smile smiles, and so on, until you erupt. If smiling evolved as a way for us to convert an implied threat into an explicit greeting, as in "I was going to threaten you, but I see it's you, so I'm smiling instead," then laughter is a way to announce that everything is okay. As the joke unfolds and the tension rises, we're on guard as though we hear a rustling in the weeds behind us. But then, the punch line comes along and we let loose with the uncontrolled cackling, a jovial "tragedy's not imminent, everything's okay; it's just Butch returning with a hippo."

7.3.3 Our subjectivity has a lot in common

How much we value things, people, or animals varies by whim and whether. We're fickle. Business, art, and science all have examples where failed works later became important.

In 1887, Albert Michelson and Edward Morley performed an experiment to measure the properties of the æther. The æther was thought to be the atmosphere of outer space, and everyone knew it had to be there.

Michelson and Morley assembled an experiment capable of measuring spatial variations with an accuracy of about 0.00000002 inches (5 nanometers), an amazing accomplishment with nineteenth-century technology. The idea was pretty simple. Light should travel faster in the direction of the aether's "luminous wind" than perpendicular to that pseudo-breeze. But their experiments kept coming up negative. Scientists at the time, including Michelson and Morley, believed that they'd failed to find it, and back to the drawing board they went, and failed again. Morley had a nervous breakdown from overwork. Either they were terrible scientists, or the æther didn't exist—but it had to exist, everyone agreed!

Unknown to Michelson and Morley, a young man working in a Swiss patent office had been spending a great deal of time puzzling over light, space, and time. Albert Einstein's special theory of relativity didn't need an æther, and the Michelson-Morley experiment became some of its first supporting evidence. Those experiments are now considered the world's most important failed experiments.

About the same time that Michelson and Morley were failing in science, Claude Monet was failing in art. Well, the parallel isn't that parallel, of course, but the subjective nature of value runs deeper in art than it does in science.

As photographic technology matured, the need for realistic images changed. Why paint a picture when you can take a photo? In 1863, at the juried Salon de Paris exhibition, the old-school realists—the folks whom Kodak would render all but irrelevant—rejected the emerging impressionists' work. A decade later, Monet, together with artists like Renoir, Pissarro, and Cézanne, formed a cooperative, the *Société Anonyme Coopérative des Artistes Peintres, Sculpteurs, Graveurs*, and held their own exhibit in a photographer's gallery. The critics unleashed on the new style, though one critic, in thrashing Monet in particular, coined the term "impressionist" and it stuck.

Is Top 40 music the best? Are bestsellers the finest literature? How about blockbuster movies?

Hold on, you say? Should I use popularity to measure quality?

What other measure is there? We just saw experts in both science and art make huge mistakes.

Van Gogh sold one painting in his life, and he cranked out over two thousand works. What his family didn't throw out with the rubbish now sells for tens of millions of dollars, but the critics trashed his first masterpieces.

Who decides what's good?

In science, good means correct, demonstrably verifiable. Einstein and Feynman were great physicists because the theories they developed predicted phenomena that really happened. Michelson and Morley turned out to be great scientists because they shot down a lame theory.

Art has critics and contests that award the "best artists" to help us decipher what we should value.

Was Thomas Kinkade a great painter because malls all across America sell his works? No other painter could boast his level of retail success, but critics hated him.

Why should we pay attention to critics? You and me, babe, we know what we like. We don't need no stinking critics, right?

But just as no single scientist can perform every experiment, make every observation, reformulate every theory, that is, just as every scientist has to rely on other scientists, neither you nor I have time to read every book, watch every movie, listen to every band, drink every beer—okay, we can make time for that, but for the other things, maybe we need some help.

The creator-beholder feedback loop is tied as tight as any. Our positions and values may all be subjective, but our subjectivity has a lot in common. A critic's job is to find that common subjective value so that we can waste less time on crappy art. Critics serve a worthy purpose, but that doesn't mean we can't continue to loathe them.

7.3.4 Right people, right place, and right time

Physics was finished in 1900. The great classical physicists Ludwig Boltzman, Henri Poincare, Henry Poynting, Lord Rayleigh, and the rest all but declared the field complete. With Newton's gravity having survived the test of time and Maxwell's recent unification of electricity and magnetism, the theory of the physical world had been reduced to five simple equations. Sure, there were a few wrinkles in need of ironing, but the big questions had been answered. Nice work all around!

Two of those wrinkles would explode under the iron within the next few years. First, Max Planck came up with an explanation for what was known as the "ultraviolet catastrophe." The wrinkle came from an old theory's prediction of the light spectrum radiated by black bodies; think of charcoal briquettes in a barbecue. As they heat up, they first glow red, then yellow, white, and blue. Not only did the old theory fail, it predicted high-intensity ultraviolet radiation from even slightly glowing coals. If it were true, you couldn't cook ribs without getting melanoma. Planck's solution predicted that light comes in discrete packets of energy. In calling them "quanta," he discovered quantum physics.

At about the same time, the pipe-smoking guy with the crazy hair in the Swiss patent office ironed out the wrinkle that killed the idea of interstellar æther.

For science to go forward, you need experiments capable of testing theories and theories that make testable predictions. Technology drives experimental progress by enabling ever-more precise measurements, and theory drives technology by providing the understanding necessary to devise new equipment, like a game of leapfrog.

Could it have been a coincidence that the quantum/relativity revolution in physics began in 1900, half a century into the industrial revolution?

You've heard of most of these people: Erwin Schrödinger, Paul Dirac, Lord Ernest Rutherford, Emmy Noether, Werner Heisenberg, Neils Bohr, Richard Feynman—okay, maybe you haven't heard of Emmy Noether, but you should have, and you will hear more in a few pages. Were they truly geniuses? Or were they lucky to be in the right place at the right time? More scientific progress occurred in the next five decades than had occurred in the previous fifty thousand years.

Allan Ginsberg wrote a poem titled "Howl" in 1955. At the time, he and a bunch of people he hung out with called themselves Beat Poets and did readings at an art gallery in San Francisco. Like quantum physics and relativity, "Howl" didn't exactly come out of nowhere. Ginsberg was well-read and wrote in the long-line style of Walt Whitman, so his poem had literary credibility. Lawrence Ferlinghetti, a San Francisco bookseller, published it. The mainstream media thought that "Howl" was obscene and generated such a fuss that the poem was banned and Ferlinghetti was arrested for selling it.

A year after the publication of "Howl," a book written by a friend of Ginsberg, On the Road, by Jack Kerouac, came out. It so happened that the New York Times book reviewer was on vacation. The fill-in reviewer loved On the Road, and said that it was "the most beautifully executed, the clearest and the most important utterance yet made by the generation Kerouac himself named years ago as 'beat,'" and it sold like crazy. The Beat Poets' notoriety grew into a counterculture movement, and thousands of beatniks took their parents' cars on the road to drive to California via Route 66.

Did destiny look down on the circuits of Silicon Valley in 1975, the music of Liverpool in 1960, the poetry and prose of Greenwich Village in 1950, San Francisco's North Beach in 1955, cars in Detroit in 1903, physics, psychology, and art in Vienna in 1900, paintings in

Paris in 1873, and religion in Jerusalem in 33 and decree that they were special? Did fate assemble extraordinary talent in these locations, or did a critical mass of passion at the right time and place fuel the talent-skill feedback loops into revolutions?

Was Allan Ginsberg a visionary? Of course he was. But would he have been a visionary in Kansas City? The odds are that no one there would have helped him publish *Howl*, so probably not. Was Freud or Klimt or Max Planck special? Damn right, but would they have been as special in 1900 Bogota as they were in a Vienna brimming with brilliance, creativity, and free speech? Were the apostles and Jesus special? Apparently they were, but could we distinguish John the Baptist from Jesus of Nazareth without the help of Judas, Mary Magdalene, John, Paul, George, and Luke? Maybe so, maybe not— and I'm not disparaging religion here, other than the George wisecrack, and I'd like credit for deleting the Ringo joke—I'm merely pointing out that something special occurred that distinguished Jesus from the other itinerant rabbis of his time; whether or not that special thing was directed from on high or not is above my pay scale.

So were these folks natural-born geniuses? Or were they in the right place at the right time with the right friends?

Lots of ingredients go into the witch's brew that generates cultural disruption. The specific people are rarely as unique as they seem. Without the right timing and place, the cauldron doesn't make the same soup.

7.3.5 Common sense is neither

Common sense is something that a group of people believes. When something makes sense, we get a satisfying feeling of certainty, but it doesn't mean that we're right, nor does sharing a conviction with others mean that it's true.

What passes for common sense in one culture might not be the same in another. We get most of our beliefs by interacting with people in our own tribes. When we examine a human trait, if we want to understand whether it's true for everyone or just for the people in a specific group, we have to make comparisons. Science demands that those comparisons stand up to the as-close-to-objective-as-we-can-get examination of statistical significance. Statisticians always sound like they're talking in reverse, so I apologize in advance for the next sentence. Statistical significance measures the degree to which an observation is inconsistent with random processes. If an observation can be produced by a random confluence of events, then that observation merits no more attention than a roll of dice. Statisticians have analyzed random processes for centuries. We have the tools to subject claims to objective tests so that we can say something like "the chances of a culture preferring long necks to broad foreheads is consistent with a random fluctuation occurring in 5 percent of similar samples."

Paul Ekman is a psychologist who has performed many cross-cultural studies of facial responses to emotions. Consider pleasure: Something tickles your fancy—literally or figuratively, battery-powered or cerebral—and certain facial muscles react much faster than conscious processes allow. He has accumulated evidence that certain responses are common to every culture; everyone smiles, everyone cries, everyone laughs—he's got a long list of others.

Linguistics has a similar commonality. When describing an injury caused by a sharp object or an injury resulting in a bruise, regardless of which language you speak, you would be able to tell which word, "cut" or "pummel," caused which injury.

But now the trouble begins. Although it takes a quarter of a second to hit the brakes, our facial responses to surprise, disgust, sadness, and anger happen almost ten times faster. We might think that reaction speed measures the amount of wetware processing required and that the less wetware involved, the more universal the response. No such luck. Reaction time is insufficient; we are too plastic!

While the responses can be universal, the causes needn't be. Our motor responses are programmed down to the lowest levels, and culture is one of the most effective programmers around.

We're all likely to be freaked out by a slithering, hissing, fanged object. But when that object is fricasseed, some of us will tighten our lips in disgust and others will salivate.

Here's an example of how comprehension can depend on whom we grew up with. Neurologist and author Robert Burton loves to show these two diagrams; which looks longer?

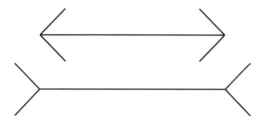

Figure 20: Dr. Burton's favorite piece of art (since I knew that you'd know that both graphics were the same length—I mean, why would anyone ask if they weren't? —I drew the bottom one a bit longer).

The bottom one looks longer, though you know me well enough by now to realize that I wouldn't ask unless they were the same length, right? Well, to folks from Europe and North America, the bottom one looks almost 20 percent longer than the top one, but to the San foragers of the Kalahari Desert, the two appear to be the same length.

To illustrate the fragility of conclusions drawn from tests performed on samples of people from undergraduate programs mostly in the U.S. and Europe, let me present an alternative conclusion to why one graphic appears longer than the other. Since our eyes are so close together, we don't see objects in their full three-dimensional glory unless they're within a few meters. To discern the distance (i.e., the third dimension) of objects far away, we rely on perspective. This figure shows how perspective conveys the illusion of different lengths.

The perspective argument provides a common-sense description for the optical illusion. It gives a cozy chin-stroking feeling of pleasure in our highfalutin, pseudo-intellectual brainpans, doesn't it? But it collapses under the weight of a single contradiction from a rare culture. See, that's all it takes. For a scientific conclusion to be deemed correct, it has to apply in every case. One failure and it's done. After

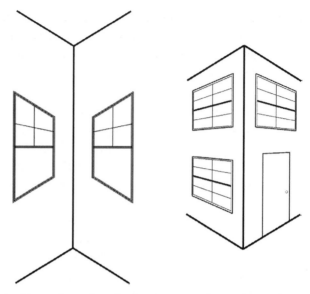

Figure 21: Alternative explanation for why we perceive one figure longer than the other—though this explanation collapses under intercultural examination.

all, the San foragers see in just as many dimensions as everyone else does.

Before wrapping up an idea, calling it done, and congratulating ourselves, scientists have to submit any test performed on humans to a huge cross-cultural population to find out if the effect is universal or culturally derived. It's not the place of science to judge the relative merits of separate cultures—that's best left to Raiders fans. And second, as Miles Dylan says, regardless of subject, "There's more to it than that."

7.4 DOES FRIENDSHIP DEFINE US?

Friendship might be our greatest achievement. How many successful friendships have you had? How many successful love affairs? Compared to romance, friendship is easy.

Our mind-reading ability, resulting from a combination of theory of (other people's) mind(s) and our immediate mirrored responses to the experiences of others, does more than give us empathy; it makes us friendly. We get each other's jokes, sometimes before we even say them out loud. How often do you have an experience that you can't wait to share? "Can't wait" means that you feel an appetite. We are drawn to each other. When we interact with our people, the tribal wells from which we draw our friends, we get a pleasant dose of oxytocin. Humans feel good about hanging with their people, but we don't get that pleasant dose when we interact with other tribes, people whom we think of as separate and different. Trouble has ensued from this trait.

Friendship does more than bring us closer together to fend off the elements; it gives us a mirror in which we see ourselves. It goes like this: Your mirroring system reproduces the experiences of other people in your mind. From those experiences, you construct models of the identities of other people. You then use those models to see yourself as others see you. Now reproduce that feedback loop for everyone you've ever interacted with, and your self-image appears.

Let me rephrase that last bit. You're standing between two mirrors. When you look in one, you see reflections of your reflections of your reflections ad infinitum. Now think of each of those images as your understanding of how another person sees you. Your first reflection is how you think you look to your partner or your best friend. Six or seven reflections further in, you'll find what you look like to colleagues and acquaintances. The really dim reflections far in the distance are how you're seen by people you barely know.

Our unique characters quite likely emerge not from quirky independence, but from our perceptions of what other people think of us.

And the wind carries away the final ashes of my rugged individualism.

Right behind the geometric center of your forehead there's a spot in your brain that lights up when you think of yourself, look in a mirror, or hear your name. It lights up when you think of other people thinking of you, when you decide how to interact with someone else, how you fit into a specific context, and when you suppress your emotions, that is, when you suppress who you "really" are.

If nature put the processors that we use to figure out who we are right behind the geometric centers of our foreheads, then neuroscience has found evidence that we figure out who we are and what we care about, not as rugged individuals controlling our own destinies, but from a feedback loop of our interactions with other people (and presumably animals). The feedback loop goes like this: We conceive our self-images by adding up our perceptions of what other people think. Some people matter more than others, but everyone you interact with has an effect.

If this sounds a bit sketchy, a bit speculative, it should, because it is.

In any case, there's no denying that our identities form to some extent or another from a self-perception that is deeply influenced by our perception of other people's perceptions of us.

7.5 SIGNIFICANCE

Our worlds are fragile.

I've had to surrender my self-image as a rugged individualist. While I still insist that I'm neither a follower nor a leader, I have this impending feeling that, no matter what I do, I'm a cog in some sort of machine, a bee in some sort of hive.

In coming together as teams, we extend our own frog-puppy-Feynman feedback loops to other people. Like everything else we do—sticks and rocks to hammers and chisels to symbols and software—it's another layer of abstraction. Organizations reflect similar structures as our own brains. Oh, it's hardly a one-to-one map, and if it were a metaphor, it would be a poor one, but nothing is tidy in biology.

Like your brilliant, top-down, at least somewhat unified consciousness, the supreme commander assembles the other generals and sends commands down the chain to an infantry of parallel processing privates. The actions of those parallel processors percolate up to higher levels, but everything the supreme commander wills depends on the actions of thousands of privates and their results. It's the rare private who boils up and catches the attention of the top-down commander. The loop is reproduced at every layer of organization.

What gives? Must there be a leader? Are the anarchists wrong about utopia emerging from the natural goodwill of humanity once they've annihilated all authority? This brings us back to hives and my mother.

In writing this chapter, my rugged individualism went AWOL and I had to realize that I'm part of a community. My mother once pointed out that community is the root from which the word communism springs.

Pardon me for using such inflammatory rhetoric, but I can't resist. "Soviets" were meant to be small democratic committees in which each member would have an equal vote in deciding the course of a community, like city councils where everyone in town is a councilperson. If everyone played a part in one or more soviets and the structure repeated across the world, then any remaining central authority would evaporate like my sense of independence. Instead, they got Yuri Andropov.

That's a butchered version, but it's good enough for government work. (See how I put a government wisecrack in a description of a government structure? Yeah, it should have been funny. Maybe the Soviet thing killed it.)

There's no organization chart among bees. The hive emerges from the actions of all of them. The queen is nothing but a well-fed worker. She doesn't have any authority other than that she's the only one getting laid.

Now let's go back to the neocortex, that repeating structure of neural circuits from which consciousness emerges. Sure, different sets of neurons assemble into circuits that perform specific tasks, and you may value one more than another, but anything resembling Eisenhower emerges from all of them acting together. So maybe your brain is a bed-wetting, god-hating Communist, or maybe not. Look, I had to abandon my rugged individuality; give me a break.

The layering of abstraction ferments everything we do together.

Baring your teeth became a welcome gesture that indicated less level of threat. Our inner drug dealers give us a neurotransmitter buzz when we laugh and hang out with our friends so we value friendship and laughter. Emoticons, the little smiley faces you embed in text messages and Facebook's "like" button are abstractions of smiles. Emoticons like :) started out as the exchange of fanged threats among primates.

We want objective value, but it doesn't exist. Value only exists when either a bunch of us, or one person who lots of others either respect or fear—damn Machiavelli—declare it. We make things significant. Either some person, place, thing, or idea is invested with significance, or there isn't any.

That we create significance need not offend your coat of ethics or moral cardigan; it doesn't imply moral relativism. The alone-together feedback loop presents plenty of common social parameters. Provided that you are extra careful in determining which are common to all cultures and which are unique to yours, you're welcome to consider them absolute.

Now that we've seen how value comes from each other, we can dig back into the gray matter and try to make sense of how neurons transmitting action potential spikes from axons to dendrites result in stuff that most of us like, stuff that's "good."

Value might be subjective, but it's not arbitrary.

But first, I give you a sad story that will prime you for my favorite chapter and a really cool section in about two dozen pages. By the way, telling you that I'm priming you primes you even more than if I hadn't mentioned it, because otherwise you'd be all, "I was told there would be neither math nor tears in this class."

8

ART & SCIENCE

SHE LIVES IN A MANY-ROOMED HOUSE ON A HILL, a house where people go to tie up loose ends and fade away. Instead of a driveway or garage, this house has a parking lot. Instead of parents and kids, this house has nurses and old people. And instead of a mailbox, there's a small sign out front that says "rehabilitation," but no one recovers and walks away from this house.

A couple of years ago, when she first moved in, she liked to joke around with the nurses and doctors, but they were too busy to laugh. From her bed, she used to watch the cars that drive by carrying people who don't have the time or take the time to listen to the stories of the folks in this house. She doesn't look out that window so much anymore. The sun shines into her room, but she sits with her hands over her eyes blocking the light.

As a little girl, she played with dolls and trucks. As a young woman she flirted with airmen, soldiers, and then scored herself a sailor. She waited and helped, and one time she even jumped out of an airplane.

I met her the day I was born. She comforted me and took care of me. When me mum went to work, she played with me; she taught me how to kick a ball, and there she was, cheering, when I buried my first goal.

I remember her standing at the head of the table and telling stories. She could make a man wink, a woman cringe, and children bawl with laughter. I remember adults telling stories in hushed tones that I was too young to understand, stories that she stopped with one withering glare.

When I was a boy, I couldn't pronounce her name, but she didn't care about that. Now I'm not even sure if she remembers it. And that's a shame because it rolls off your tongue like water in a stream.

Watching her in that sunny room, you see the nurses go by. Now and then they stop and leave some food or steal some clothes or jewelry that she'll never miss. She doesn't move, just sits in her own darkness.

Do you think she's hiding? Do you think she laughs when the nurses come and go?

She used to laugh so often, a merry laugh that would light up your heart if you could hear it now. She taught me to laugh in the face of crises and smile in the face of tragedy. And she always had an illuminating quip at hand, something she managed to balance on warmth, insight, and irony.

Does she relive the decades? Is that what she does in her place in the dark?

You know how time slips away. Does she cling to the years, the lovers, the children, the cousins, and does she remember me?

I remember a picture over the mantel in her warm, frilly house, a picture of her with the ghost she loved but barely knew.

Sixty-five years ago, she lived on Kings Road. She helped the wounded and she cleared the rubble while her young man sailed across the Channel with her picture next to his heart.

She woke up this morning and said his name. In that instant, the clouds cleared and she remembered that he never came back across that channel. Now she sits without a sound, without motion, and no one knows what happens in her mind. No one knows if anything goes on in there at all. She has so much in her life to relive, to wonder about—the way children look into the future and wonder where they'll land; does she wonder where she flew?

She closes her eyes again and I wonder if she's gone to hide.

A nurse comes in with ice cream because it's cold and sweet and easy to eat and says, "Here you go, Valerie." She says it with care, but it's different from the name she used yesterday, Victoria, I think it was, and Verona or Virginia the day before and Violet last week.

Her eyes flutter at the name, and it comes back to me.

I remember the boy I was, going to her door and mispronouncing her name. I remember the look on her face. That sparkle in her eye when she took my hand and said, "You can call me anything you like, but my name is Veronica."

8.1 THE GOOD, THE BAD, AND THE VALUABLE

So far, at this point in each chapter, I've conveyed to you how the opening story indicates where the chapter is headed. I'm not doing that this time, other than to tell you that the story of Veronica is mostly fiction. What's not fiction is about someone else's grandmother, not mine. You'll see whose in a few minutes, and you'll be psyched.

This is my favorite chapter because we're finally going to start pulling concepts together into tools that we can actually put to use.

8.2 IN IT FOR THE BUZZ

We tend to think of science and art as widely separate fields. Some people might even think of them as opposites—though I suspect those folks have little experience doing either. To understand how science and art feed each other, we need to look at what brings value to the fields, how they're performed, and what their goals are, but first, let's consider the people.

Artists and scientists have a lot in common. As highly educated people, scientists tend to appreciate the classics in art, literature, and music. Artists, working with color and sound and materials, employ scientific analysis in the daily process of making art.

There's no question that science is better funded than art, but the tiny fraction of well-paid artists brings home far greater riches than the highest-paid scientists—after all, the highest-paid university faculty are football coaches. On the other hand, if you pick a random scientist and a random artist, odds are the scientist makes a six-figure salary and the artist a five-figure salary. A scientist grinding away in a lab, digging through data, searching for a discovery, or struggling with equations to assemble a theory can double her salary in a month by bailing out of research and signing on with industry.

A struggling artist, whether cranking out novels, paintings, sculpture, or playing gigs at bars and coffee shops, can easily make more money by getting a "real" job. Indeed, few of the people who think of themselves as artists actually file their taxes as artists.

Artists and scientists do what they do for the buzz.

When you stumble onto something that no one else has seen before, you get a jolt of excitement, joy, satisfaction, elation, and even fear. After all, if you make a mistake, your so-called discovery will reveal it to everyone you respect. Creating a work that you know to the depths of your being will alter people's perspectives or move them to laughter and tears, outrage and contentment, brings the same buzz of joy, satisfaction, elation, and, yes, fear—because no one experiences self-doubt like artists experience self-doubt.

8.2.1 The glorious hopelessness of art and science

Here's my favorite definition of art: the distillation of pure experience. What do you think pure experience even means? It sounds to me like the rush of being alive in the moment, truly experiencing existence, a feeling that you might never achieve but can always get close to. When an artist creates a masterpiece, he imposes his own experience of the world in all its meaning and feeling, culture and politics, oppression and exultation, glory and despair on us, the beholders. Artists insert us into different subjective realities, in one way or another, to help us understand what it's like, whatever "it" may be. Sharing one person's raw subjectivity with another is, of course, impossible. That artists pursue the impossible is in itself beautifully artistic.

On the other hand, scientists pursue objective descriptions of impersonal reality that should make sense to any sufficiently capable and curious being—human, alien, or beast. Scientists insist that their descriptions and predictions of nature's phenomena be independent of their personal viewpoints. Galileo's formulation of relativity, identical to Newton's, provided equations for assuring that we could switch reference frames without altering the theory. Einstein's relativity does the same thing, but with the caveat that the speed of light in a vacuum must have the same value, regardless of the point of view of the observer.

Scientific results must be independent of the moods of the scientists, right?

Well, no, not quite. Science begins and ends with feeling, just as much as art does.

One of the keystone discoveries so far uncovered by neuroscience, a foundational observation that I'm confident will survive with only fine-tuned modifications as the field stabilizes, is that we don't understand anything without feelings. Before we can realize our own understanding, we have to get the feeling of knowing.

The feeling of knowing drives a scientist on the path to discovery, but it also compels artists to push harder in their search for the perfect metaphor, whether in sound, on canvas, or in stone.

That scientists and artists both pursue impossible goals—pure objectivity on one hand and pure subjectivity on the other—carries a divine justice or a melancholy hopelessness, depending on your mood. As hard as they try to transcend their limits, artists and scientists are just blood-pumping, milk-nurtured, air-breathing, laughing-crying mammals, not so many steps up the ladder from the dogs lying at their feet or the cats scratching their furniture.

Scientists have proven that true objectivity is impossible because the experimentalist can never be removed from the experiment. Heisenberg's uncertainty principle gives a precise, dare I call it objective, measure of the minimum possible level of subjectivity. Isn't it just like science to be so objective about its subjectivity? Those scientists are so cute.

Art has nothing like Heisenberg's uncertainty principle. Artists will fly ever closer to the flame, forever distilling meaning into feeling and sharing it in more ways, despite their absolute, primal understanding that they can never make the perfect connection.

Quite appropriate epitaphs for each, don't you think?

Figure 22: (a) The scientist and (b) the artist.

8.3 NEUROAESTHETICS IN ART AND SCIENCE: RAMACHANDRAN'S RULES

Along with neuroeconomics, neuromarketing, neurowrestling, and neurophilandering, neuroaesthetics is an emerging field that claims to be able to cite specific features of art that render it popular or perhaps even good—in the sense of "subjective, sure, but 'good' to every subjective human."

Neuroaesthetics sets out to determine a set of guiding principles to understand how and why, though not what, art pleases people. Trying to figure out what makes a masterpiece or a bestseller or a top-of-the-charts hit is nothing new. One could even call it the siren's wail of record executives and publishers. Gallery owners seem a bit above the fray.

V. S. Ramachandran, a professor at my alma mater, the University of California, San Diego, and one of my favorite neuroscience authors, has composed a set of criteria accompanied by neuroscience-based explanations for why some metaphors explode with the clarity of the Hope Diamond while others are peanut butter sandwiches that take too much chewing to get to the point.

Don't concern yourself about artistic beauty being reduced to a set of rules that Madison Avenue can use to "create" masterpieces in sweatshops. Worked out to its logical conclusion, neuroaesthetics applied to marketing would undo itself. The role that novelty plays in value requires scarcity, so any success in mass-producing breakout art would be short-lived. It's sort of an economic version of Heisenberg's uncertainty principle: The instant that someone develops a perfect system for predicting what sells, the market self-corrects in a way that ruins the system.

That said, it's perfectly reasonable to peek under the hood and try to glean common elements of successful art in terms of brain architecture and response—be it paintings, sculpture, music, literature, craft beer, whatever. To this end, let's work through Ramachandran's nine laws of aesthetics. Dr. Ramachandran cheerfully agrees that some of his proposed laws seem to contradict each other and are redundant in some ways. Rather than defend these deficiencies, he suggests that we have to start somewhere. I'm down with that.

Instead of calling them laws, let's call them rules; laws should be reserved for the inviolate laws of nature. Rules, on the other hand, are made to be broken.

Ramachandran started from the Sanskrit word *rasa*, which means something along the lines of "capturing an essence in order to evoke a specific response." The secret to deriving an aesthetic buzz by applying Ramachandran's rules requires balance in the push and pull of very nearly contradictory concepts.

8.3.1 Ramachandran's rule of grouping—dissonance to consonance

Common themes within a work percolate patterns, clues of what the work is about, without screaming in your face. In paintings, you'll find the same color repeated here and there; melodies are built on a riff that's repeated at different scales with different emphasis; themes infuse depth into literature and enforce concepts in popular science. Visually, groupings settle the eye, provide regularity, and build up from behind the scenes into the whole.

Consider the pieces of a really easy puzzle.

Figure 23: Incoherent drawing.

As you look at the pieces, your visual processors check each one independently. Your left brain compares the pieces, searching the edges to determine how they attach to each other. Your right brain is annoyed by the dissonance and automatically backs off to ponder the whole. Signals relay across the left-right divide as though debating the prominence of the pieces versus the whole. Action potentials fire almost at random between your senses and symbol processors until the instant when you recognize the whole. In that instant, they begin firing in a coherent, synchronous resonance, and you see how the pieces come together.

The pleasant sensation when you decipher a puzzle comes from the transition between random and coherent neural activity, that is, from dissonance to consonance.

Grouping comes from our fine-tuned ability to recognize patterns even when they are hidden; that is, to see through camouflage. Since that ability allows us to find apples in trees, spot hidden saber-toothed tigers looming behind boulders, and recognize talking points from politicians of the opposite stripe, it generates satisfaction. Just as with everything else humans do, we get the same buzz from more abstract grouping: by using metaphors that follow common themes in literature; similar, carefully positioned colors in art, fashion, and design; and melodies that expand the complexity of a riff. Creators draw the beholder to certain features of images, structures, or songs; the more complex the pattern, the greater the satisfaction—as long as we can make the transition from dissonance to consonance.

You can see the risks that artists take by grouping complex patterns in a work. The juice in literature comes from putting the reader into the experience of characters, and that juice gets even sweeter as the author backs off and lets the reader interpret the world presented, solve its problems, and decipher its mysteries—but if the work isn't clear and the reader has to pause and go back pages to figure it out, they're likely to set the book aside. Too much complexity, and it collapses like a lead zeppelin; get it just right, and it soars like Led Zeppelin.

Now let's look at Ramachandran's law of grouping in the context of science.

Figure 24: Coherent drawing

Science begins with assumptions. Rather than fret over whether an assumption is reasonable, scientists move forward knowing that some of their assumptions will not hold, and they'll have to deal with it. That's okay, though; they like to deal with things. Maybe the best scientific example of grouping is the periodic table of the elements. More than a hundred years before quantum theory explained why certain elements have similar behaviors—like carbon and silicon, neon and argon, silver and gold—alchemists and early chemists grouped the elements by their similarities. The patterns within the groups and subgroups aided the development of atomic theory even as atomic theory explained the origin of the common themes.

In the first half of the twentieth century, nuclear physics experiments produced hundreds of particles. Theorists used the mathematics of group theory to provide order to the so-called particle zoo. Making use of these patterns led to the quark model almost a decade before quarks were discovered. I say this with an air of celebration—and how could I pass up using group theory as an example of grouping?—but in the back of my mind, I wonder how our prejudice for things that fit in groups might be directing what we do and don't discover.

8.3.2 Ramachandran's rule of peak shift—exaggeration

We like a twist in our martinis. We like pushup bras. We like big muscles. We like tight jeans. We like extra emphasis on the things we like. We season food to get as much taste as we can. We apply perfume. We attach shiny metals and glittering stones to our bodies, sometimes at the cost of cutting our very skin! We like beer, of course, but we also like scotch. We decided that gold, in all its untarnishable shininess, would be our symbol of value, the soft, malleable, rare, and most metallic of metals.

We seem prone to enjoy a bit of excess: excess in all things, but not excess in all details.

Peak shift excites our inner puppies, making it easier for our inner Feynmans to latch onto the features we like. Overemphasizing certain facets of an object fires up our internal models of those objects and gives them motion and reality.

Every color we see is a combination of the three primitive colors our eyes detect. Peak shift emphasizes the primitives, the fundamentals, the magic parts, the aspects of the thing that give it its thingness. When you see the peak, you can figure out the rest. Peaks are primitives.

Abstract art separates the peak from the object itself. Mathematics separates the peak of a natural principle from reality.

Ramachandran's laws of neuroaesthetics are a picture-in-a-picture example of peak shift. When these nine rules have been reduced to the minimum number of coordinates that explain all of aesthetics—okay, IF these nine rules turn out to be on the right track, and IF we eventually discover aesthetics' red-, green-, and blue-like primitives—then those coordinates themselves will be the aesthetic peaks of aesthetics.

It's not just people, either. Nikolas Tinbergen did a bunch of experiments with seagulls in the 1950s. First, he discovered that hungry seagull chicks focus on a little red dot on their mothers' beaks. When a chick pecks at mom's dot, she feeds it. So Dr. Tinbergen made a little puppet with a yellow beak and a red dot. The chicks pecked, and he fed them. Then he switched from a beak puppet to a stick with a red dot.

The chicks pecked the dot, and he fed them. He made the dot bigger, much bigger than the dot any seagull mother would ever have, and the chicks became very excited, pecking away like it was seagull Thanksgiving. Then he went for the peak. Instead of a dot, he put three red stripes on the stick. Even though it looked nothing like a seagull beak, the chicks went crazy. Dr. Tinbergen found the peak, the seagull broad shoulders, the seagull cleavage, seagull candles and champagne. The seagull chicks got the munchies, and Tinbergen won a Nobel Prize.

Science is built on peak shift. The entire goal of physics is to determine the bottom line, the primordial rules that dictate how the universe works. Newton's laws are an abstract peak of motion.

8.3.3 Ramachandran's rule of contrast—boundaries

Our visual processors seek boundaries first.

The brighter the boundary, the faster we can recognize the pattern, and the more easily that pattern boils up into consciousness. When an author switches from a tranquil scene to an action-packed one, he makes an abrupt shift from long, metaphor-heavy sentences close to a character's point of view to simple, short, sharp sentences that let the action tell the story. Arguments rely on contrasting pros and cons. The universe has matter and antimatter, and the fact that there's so much more matter than antimatter drives physicists nuts.

Dark orange against a muddy red background looks just as orange as bright orange against a bright red background, but that dark orange would look brighter and better against a blue background.

Some pairs of colors go nicely together. Color-value pairs, like yellow and purple, red and green, orange and blue, and silver and black convey day and night, apple and tree, flowers and sky, and just win, baby! They accentuate each other. Such colors capitalize on the origin of our color-detector wetware. Natural selection made red and green go nicely together so food would look good, not for Christmas decorations.

In music, chords are combinations of separate notes that go nicely together. Sets of three to six different notes combine in pleasing ways, similar to the way colors pair up. Combinations of different notes cause different audible experiences. Two close-together notes create beats at a frequency given by the difference of the frequencies of the neighboring notes. Most cultures find anharmonic beats annoying. If the notes composing a chord have frequencies that are far-enough apart that our frequency-detecting cochlea can't detect the beat frequencies, then those combinations tend to come together nicely in a consonant sum. Musicians manipulate their audiences by grouping pleasant and unpleasant sounds to evoke certain responses.

When the rule of grouping means grouping in a broad (and not necessarily neighboring) sense, contrast emphasizes two neighboring characteristics. Artists of every type learn how to use contrast to focus your attention where they want it.

In science, contrast leads to discovery. Signals tend to be buried in noise. Of course, one boy's noise is another girl's signal, but the trick to finding something new is looking at a set of data in a way that gives maximum contrast. Scientists and engineers design equipment to provide the greatest contrast possible between what they want to see, things they don't yet understand, and what they don't care about. Biologists use dyes to distinguish cellular structures. We switched from analog signaling to digital for many reasons, but the biggest reason was contrast. Digital signals impose a step above the noise.

8.3.4 Ramachandran's rule of isolation—heuristics and approximation

A simple sketch, a bare outline, a single brushstroke, one tell-tale note, and a single character overcome by a single emotion all demand attention and make powerful, long-lasting impressions.

To get your attention, an artist has to give your brain something that's either unexpected, so it boils up from your parallel processors, or strikes a note so clear that you can understand the whole without assembling it from its parts. Isolating features of a work draws the beholder's attention and simplifies the point.

Simple, isolated objects resonate because they're easily matched to our stash of recognizable patterns and, because they're so easy to latch onto, they feel louder, brighter, and more archetypical without actually being louder, brighter, or more archetypical.

While Ramachandran's rule of peak shift relies on exaggeration, isolation relies on simplicity.

Understanding the universe is difficult because there's so damn much going on. Reductionism is a form of isolation. By isolating components of a system, we have a fighting chance to understand complicated systems. What's more, when we really understand something, that is, when we have a complete mathematical description that unfailingly predicts everything that a system does, we still need a way to really understand it conceptually. I know how stupid that sounds, but whatever truth there is to a physical theory is in the mathematical prediction, and sometimes the translation to language, to a concept, leaves crucial details behind.

Isolation provides the powerful tools of hand-waved descriptions, back-of-the envelope calculations, and rules of thumb, heuristic descriptions that help us internalize a complex theory into a satisfying concept. Once we have the concept, we can develop intuition for how things work. Without isolation, a mathematical theory doesn't provide the satisfaction of understanding, the feeling of knowing that is, after all, why scientists play in their respective sandboxes in the first place.

8.3.5 Ramachandran's rule of peekaboo—bait

Peekaboo is another way to get someone's attention, this time by understatement. It's such a powerful concept that you'll grasp it in one word: striptease.

The world's great theatres have no microphones, amplifiers, or speakers; instead, they have wonderful acoustics. Good acoustics don't make the sound louder; they make the sound clearer. Storytellers and stage directors understand the value of soft, low-volume speech that forces the audience to pay extra close attention. When a simple, subtle puzzle is embedded in art, a fragment of a guitar riff hidden in a rhythm, a swirl of yellow in a tree trunk or pond, a quirky minor character or clue in a novel, the beholder is sucked right in.

Novelists create suspense by suspending the story and withholding information to draw your attention, sometimes without your even knowing it. As the saying goes: Make 'em laugh, make 'em cry, but make 'em wait.

When baited, we look closer, and that means we're aroused.

Unlike isolation or contrast, the peekaboo rule acquires your attention by hiding the goods and engaging your participation in the song, story, painting, or structure. The extra attention requires some work on your part, an investment, and when you invest in something, you feel like you need to own it.

Isolation draws your attention, but peekaboo entices you with hints to look closer. Isolation gives immediate top-down gratification when you "get it." Peekaboo engages your bottom-up parallel processors by hinting at something, creating just enough dissonance to draw you in, but not so much that you're confused. Isolation fails if you don't get it, but peekaboo is even more effective. Brain scans have shown that anxiety is greater when we're not conscious of its cause. The lingering anxious doubt plays right into artists' hands.

Scientists take pride in their ability to figure stuff out with ever-greater subtlety and finesse. The three-volume set of lectures that Richard Feynman gave to his freshman physics class at CalTech in 1962 are the bestselling, most loved physics texts in history. He explained things in clear and simple ways but without spoon-feeding the reader the details; Feynman left plenty for the reader to figure out on her own.

8.3.6 Ramachandran's rule of abhorrence of coincidence—bullshit meter

Your brain combs through the incoming stream for patterns and, when you find one, your bullshit detector is primed for anything suspicious. Our ancestors spent lots of time among forests, hills, and tall grasses looking for food and avoiding predators. Predators want us to feel comfortable, fat, and lazy—off-guard. So when we come upon something that seems too good to be true, like a still, clear pond in the middle of an empty clearing, we get suspicious. After all, those of us who walked right into traps never got laid, so we survivors have well-primed bullshit meters.

A painting or sculpture that offers a unique rather than seemingly common or random viewpoint must somehow rationalize that special orientation by intimating extra context, or it just looks fake and contrived. In *Following the Equator*, Mark Twain said, "Truth is stranger than fiction . . . because fiction is obliged to stick to possibilities. Truth isn't." Remarkable coincidences are acceptable in memoirs but not in novels.

It's no different in science. When things fit together too nicely, we get suspicious, and we get to work.

Physics is plagued by "naturalness" and "fine-tuning" problems. Einstein's cosmological constant has exasperated physicists for almost sixty years. It seemed like the cosmological constant was zero with an insane level of precision, a level of precision that bothered physicists. Zero meant that the universe was flat, which was annoying; let it expand in all its glory eternally or give up and collapse eventually, but straddle the teeter-totter in a perpetually flat, static tedium? Yuck. In the late 1990s, the first evidence appeared for "dark energy," which required that the cosmological constant be a positive number, an expanding universe. No one knows the source of dark energy, and results continue to accumulate that reinforce a positive cosmological constant. We can safely assume that cosmologists will continue in a state of disagreeable moodiness until they solve the puzzle.

Coincidence causes dissonance between your delusional left brain and your overbearing right brain. Your left brain is perfectly happy with a coincidence—it doesn't even have to think! But your judgmental right brain doesn't trust it. When the two halves of your own brain don't get along, you can't relax. Coincidences suck.

8.3.7 Ramachandran's rules of orderliness and symmetry

Ramachandran distinguishes between orderliness and symmetry as separate rules of aesthetics. I'm not comfortable dicing the tomato into such narrow pieces. The seeds get everywhere. Symmetry seems like a special case of orderliness, so let's consider them together.

Sensations that fit tidily within our expectations provide rhythm. Rhythm doesn't wake us up; it relaxes us.

Here's a silly trick to play on your significant other when you're asked to tidy up or put your stuff in that mythical place referred to as "where it belongs." Don't pick anything up; just rotate it so that it's parallel or perpendicular to the other stuff in the room. A cluttered table, desk, or hearth, will appear tidy even though it has just as much crap on it as before.

Any piece of art—rich music, a textured novel or poem—requires a background. Those backgrounds provide the setting for grouping common themes, a place to isolate features or to shift peaks, where contrasts can emerge and puzzles can hide. We can't pay attention to everything, but we require context, and contexts that aren't orderly require too much attention. Everything that provides the background needs to fall into the background. It's why we hate jazz. Seriously? Even with brushes instead of drumsticks?

As I was saying, it all boils down to predictability. Since the flow of your reality is predicated on how you predict the future from the past, "good" art interrupts our rhythm with a purpose. The regularity of a melody soothes the soul, cleanliness is ethereal, and a steady backbeat converts jazz into rock.

People associate beauty with symmetry. Ramachandran explains this phenomenon by pointing out that we are symmetric and the animals we eat, as well as those who would eat us, are also symmetric, so we're naturally selected to take note of things with bilateral symmetry. Plus, broken symmetry can indicate the presence of disease, and disease is not attractive. Maybe nature uses broken symmetries in her self-portrait to draw our attention, to tease us.

In art, symmetry provides a way to bury artifacts and thereby enrich context. Similarly, carefully broken symmetry pulls your attention to where the artist wants it.

The rules of orderliness and symmetry go a bit over the top in science, indicating that the lab-coated might be fastidious.

Physicists demand symmetry at ever-higher levels of abstraction. You've heard of superstring theories that might someday lead to a theory of everything. Well, superstring theories are built on an abstract concept of symmetry. The first evidence for superstrings would be the discovery of super-symmetry.

The scientific method is predicated on Newton's first rule of reason, also called Occam's razor, a giant pragmatic prejudice: When presented with more than one description of a phenomenon, we assume that the simplest description is closest to the truth. That is, we use the theory built on a foundation of the fewest, most straightforward assumptions until it breaks down. We prefer tidy, elegant theories at the expense of cumbersome, complicated theories.

Science has worked pretty well, but I wonder if our prejudice in favor of simplicity might cause us to gloss over messy phenomena. Here's a particle physics example: The big money is spent on high-energy experiments capable of making fundamental discoveries that try to organize our understanding of the constituents of matter and energy. In the process, we've left behind lots of complicated systems as though we're not interested.

Grouping the particles formed in nuclear reactions led to the quark model, which led to the discovery of quarks; the up, down, and strange quarks were first. After those three, the hunt was on for more. We plowed ahead and discovered the charm quark in 1974, the bottom quark in 1977, and the top quark in 1994. During that twenty-year span, we didn't put nearly as much effort into understanding the grimy details of how the first two quarks, up and down, form neutrons and protons and how those bind together in atomic nuclei.

I'm not arguing that physics should abandon pursuit of the keystones of nature; I'm just wondering if our prejudice in favor of puzzles with tidy solutions holds us back as much as our appreciation for tidy grouping draws us forward.

8.3.8 Ramachandran's rule of metaphor

If this thing starts snowballing, it could really catch fire—some metaphors work better than others.

Descriptions that use adjectives and adverbs portray a scene more accurately than a metaphor, but a well-wrought metaphor does a much better job at conveying mood, tension, and color, along with whatever detail the author's sharing. Which do you think makes the point better: "my daughter's hair is a sort of reddish, dark brown" or "if the bark of a two thousand year-old redwood tree could be spun into silk, it would be the color of Heather's hair."

Candles make awesome metaphors for life, death, memory, and our association with the past: "a candle burning bright," "a flame just extinguished," or "the wax of his candle has nearly run out."

Modern sculpture and abstraction of form are nothing but metaphors.

In music, the tempo, bass-treble mix, complexity of melody, harmony, and rhythm combine in a complex auditory metaphor to relate feelings, scenes, and experiences from musicians to listeners. The long, intermittent riffs of the blues convey melancholy. Rapid, high-pitched punk melodies translate into raw, euphoric energy. Heavy metal chords put the oomph in a headbanger's heart. Yet none of these sounds has anything to do with what they convey, or do they?

Ramachandran argues that metaphor generates a synesthetic effect, crosstalk between different senses. Metaphors use one sense to describe another. Painting the town red, cranking up a color, tasting life's bitterness excite neurons in those senses. When the processing centers for the senses used in the metaphor are physically close to the processing center for the sense or feeling being conveyed, you get effective metaphors. If they're too far away, you get confusion or puns.

Metaphors are at once lower and higher levels of communication.

In chapter 6, we talked about synesthesia as a literal example of lateral thought. When they work, metaphors relate separate processors, tying tactile, nasal, auditory, visual, and tasty imagery together with emotion in a direct connection that either reduces or eliminates the need for words.

"That ship has sailed" generates an image of opportunity passing over the horizon, into the sunset, and out of reach. What opportunity? Any. For Johnny, playing the guitar is as easy as ringing a bell.

We use metaphors in science to make sense of how stuff works. Ribosomes are the components of cells that synthesize proteins by encoding the genetic recipe of amino acids in the right order. I know this because, over thirty years ago, my biology professor described them as tiny heads on cassette recorders. You might ask, what's a cassette? And I might answer, analog memory technology based on thin reels of magnetic tape. To which you might reply, "And this archaic technology somehow helped you remember how ribosomes synthesize proteins?" And I'd say, "Yes."

Metaphors relate a pattern that is well-worn in your brain, an easily retrieved association, to a similar pattern. Ribosomes reproduce sequences, recording and playing proteins the way cassette recorder heads record and play music. My description of my daughter's hair color stretches analogies by pulling together the textures of tree bark and silk, the grand status of an ancient life form, and the common ground of combing. A candle's flame replicates the tenuous relationship between a flame on a wick and our few decades of awareness.

Doing science means figuring out how things work, but we can only understand things in terms that make sense. And terms that make sense are patterns that we already know. I used the metaphor of river and canyon formation to convey the pros and cons of tightly focused analysis and wide-open creativity in chapter 6.

More than that, in teaching science, we wave our hands around to give heuristic descriptions. We use isolation to pull a concept out of context, make sense of it, and then put it back into context. When the process of making sense involves metaphors, students get it. And we're all students.

The best example of all, maybe ever, is the Feynman diagram.

Before Richard Feynman understood quantum electrodynamics—

which is electricity and magnetism at very small distances—it took weeks, sometimes months of calculations in quantum field theory to predict how electrons interact. Then Feynman drew diagrams of how he pictured the physical processes. Let's stop here for a second, because there's an important metaphor in that last sentence: He pictured the physical processes. To literally picture something, it must either radiate or reflect light in the optical spectrum—right? That's how images get into our eyes, down our optic nerves, and into our heads. Feynman visualized the processes through an extra layer of metaphor and, in the process, performed magic: He provided both a conceptual understanding and a method for speeding up those calculations. He invented Feynman rules.

Here's the simplest Feynman diagrams for the interaction of two electrons.

In these diagrams, time flows from left to right. The two electrons

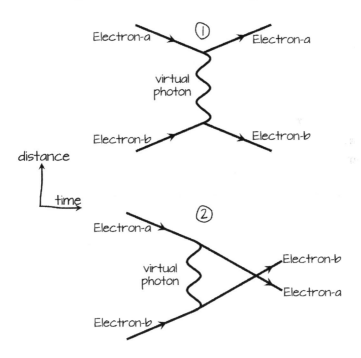

Figure 25: First-order Feynman diagrams for the interaction of two electrons.

are indicated by the solid lines approaching each other, one from the bottom going up and the other from the top going down. Then they exchange a photon, a tiny quantum of light indicated by the wiggly line.

Check out the caption. Remember Starla and the rainbow? How her first-order understanding of light was light/dark, then her second-order understanding was the rainbow spectrum, and so on? There are Feynman diagrams for the second-, third-, and so on–order interactions of electrons too, and the calculation gets more accurate with each term.

8.3.9 Ambiguity

Ambiguity is not one of Ramachandran's rules of neuroaesthetics; we don't require that something be vague to be appealing, though it does play a role in art. Science, on the other hand, can be described as the elimination of ambiguity.

Ramachandran's rules of peak shift, isolation, and peekaboo each recognize the value of balancing contrast and ambiguity in different ways to fire up the beholder's internal simulators. Demanding that the beholder solve the details forces her to complete the work within her own context and life, where she can find meaning.

These two images demand that you make a choice.

Figure 26: (a) We can't really see both the old woman and the young woman simultaneously, but we can switch back and forth; (b) once you see the Dalmatian, you can't unsee it.

In the first case, you can see either an elderly woman or a young woman, you can switch back and forth, but you can't see both simultaneously. In the second, you have to decode the Dalmatian from the dots. Once you see the Dalmatian, you can't unsee it. But once you've solved these images, the ambiguity evaporates, and so does their potential to engage you.

Great art continues to demand your participation, to evoke feeling, to encourage you to keep searching.

8.4 VERONICA

The tension and release, the awe and joy, the power of music provides a perfect example of the melodic interplay of prediction and surprise that gives art the power to move us, literally move us, to dance, to head-bang, to sing, to take up the air guitar and thrash.

Elvis Costello's song "Veronica" has all the necessary components. Not to impose my taste on you; although "Veronica" is on my top-twwenty list of favorite songs, I picked it because the components are easy to decipher, and it's probably not a song you have on heavy rotation. So you're probably not sick of it. Besides, if I pretended to be qualified as a music critic, neither of us could keep a straight face.

As an art form, music precedes all others. We had music before we had speech. Birds and the other mammals appreciate music but not paintings or stories, though birds do have some affection for sculpture.

Here's how it works, then we'll listen to "Veronica."

8.4.1 How music works

Music doesn't have to grab your attention; it soothes your inner beasts whether it boils up to consciousness or not. Take that, all you music producers who demand that songwriters open with a strong hook. Soothing is one thing; it'll put you to sleep, but "Veronica" is the kind of song that moves you to howl at the moon and cry out into the nothingness and everythingness and to both embrace and deplore the sheer finiteness of existence within the infinitude of possibility.

Music is sound, compression of air at frequencies from 20 to 20,000 Hertz—remember that 1 Hz is 1 oscillation per second. The top string on a guitar, that is, the low E string, vibrates at 82 Hz. Translating that raw data into tears requires a lot of processing. The components—volume, pitch, rhythm, melody, harmony, and lyrics—are processed in different brain regions simultaneously and reassembled in a continuous multidimensional train. Your inner puppy understands the emotional tone; it gets happy, sad, bittersweet, or euphoric independent of the lyrics.

Like life itself, a rich melody sets up expectations. You have an idea of what comes next, the chorus, the riff, the bass line. Sequences of small surprises, diversions from the melody, make you soar or blue, and then, like an unfolding triumph or crisis, an abrupt departure grabs your attention. As in life, the triumph gives you a dose of oxytocin and you soar; the crisis sucks the oxytocin up, and melancholy washes over you. Eventually, the melody returns and you settle into a slightly different rhythm; parallel but separated from the original melody by experience.

The melodic sequences and shifts of harmony set up expectations for a particular resolution and then delay or subvert it: relaxation-arousal-tension-relief-relaxation-arousal. It's copacetic, just telepathy from musician to dancer, shredder to headbanger, punk to punk, heartbroken artist to heartbroken beholder. Our brains mirror the artist's intent. At live shows, you can feel the feedback from stage to audience and back and forth. From the air guitarists to the mosh pit, a positive feedback loop builds up and levels off. Performers like Bruce Springsteen are masters at making that connection.

Have you ever noticed how you appreciate a song more after you've heard it a few times? When you know the song, the carefully grouped, orderly, symmetric melody can fill up the background, and its contrast, isolation, and peak shift can direct your attention. Great music draws your instincts, your inner frog, back to the wild, simulating sounds from your prehistoric glory.

So let's crank up a good song.

8.4.2 Elvis Costello's "Veronica"

I think that "Veronica" is better listened to alone because it tells a deeply sad and wonderfully melancholy story of the end we all fear and the journey we all cherish.

"Veronica" was written by Elvis Costello in collaboration with Paul McCartney as an ode to Costello's grandmother. I opened this chapter with my visualization of this song.

I want you to connect to your favorite music site and buy "Veronica" from Elvis Costello's 1989 album *Spike*. If you don't feel like dropping the cash, hie thee to YouTube.com and search for Elvis Costello's "Veronica." There's a music video, but don't watch it! Let's just focus on the music here; you can watch whatever you want on your own time. And no, not the "unplugged" version either; we need our watches synchronized. We need the album version with all the pieces, from Costello's voice to McCartney's bass to that oboe or bassoon, I don't know, maybe it's a keyboard effect.

Listen to the whole song with eyes closed first, and then we'll pay attention to how it works through the lens of Ramachandran's rules.

Ready? Press play.

It starts with a strong melody. Our right brains catch the context within seconds, transmitting expectations across our cortexes. The lyrics come on quick and sound light and fresh with nice, regular ups and downs, a pleasant melody with a rock 'n' roll beat. But as we take in the lyrics, a contradiction grows. Grouped within the melody, the first hint that there's more to it than carefree rock 'n' roll, come the lyrics ". . . what goes on in that place in the dark" and the story takes another turn.

A little oboe (bassoon?) riff peeks over the melody at the end of the first stanza, not quite twenty seconds in: a simple, sad contrast to the essential melody. The next stanza maintains Costello's new-wavey style, consistent with our predictions, but now our right brains are on alert. Toward the end of the second stanza, around twenty-five seconds, a glockenspiel chimes in, an understated, isolated swirl that warns of another shift in context.

Then, half a minute into the song, the chorus erupts in a cry to the stars, the universe, everything and nothing. Costello's high-pitched whining lilt carries the melody to a different place. We can't understand the lyrics, but we don't need them. The wailing contrast to the cheerful rock 'n' roll that led us to this point sucks back oxytocin from our synapses, and melancholy invades our souls. As we cry out and feel the shivers along our spines, maybe a tear-drop falls, more likely on your tenth listen than your first. Then, the difficulty we experienced trying to understand the chorus lyrics gets our attention. Primed and ready, the next lyric you can decode is the answer: Veronica.

Now, short of fifty seconds into the song, we hear another little overlay, a sort of "di-deet-dee" isolation that makes everything a bit softer, a bit easier to take. But then another peak shift comes: The drums rest and you relax as Costello wails, the glockenspiel spiels, and a snare drum awakens us to the moment of peace before: Bang! The backbeat drops us right back into the melody, the grouping. Like reemerging from heartbreak, knowing we have to go on despite the loss, we settle in and go forward. No coincidence here, just back into the river of time, the inescapable continuity of experience.

The next stanza poses vague images of doubt and wolves and wondering, and then that bassoon (oboe?) comes back, with just a little bit of peekaboo to tease us into thinking we're going somewhere. The next stanza, at about 1:10, settles into the narrative, giving images of a woman's life, of her husband going off to war sixty-five years ago. The damned oboe (bassoon?) paints enough melancholy contrast over the melody to reinforce the nostalgic sensation of the finite time-capsule nature of life, but not so much that we fall into the blues. No, he's saving that, the bastard.

Now, not even 1:25 in, the melody takes a dramatic shift. Along with Sir Paul, the drummer switches to half-time, kicking us out of that nostalgic coma. The peak shift warns us that this chapter in Veronica's life does not end well. The next verse, with lyrics that are finally orderly and understandable, confirms it.

Halfway through the song, the melody all but comes to a stop, setting us up for the big contrast that's heralded by two sharp drumbeats. But it's the one missing beat that launches us into that soaring, crying chorus with lyrics we still can't make out. The melancholy washes over us again. It relents a little when we get to her name, Veronica, and then we're back into that tightly grouped rock 'n' roll melody—except, not so fast. It's the same melody, but a bit quieter, a bit older and sadder. With no snare, just the low-bass kick drum, the chorus is different this time. It's like the melody we predicted but isolated enough to pull us out.

Now, at 2:10, we're in the convalescent home with Veronica at the end of her life. Costello backs off from his trademark new-wave crooning, using contrast to draw us in and isolation to put us on alert, not on guard and not in fear, but in anticipation of the inevitable. He groups the metaphor of his softer, quieter voice, with the lyrics "quiet and still."

The nurses and caregivers call her by a name, but not her name, not Veronica. Now, so soft that we wonder if the song is over, he sets us up again for another peak shift. In comes the snare drum, and we're back into bittersweet nostalgia. He contrasts who she is now with who she used to be. We're taken back and remember her sense of humor, what she was like.

Now, when the glockenspiel peeks in, it sounds cheerful in contrast to the sad ride we're on that we know is ending soon. The chorus comes in for the third time and we see it coming. The crying out becomes cathartic, orderly, predictable, sad but in the way the blues makes being sad somehow okay.

All in just over three minutes, holy shit.

8.4.3 Musical resonance

When you pluck a string, you excite a note. That note is amplified by either an amplifier or an acoustic guitar's hollow body (a resonant cavity). The sound comes out and excites the string some more, which then excites the note, and so on—a positive feedback loop that sustains the note. If not for the negative feedback of air resistance and friction, it would sustain forever.

That feeling of being absorbed in a song or carried away in a work of art is the sustain of neural circuits. Your audio processors first associate the notes in a melody and lyrics in a story. A step higher in sophistication, you associate the song with experiences. The more the song affects you and the more associations it produces, the more layers of feeling spread across your brain and the more your heart fills. The sustain primes you. It carries on after the song ends, until the negative feedback of some annoying crap, like bank fees, crushes it.

8.5 ART & SCIENCE

Science and art, like the other this-and-that dichotomies I've been using for chapter titles, feed back to each other. Science requires art; art requires science. Advances in one tend to produce advances in the other, usually with some engineering between them. Photography led to abstract art and the discovery of x-rays. Communicators in television's *Star Trek* influenced the design of cell phones, and Dr. McCoy's diagnosing tricorder preceded the creation of smartphones.

Our affection for music demanded recording and amplification technology. Electrical amplification allowed neurologists to detect the tiny electrical signals that make up the marrow of our thoughts and made guitars as loud as trumpets, relieving us of big bands and introducing four-piece rockers. Ideas, opinions, stories, and religion all led to printing and information technology that periodically disrupts culture with inventions like Gutenberg's press and Berners-Lee's World Wide Web. Kip Thorne, a general relativity theorist at CalTech, helped a computer-generated imagery artist create black holes for the movie *Interstellar* and, in the process, came up with new ways to think about gravity.

Rather than being woven together in an inextricable knot like talent and skill, the practices of science and art have a lot in common, but they have a lot of differences too.

8.5.1 Good work if you can get it

Like any other job, they can be boring.

Let's face it, when Michelangelo carved *David* from a block of marble, he spent most of his time chipping away at stone. The day-to-day grind probably wasn't all that different from the experience of a bricklayer: lots of dust and grime. Van Gogh may have poisoned himself by ingesting lead paint as he chewed on his brushes like a bored third-grader gnawing on a wooden pencil. Discovering the Higgs boson required decades of running cables, soldering electronics, and debugging software, and months puzzling over enticing hints in the data. Musicians spend years writing songs, fine-tuning licks, and then playing them over and over again in recording studios and in front of audiences.

The truth is that the actual performance of art and science looks pretty much the same as most other jobs, except for the buzz. And it has to be that way, or the buzz wouldn't give you a buzz. If you feel the buzz everyday, it goes away.

Behaviorists refer to our ability to adjust to damn near any condition as hedonistic adaptation. Lottery winners fly high for about six months before realizing that money really doesn't buy happiness. Once our wealth surpasses the minimum requirements for food, shelter, and health, happiness is as elusive for billionaires as thousandaires. Prisoners adapt so well to their constraints that some of them never want freedom.

But it's all worth it when a songwriter, poet, or novelist writes down the perfect metaphor, when Johnny stumbles across the perfect riff, when Brandi catches the perfect wave, or when Butch pulls a dead hippo into camp on his wheeled wagon.

When you add it all up, we're nothing but dopamine, oxytocin, and vasopressin junkies, and maybe that's not so bad.

8.6 WE HAVE A LOT OF SUBJECTIVITY IN COMMON

Lateral thought, novelty, and abstraction all play key roles in creativity, but only when other people appreciate the results. In chapter 7, we concluded that people are significance investors, that value is subjective, and it only comes from the significance that we invest. The ultimate goal of artists is to relate their own, purely subjective experiences to you, their audience. The most successful artists don't perform market analyses before working on their next masterpieces. Sure, van Gogh studied everyone and tried everything, but if his primary goal was to please other people, he didn't accomplish it while he was alive.

Within a culture, our similarities outweigh our differences and, when viewed by a Flintstoner from Andromeda, the humans don't just look alike, they seem almost identical. So it shouldn't come as a surprise that, when it comes to what we value and why, we have a lot in common.

We also have a lot in common with other animals. Explanations for why people like music include seduction and the tightening of social bonds through song and dance, and that it's an exaptation. Yelling and screaming started out as warning systems that were easy to refine into singing and joking seduction techniques, so we kept refining them. There are many other descriptions too. Maybe we like music because birds like music. Maybe our music-appreciating wetware came from some ancestor we had in common with birds. Maybe natural selection didn't prune away our ancient music-loving networks. We've still got wetware from our reptilian past, so why not a few algorithms too?

Now that we have an idea of what creativity is and why so many of us can agree that some things are better than others, let's turn to innovation and discovery, two acts built from optimizing our interactions alone and together, meshing creativity and analysis, fine-tuning intelligence and intuition, and making the most of our talents and skills. Our ability to innovate and discover solutions to the problems we face on every scale—as individuals, members of communities, citizens of countries, and inhabitants of Earth—will dictate how long and how well we can survive. This takes me to Emmy Noether, a woman who faced big problems and flourished despite them. If there ever was a rugged individualist, it was Emmy.

9

INNOVATION & DISCOVERY

IN 1882, AMALIE NOETHER WAS BORN IN THE KAISER'S
Germany to a Jewish family. Everyone called her by her middle name
Emmy. A friendly, near-sighted girl, Emmy spoke with a slight lisp
and loved to dance. She showed little academic promise, but she could
solve complex puzzles quickly.

In 1900, after receiving her teaching certificate—an acceptable
intellectual achievement for a properly demur young lady—she chose
to study mathematics. Of course, she was not permitted to enroll
at the university because she was female. The Academic Senate of
the University of Erlangen considered her case but concluded that
"allowing coeducation would overthrow all academic order."

But Emmy went to classes anyway. Since her father taught mathematics at the university, the professors knew her, and most of them let her audit their classes. She worked through the course material without the allure of a degree on the horizon. Then, having completed the program, she was granted a boon. Few of us would think of an opportunity to spend four hours a day taking grueling mathematics examinations as a gift, but Emmy did.

The dawn of the twentieth century brought new liberalism to many institutions and so, having passed the exams, Emmy's application to the graduate program was accepted. In 1907, Emmy Noether was one of the first women in Germany awarded a Ph.D. degree.

The only obvious career path for a mathematician at the time was to continue in academia as a researcher, instructor, and then a professor. The Kaiser's Germany had no high-tech algorithm development or big-data analytics jobs. The only place she could expand mathematical symbolism along ever-more-abstract coordinate axes was from the sanctity of the ivory tower. But again, lacking the crucial y chromosome, Dr. Noether could hardly be considered for a university faculty position.

We don't know how she felt when her head hit these glass ceilings, but her actions demonstrated a determined and undaunted nature. Just as she took classes even though the university rejected her application, she went right ahead and pursued her research. The men she worked with described her as someone who laughed off obstacles, at least outwardly. Perhaps, like Frank Ransom, she wept alone.

At the time, the center of the mathematical universe was at the University of Göttingen. The Göttingen mathematics faculty were impressed by her Ph.D. dissertation (which she once described as "crap"), and she accepted an invitation for an unpaid research position. She taught as a guest lecturer and lived on her small inheritance. Her older brother, fully equipped with that all-important y chromosome, inherited the lion's share of their parents' modest wealth.

As with everything she did, Dr. Noether's teaching style didn't fit accepted norms. Rather than deliver passive lectures to a silent audience, she proposed mathematical questions and invited students to solve them. Soon, Dr. Noether acquired a following of students who would come to be known as "Noether's boys."

In 1916, Emmy Noether derived and proved Noether's theorem, which, I think, ranks with Einstein's relativity and Max Planck's discovery of quantum physics in its impact on scientific progress. Nobel laureate physicist Leon Lederman once referred to it as the physics equivalent of Pythagoras's theorem.

Noether's theorem relates what had been considered simple facts like Newton's laws of motion and the laws of thermodynamics to the geometry of space and time. For example, the first law of thermodynamics, which states that energy is neither created nor destroyed but can only change form—called conservation of energy in the trade—arises from the geometry of time.

When World War I ended and her inheritance was running low, her colleagues at Göttingen, including mathematical superstars David Hilbert, Felix Klein, Herman Minkowski, and Ernst Mach, nominated her for a low-level but paid instructor position. The department of philosophy opposed her: "What will our soldiers think when they return to the university and find that they are required to learn at the feet of a woman?"

To this, her friend and mentor, Professor David Hilbert, replied, "I do not see that the sex of the candidate is an argument against her.... After all, we are a university, not a bathhouse." And so she got the gig.

Dr. Noether spent the rest of her life studying and developing abstract algebra. She's well known within the halls of mathematics and theoretical physics, but did you ever hear of her?

She never married and there's no record of any intimate liaisons, but she certainly had lots of close friends. She didn't care much about appearances, and when her long, unkempt hair broke free of its pins, she let it fall and kept right on discussing mathematics with a well-recorded passion. In every photo I've seen, she's either grinning or laughing. Even in the formal shots, you can see a twinkle in her eye.

Though she wasn't politically active, she was a liberal pacifist in an increasingly aggressive and militant Germany. In the 1930s, some of her students came to class dressed in Nazi Brownshirts. She laughed it off at first, but she was soon one of the first Jewish professors to be fired by the Nazis. In 1933, Albert Einstein convinced the Rockefeller Foundation to match a grant from the Emergency Committee to Aid Displaced German Scholars, and Emmy was granted a one-year instructor position at Bryn Mawr College in Pennsylvania.

The time she spent at Bryn Mawr seems to have been the happiest of her life. But after two years in the U.S., she died of complications from surgery to treat uterine cancer.

9.1 FACING CHALLENGES

Emmy was denied at every turn, but she just kept going, trouncing challenges and breaking down walls. Emmy Noether was a badass. By all accounts, she was also quite happy and felt no bitterness.

Some psychology experiments have correlated happiness with problem-solving ability. Are happy people better problem-solvers, or does solving problems make you happier? I'm going with the egg on this one: Confidence in your ability to meet challenges makes challenges feel less challenging. That confidence starts with the first challenge you conquer and, as we've seen, first impressions have disproportionate influence on our pattern-recognition wetware.

Life is all about challenges.

9.2 MAKING BETTER USE OF OUR BRAINS

Let's build a model for challenges, the quests that we all face. These can be any kind of challenge, pursuit, or desire, that is, a quest for whatever grail you're after. Monet had his lily pads and bridges, Michelson and Morley had the interstellar æther, van Gogh had starry nights, and Einstein had spacetime; everyone's got something.

Before we row into this endeavor, I feel compelled to offer somewhat of a disclaimer. I apologize for not having solved the ultimate question of how humans can achieve perfection. My wife and my dogs will attest that it is an answer of which I am not burdened. Surely you didn't expect the ultimate answer for less than thirty bucks (twenty pounds/twenty-five Euros).

Instead of THE ANSWER, let's try to put everything together into an encompassing concept and dig up some techniques that might help juice the process. You'll think that some of the juicing ideas are stupid (I certainly do), but we're attempting the impossible here. And it really is impossible. If we came up with a recipe for confronting challenge that actually worked, the idea would spread until the nature of human challenge would shift, and the recipe would no longer work—the marketing version of the Heisenberg uncertainty principle. Let's do our best anyway. It would help if you could offer ideas from the other side of this page and whatever future from which you're reading this. Oh well.

I hope that our model will help us each boil up better ideas a bit more often so that we can solve bigger problems, create more valuable things and ideas, raise better people, and bring more peace and harmony to our world—and I'd like a little credit for typing that last bit with a straight face.

Everything we do in this section should scale up from individual efforts to teams, organizations, and all the way up to, dare I say it, entire hives of human endeavor.

9.2.1 The quest

We turn to a young woman who grew up in the outback of Cornwall. Percifal loitered around Camelot until King Arthur noticed her. To get rid of her, Arthur told her to go find a grail. Any old grail would do. Art was actually thinking of a nice coffee mug from Tintagel, but he didn't tell Perci that.

Perci spent her life to this point preparing for her quest without ever knowing it. She went to school, hung out with good kids and bad kids, had a few jobs, got into some trouble, went to school again, and got into more trouble, and so on until she was confronted with a life-altering challenge. She got pretty wound up when the challenge appeared. After all, it seemed impossible: How and where will she find the grail? What if it's too heavy or she's too weak? What if she can't get past the guards? What if this? What if that? At first, her inner puppy just wants to chase something and bark at the problem.

No challenge arrives without stress from the demons of self-doubt.

Eventually, she accepted the challenge and consciously pushed back the stress and anxiety. She distanced herself from the stakes so that she could think clearly. (This step is no mean feat, by the way.) Now able to concentrate, she reduced the problem to pieces that fit into her working memory and commenced her analysis.

Once she broke the problem down, she started coming up with ideas for solutions. She searched for people who could help her. She used the power of crowd-sourcing, but took care to avoid situations where the loudest guy's opinion dominated. She also used the power of internal crowd-sourcing: letting ideas percolate up from her individually-stupid-but-brilliant-as-a-team bottom-up processors. During this stage of the process, she didn't appear to be working.

While defining the problem and recruiting resources requires disciplined, focused attention, great insights rarely occur when we're focusing. Perci may have looked like she was staring into space, daydreaming, going out dancing, wandering around wasting time, but she was actually working with utmost efficiency.

Convinced that Percifal was lollygagging, Arthur resigned himself to drinking from ox horns.

The process of thinking laterally, blending different ideas into all-new concepts, only sporadically resembles what we think of as work. She primed her team to maximum creativity both internally with her bottom-up processors and externally with her assembled colleagues. Trying different perspectives and generating pieces of the solution, she waited, hoping and trusting that she would experience the upsurge of insight.

When the insight finally lit her flame, it came with that wonderful feeling of knowing that the solution had arrived. But most insights are lame; even great ideas come to us half-baked. Evidence from fMRI tests indicates that the "aha!" feeling arrives a fraction of a second before the idea comes to mind.

With the candidate idea on the tip of her consciousness, Perci dove back into focus and set about evaluating it. The king was pleased to see her back at work, though he did look at his watch.

Evaluation means assembling a context and imagining how the idea will work once it is implemented. For the most part, this is the crappy-idea burial ground.

The process of insight à evaluation à insight doesn't so much repeat as continue, like throwing mud against a wall until Perci had a fully baked solution. Having worked it through in her imagination, she knew what tools she needed: physical tools like armor and swords, abstract tools like directions and strategy, and organic tools like knights and horses.

Finally, our heroine set out on her quest.

Now let's take a look at the pattern. In the process, we'll be engaging our bottom-up processors and, when we walk away from these pages, those processors can resonate among themselves and make us all better at whatever we do. That's the plan anyway.

The pattern of meeting a challenge involves both focusing and defocusing.

As citizens of countries that prize hard, focused, and productive work, our education and business structures err on the side of focus, and so do our role models. Coming from this background, when we try to formulate practices to improve our ability to innovate, we're likely to err on the side of defocusing. I'll try not to.

Here's a simplified feedback loop for creativity and innovation. The key piece is the amplification loop of contemplation and distraction.

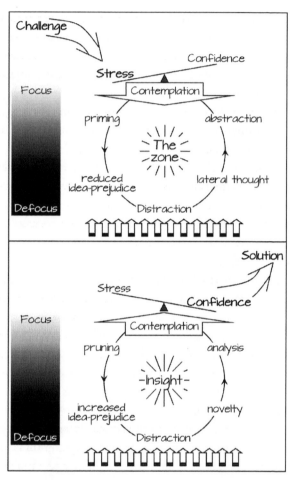

Figure 27: Models for figuring things out. And don't forget to shower.

9.2.2 Stress and focus

Before you can innovate, you need to suffer; Emmy Noether certainly did.

Every challenge, however trivial or grand, begins with a mix of desire and need—a compulsion to achieve, a problem to solve, and the stress that goes along with the need to solve it ASAP. If the problem doesn't boil up, it will never engage you.

You know the feeling you get when you're drawn into an argument? A flash of passion raises your hackles and prepares you for the fight, but just as often, it prevents you from debating effectively. How often do you think of the perfect comeback in the heat of an exchange? For me, it always comes an hour later.

Our ability to abstract visceral, emotion-heavy, and reactive thought into principles and concepts allows us to reason. There's a rub, of course, and it rubs both ways. On the lackadaisical side, if you don't care about something, then you're perfectly capable of analyzing the problem, but you'll never have the passion required to solve it. On the paranoid side, if you care too much, the stress can inhibit you too much to listen to your bottom-up processors, much less perform top-down analysis. The churning dissonance defocuses us and, instead of solutions, the consequences of failure percolate up.

Before we can solve the problem, we need to cool off and focus.

Remember from chapter 5 how the ability to delay gratification turned out to be a better predictor of a kid's future success than her IQ? Being able to delay gratification also may indicate that you have the self-discipline to delay panic. Several low-statistics, difficult-to-control tests have indicated that we might have fixed allowances of self-discipline to spend each day. If so, you should cash some in right now.

Artists who wait around for a cherub-like muse to shoot them full of inspiration don't get a lot of work done. Inspiration isn't a thing; it's a state of being, a mood that you experience when you're in the zone. So the muse must be whatever it takes to get you into the zone.

We talked about the zone in chapter 6. It's not your comfort zone. If your comfort zone is a nice chair, being in the zone is the state of engagement and balance you find at the edge of your seat.

The zone is not a state of relaxation, though relaxation can help you get there. Self-discipline and its disciple, determination, might be enough, but it's also possible to use defocusing techniques to cool off. We'll talk about some techniques in a minute. I'll warn you in advance: I'm going to use the word meditate, though I'll also say head-bang. By blowing off steam and cooling off, we let our inner puppies help by giving us hope and confidence.

When you're in the zone, ideas simmer up, and you're in position to apply them consciously. Picture a quarterback running the two-minute offense (a forward dribbling the ball downfield with the striker forty meters across, sprinting to the net). The zone is intense engagement, including the rush of high-pressure situations with limited time and dubious hope, situations conducive to both letting go and going for it.

The exhilaration of surrendering to the situation in a way that is anything but surrender has always been a part of us. That moment of release as you run from the saber-toothed tiger, sprinting along the cliff above hopelessness, you engage in the instant and start to feel that your plan might just be crazy enough to work.

Now that the immediacy of anxiety is past, it's time to analyze the problem. Now you can use intellectual tools like reduction and abstraction to slice it into pieces that you can contemplate. Remember, your brilliant, top-down, conscious thinker can't hold more than three to ten concepts in working memory. Your top-down thinker may be brilliant, but it's limited.

Analyzing the problem achieves two goals: First, you get a clue of just how hopeless the situation is, but more importantly, you recruit your bottom-up parallel processors for the effort. Where your brilliant, serial, top-down consciousness can't entertain more than a handful of ideas at once, your stupid, parallel, bottom-up processors are, for all practical purposes, unlimited. Taken one by one, they're not very good, but when you put them *all* to work, they'll blow you away.

You may have heard of this New-Age-y thing called "the secret" or "the law of attraction." The idea is that by asking something of the universe, you will attract the answer. Here's its most valid kernel: When you analyze a goal, you engage the power of your whole brain. Your parallel processors work below consciousness and, once attuned, they will notice everything you come across that can help your cause. It's powerful, but it's not a secret; it's an example of priming.

The idea scales up to the team or organization level. Getting everyone engaged distributes the workload. With everyone on the team primed, you have a much wider swath of fertile imagination than you do with an individual, though managing them can be a hassle. Personalities can influence the perceived value of ideas—the echo-chamber effect.

Where do you get your best ideas? In the shower? At the beach? In bed when you wake up in the middle of the night? I'm pretty sure it's *not* while you are at your desk pounding your head against a problem. Why do we even have desks? Workstations should be in shower stalls, not cubicles.

Notice something ironic about the process at this point. Now that you've engaged the full power of your bottom-up processors, you need to be in position to listen to them. Instead of continuing to hack away at a problem, you need to kick back and stop analyzing. It's a counterintuitive irony that we all experience. Software developers have an intimate relationship with this stage. You can grind away for thirty hours straight and feel like you're getting nowhere. Then you go for a walk, and a dozen ideas come bubbling up to the surface. Most of them seem obvious, but none of them came to mind in the heat of analysis.

9.2.3 Defocusing into insight

"Perspective," Miles Dylan once said. "Use it or lose it."

Galileo assembled his telescopes from magnifying lenses by looking through combinations of lenses with differing focal lengths and pointing them up at the night sky. Adding a layer of complexity is all it took. Monet invented impressionist art by changing the focal length of his paintings. Seriously, when you stand up close to an impressionist painting, it just looks like paint; you have to stand back and look not just at but *into* the painting, that is, you have to focus and defocus to fire up your mirroring wetware and get his message.

In retrospect, these innovations seem like small alterations, but they changed everything. Why, then, are such small changes so hard to come by? Have you heard the story of Native Americans who couldn't see Columbus's ships as they sailed toward shore? It goes like this: A bunch of indigenous people are hanging around the beach, hunting crabs, body surfing, spear fishing, playing an early version of volleyball, and weaving baskets; you get the picture. Columbus's three ships sail over the horizon. It takes hours for the ships to make their way to shore. The folks look up from their tasks and out onto the horizon, and even though the ships are right there, getting larger every minute as they approach, the people can't see them. Their eyes take in the light, but since they have no pattern for identifying ships, no concept that anything could possibly approach in this fashion, the ships are so out of context that they might as well be invisible.

The only way this story could be true is if all the Native Americans lacked the right hemispheres of their brains. Sure, the left brain, completely focused on the basket, fish, and volleyball, could ignore the ships, but the right brain would see them and bark like a frightened terrier. Still, the point is that sometimes we can't see something when it's standing, or sailing, right in front of us.

We spend our lives developing our own unique perspectives and, for the most part, along the way, we achieve all we can from that perspective. When something new comes along, we need to break out of the rut. We have to look at things in different ways, from different angles.

Your bottom-up processors constantly throw ideas in the general direction of the target for which you prime them, but the ideas that make it to the surface, the ones that we unconsciously judge to be good, are those that conform to our prejudices. The wetware is automatic. Our pattern-recognizing, categorizing brains, like the mythical people on the beach, can't see past their prejudices to the novelty, and the impending doom of smallpox.

Idea prejudice is the lazy thinking that inhibits lateral thought, and lateral thought is the key to innovation, novelty, and originality.

Lateral thought, as we discussed in chapters 6 and 7, is the process of blending diverse thoughts. Getting a joke is my favorite example—you have to connect the straight lines with the wiggly ones. You might call it converging divergent thoughts, but let's not.

The point is that to make the most of our brains, we need to entertain diverse thoughts, thoughts that we would not entertain unless we consciously primed ourselves.

To reduce our idea prejudice, we have to increase diversity of thought and diversity of viewpoint, which boils down to diversity of experience.

This idea also scales up to the team and organization level. If you already have a science writer, novelist, and high-tech consultant with a background in particle physics who drinks beer and yells obscenities at Oakland Raiders football games, you shouldn't hire me. Bring in someone who can enhance your organization, someone whose skills and background are different from anyone else's skills in your group. The idea is to supplement, not supplant or fortify, but rather complement your staff so that you can get another perspective that can take you to another level.

When you look at job descriptions from human resources departments, it's pretty obvious that companies try to clone the staff they already have. If your entire staff consists of electrical engineers from MIT, hire someone from Reed College—they don't have an electrical engineering program, but they did have Steve Jobs for a while.

One easy way to achieve diversity of thought in a group is to assemble people from diverse cultures. They automatically bring new perspectives to your team even when they have similar educations.

More irony comes from the other kind of prejudice, simple bigotry. Our pattern-recognizing, categorizing, judgmental, lazy-thinking natures can make it difficult to hire or work alongside an alien. Now I'm sure you don't have any personal grudges against silicon-based life-forms, but I think they're weird. That intuitive, gut feeling that the other is somehow off, somehow not quite as it should be, is an ancestral remnant that will reduce your personal effectiveness. It will cost you, personally. There's nothing politically correct or incorrect about wanting to be your absolute best. The simple fact is that idea prejudice and prejudice toward others reduce your ability to do original work, invent, innovate, and create wealth.

So when you find yourself working alongside a silicon-based life-form from Andromeda, you might have to reduce your inhibitions so that you can learn from them. But I do get it. Andromedans are dusty; they scrape their feet and leave sand all over the place; their voices grate like shovels scraping on concrete; and don't get me started about their rock-grinding eating habits. Just try to remember that those guys really know how to get stoned.

If dogs can accept cats into their packs, then surely a Protestant, a Hindu, a Buddhist, a Muslim, and an atheist can come together in a team. They just need time working toward a common goal.

To reduce our inhibitions to the other kind of diversity, diversity of thought, we arrive at meditation. By meditation, I don't necessarily mean sitting on a mountaintop in the lotus position while wearing a robe and sandals—though for most people, that might work pretty well—I mean any activity that opens you up, calms you, and helps you appreciate your world and where you fit into it. For some people, I can attest, reducing idea prejudice can include yelling obscenities at football games, banging your head in the tradition of heavy-metal enthusiasts, running, singing, bicycling, writing, surfing, playing an instrument, or even meditation. For some people, it might mean zoning out to jazz.

9.2.4 Meditation and prejudice

As the Zen master Shunryu Suzuki says in his book, *Beginner's Mind*, "If your mind is empty, it is always ready for anything, it is open to everything. In the beginner's mind there are many possibilities, but in the expert's mind there are few."

I've mentioned Allan Snyder a few times. He's the Aussie shrink who believes that electrical stimulation that reduces inhibitory neurons can unleash your inner savant, crank up your creativity, and unveil talents you had no idea you were carrying around. Snyder's work is controversial, so I don't recommend plugging your head into an outlet just yet. But the concept behind it is not controversial.

When a neuron receives signals, it can do one of three things: emit an excitatory action potential, emit an inhibitory action potential, or do nothing at all. When we're peaked and focused, those neurons are firing like crazy from your top-down consciousness. You're doing what you do well, what you know how to do, what your neurons have trained for all your life. You're also at your most prejudiced. It's the rut we live in, but it's also the rut that pays the bills. It hasn't been such a bad rut, but it can suppress your greatness.

The expert is the river that has carved a canyon; the beginner is the snow falling on the mountaintop.

Defocusing, opening up, settling down (choose your favorite metaphor)—no matter what you call it, in one way or another, it's meditation and we need to make time for it. I know, I don't have time either. The reason that I don't have time is that I spend so much of it focused on challenges, grinding my head against computer screens wasting my time. Maybe I can be more effective in getting my message across by yelling: DEFOCUSING, RELAXING, AND ENJOYING YOURSELF IN THE PRESENT INSTANT WILL MAKE YOU MORE, NOT LESS, PRODUCTIVE!

It makes sense. Sinking into a state of relaxation, absorbing sensory input without analyzing it, concentrating on deep breathing, and taking in just the current instant quiets your thoughts. With no voices yelling in your head, unconscious processors have a better chance of getting your attention.

Dr. Emmy Noether spent lots of time walking around campus in a daze, and she built the foundation for modern physics.

9.2.5 Perspective-altering techniques

The most obvious way to let your imagination run wild is to alter your perspective. Brandi the surfer tends to think that reality is a wave; Johnny sees his life as a riff in reality's song; Butch realizes that life is a great hunt; Starla sees color everywhere; whales "see" by projecting sound and then reconstructing echoes into what we think of as images. By looking at the world through each of these lenses, we can see things that we've never seen before. Pieces come together and enable innovation and discovery.

Language itself can put blinders on us. Asking whether behavior is determined more by nature or nurture, instead of asking how they interact, leads to a simplistic dead end. One way to find a different perspective is to reframe the question.

We've seen that first impressions carry inordinate weight in developing our pattern-recognition wetware. One way to fight this effect is to impose different patterns on a given problem by using analogies. If reality is like a wave, is it a wave in water? A sound wave? Or a politician waving her hand from a passing float in a parade?

Imagine parallels, extensions, themes, relationships, and similarities to other systems. Build metaphors for each part and reassemble them into a new whole. Think of how people in different historic epochs, both past and future, might approach a situation—anything to climb out of the canyon and up to the mountaintop where we have a clear view.

Diagram your quandary. Draw charts and cartoons, maps and schematics, doodles and brain-dumps on paper or whiteboards so you can draw lines to link ideas together and scribble in notes. Then shift your perspective by looking at them upside down and backward—a literal perspective shift. It worked for Feynman and his diagrams.

Another approach, one that's used extensively in physics and one that we've used a few times in this book, is to look at a situation in its extremes. Asymptotic analysis uses extreme cases to see how different parts of a puzzle fit together. All hops, yeast, and water with no malt makes a bitter brew; all malt and no hops brews a dark, sweet, but boring ale. The worst and best situations constrain the possible, making it easier to narrow in on the most likely or best.

Delve into the absurd. Most attempts fail, but something that fails in one instance stays near the surface, ready to boil up as the solution to another problem.

A particularly effective way to gain perspective is to mimic natural selection. Monte Carlo techniques use random numbers to find solutions. Using random processes is a standard technique in computational science not just because it's easy, but because in most cases, it turns out to be more efficient than using considered choices.

Think of it like this: Given a long list of ideas, it's easy to cherry-pick the good ones. So the faster you can generate that list, the faster you can start stroking your chin and evaluating.

In the preamble to chapter 3, the story about the Andromedan who had to predict the forms of life on Earth from nothing but atoms and their positions, I described a Monte Carlo simulation technique. When we don't know anything, trying things at random is as good as we can get. When we do know something, but that knowledge might prejudice us, trying random things that are consistent with the facts can be more effective than rowing down the same old river.

Sometimes the best way to imagine something new is to let loose, let your mind float, deny nothing, spout gibberish, and see what floats up. It might be best to practice this technique in your underground lair rather than seated at a café in town.

9.2.6 Insight comes half-baked

Once insight boils up into consciousness, it has to be evaluated. Evaluation puts us back into fully engaged, focused analysis. Analysis is a search within the valley. The left brain is unleashed to pursue solutions along the cozy corridors of its own canyon of understanding, while the right brain keeps the left brain on task and watches out for falling rocks.

Evaluating an insight requires imagining a reality where the insight comes to life, imagining how it will play out, pruning possibilities into probabilities, looking for holes, contradictions, and paradoxes so that we can either discard a weak idea or assemble the necessary tools to implement a strong one.

Conveniently, we spend each waking moment of our lives evaluating objective reality by imagining subjective reality, dancing along the line between what we perceive as fantasy and what we believe is reality. Every thought of the future—planning, setting goals, even worrying—comes from our imaginations. Just as infants fine-tune their senses through neural pruning, we evaluate insights by imagining how they'll play out, which amounts to pruning them down to ideas that jibe with our expectations of reality.

Once the insight has been baked into a plan, it's time to come up with tactics, to assemble tools and people and implement it. At this point, you find out something about the value of your insight. To get others on board, you have to sell it—by the way, I was told there should be no marketing in this book. Selling and marketing form the interlaced feedback loop between perceived value and proposed value.

Whether or not your plan is a good plan comes down to the degree that other people empathize with it, which depends on how it is presented. In not confirming the existence of the æther, the Michelson-Morley experiment failed, but what if they'd declared that the æther didn't exist and stuck to their guns? The world welcomed Einstein's relativity because it solved problems that his colleagues considered to be important. What if his solution had preceded his community's recognition of the problems? A fill-in critic loved Kerouac's *On the Road* and, despite its unconventional style, it sold over three million copies. Would it have done so well with a bad review?

9.3 INVENTION & DISCOVERY

Let's get back to Emmy Noether.

I want to climb the abstraction ladder of Emmy's reality so that I can ask you a question about invention and discovery. Emmy's immediate reality consisted of her family within the Kaiser's Germany, a setting that set constraints on her goals that she cheerfully ignored. Then she found herself in Hitler's Germany, which pushed her to the United States. By staying in a mathematical ivory tower, Emmy added a layer to her family, political, and social structure. Sure, they tried to kick her out the tower window every chance they got, but from her work and the comments of people who knew her, I'm convinced that she spent far more time and energy in the symbolic, synthetic world of mathematics than anywhere else. And this brings me to the difference between discovery and invention.

Noether's theorem connects the symmetry of geometry of space and time to the laws of nature. Did she invent or discover Noether's theorem?

It most certainly came to her in some form before she wrote it down. She was known to take long walks around campus away from the keyboards of her time—pencil and paper, chalk and blackboards. It's easy to imagine Emmy wandering around campus and stopping short as the relationship between abstract symmetry and nature's laws boiled up into her consciousness. Linking the essence of space and time to how stuff behaves within that spacetime must have tasted like discovery, yet Dr. Noether formulated and proved her theorem. A theorem's validity can be proven or disproven only through symbolic manipulation. You can't test it in the lab. A theorem is either consistent with the definitions of a specific system of logic or it isn't. A theorem is not a thing; it's an idea, a creation, an innovation.

On the other hand, by linking geometry—which is nothing but an imaginary set of ideals in an imaginary space and time—to the rules that matter follows, Noether's theorem provides a hint of what makes nature tick.

If we could ask Dr. Noether whether she discovered or invented her theorem, I'd bet your bar tab that she'd say that it felt more like a discovery than an invention.

As she played around with her symbolic tools, manipulating imaginary constructs, the repercussions appeared before her. Surely she felt the awe of discovery shared by Prometheus when he first controlled fire, Ben Franklin when he realized that lightning was electricity, and Tony Magee when he kept on adding hops to his IPA brew.

9.4 FINDING THE PONY

Innovation and discovery aren't like destinations on a map. The route from where you are to accomplishing your goal is a swirling, loopy, messy thing with lightbulb moments that are both bright and dim and packed with seeming insights and realizations that turn out to be wrong. Deciphering the wheat from the chaff, the buds from the stems, the clever from the stupid is as much a part of the process as the "aha!" moments. The process requires balancing focus and defocus, chilling and gelling, and the amazing conclusion, at least here in the overworked West, is that defocus makes you more productive.

The real trick to innovation and discovery is the ability to latch onto nuance, the tiny differences between two similar patterns and the tiny similarities between vastly different patterns. Strum the strings way up the neck of your guitar. Compare the acceleration of a car with the acceleration caused by gravity. If you want to study mathematics but you lack the requisite y chromosome, sit in on the lectures anyway.

To develop a reservoir of identifiable patterns, we need to expose ourselves to as many ideas as possible. The greater our answer resolution, the more archetypal patterns we can access, and the more accurate our imagined replica of reality is.

Immersion sounds great, but we're already inundated. Every device we have demands attention, and most of it is noise. The reason we're prejudiced against some ideas and their sources is because they truly suck.

How do we crank the signal up out of the noise?

We have the ability to surround ourselves with quality input, at least to some extent. You and I might not agree on what has quality and what doesn't, and that's fine. The answer must lie in where we choose to immerse ourselves. I don't want to waste my time wallowing in manure, but I don't want to miss out on the pony either.

We only get a few decades of awareness, so we need to choose carefully.

Some approaches for choosing signals are obvious: Take classes in subjects in which we're ignorant. Follow and feed curiosity. Check idea prejudice by seriously considering subjects that don't immediately spark your interest. Museums are great places to improve answer resolution. Traveling to different places and hanging out with different people are pretty obvious too. Art and history are king for me, especially since most of my education has been in science, mathematics, philosophy, and literature.

Before I started researching this book, I knew enough about art to enjoy a few days at the National Gallery. Landscapes used to be my favorites. I liked to space out and wonder what it would be like to live in those landscapes. I still love landscapes, but they're not my favorites anymore. Before I clued in on the relationship between empathy and value, art never freaked me out. Landscapes rarely freak me out, but some artists affect me more than others. My favorite artists engage my empathy.

High art is fine, but it isn't enough. Dive bars, sports events, mountains, valleys, ranches, and beaches all go well with opera, lecture series, and theatre. I've learned a lot from hanging around the Oakland Coliseum parking lot on autumn Sundays. Concerts are terrific of course, and good places to blow off steam too. I'm taking my first meditation class next week; it takes a conscious effort to push down my own cynicism. Writing this book even got me to listen to jazz, and I think I figured out why I hate it.

One sure-fire way to both reduce idea prejudice and acquire greater answer resolution is to hold fewer opinions. Sure, our opinions help us distinguish signals from noise, but they're essentially idea prejudice. They inhibit us from entertaining vast regions of idea space.

I feel very strongly that people should be less opinionated.

10

STARING AT A PICTURE
WITHIN A PICTURE
WITHIN A PICTURE

MOST OF THE IDEAS WE'VE SEEN HERE WILL SURVIVE to some extent and in some form as neuroscience matures. Neuroscience in 2016 is at a state similar to where physics was in the middle of the nineteenth century before electricity and magnetism had been combined into electromagnetism but after Newton, Leibniz, Gauss, Fourier, Laplace, Hamilton, and hundreds of others had developed the symbolic tools and techniques that would lead to the huge advances from 1850 to 1950.

Neuroscience is right around the point where Starla first saw the rainbow, the instant when she realized that there is more than on/off, light and dark. Neuroscience has just discovered its rainbow, and our perspectives on the brain, mind, and consciousness are forever altered.

Neuroscientists will soon decipher colors in that rainbow and then figure out the colors that seem to glow on the black-light posters of our minds.

Shards of the first-order, on/off observation that the left brain analyzes and the right brain creates have evolved to second-order, colored complexity. Now we have a concentrating, focused, but occasionally delusional left brain and a vigilant, wide-eyed, but occasionally depressed right brain. The progression from a conclusive statement to "well, there's something to it, but you have to be careful" isn't a flaw; it's a method.

Science seeks the truth through a succession of improved understandings. By figuring out what and how, we try to unravel why. We may never get the exact answer, the stand-alone, wave-the-flag-from-the-top-of-the-hill truth, but as we peel away ignorance, we get ever closer to the truth until the distinction between theory and truth is akin to the distinction between the realities we reconstruct from our senses and the reality that's out there, independent of our own experience.

10.1 LEFT-RIGHT, DOWN-UP, FRONT-BACK

We started this book by upgrading the roles of the left and right hemispheres, but the primary functional distinction of brain geometry is not the difference between left and right; it's the hopping frog, affectionate puppy, and intellectual Feynman. This down-up construction of our brains follows the brainstem à limbic system à neocortex timeline of evolution. Still, the behaviors we inherit from the three are pyramidal: a heartbeat, a feeling, an idea. They build on each other but are so intimately interdependent, feeding backward and forward, amplifying and suppressing, that making distinctions can lead to mistakes. Don't let the metaphor get in the way of the science.

We can play the same game in the longitudinal direction. Front-to-back thought within the neocortex makes associations. We haven't spent much time on brain anatomy. If we had mapped out the anatomy, lent names to each region of the neocortex, each nodule of the limbic system, and the primary features of the brainstem, this book would be ten times longer and three times more boring. Plus, you would have had to drill me with flash cards so I could remember the details. So let me just state that there is no oversimplification for longitudinal thought. If pressed, I'd be tempted to say that sophistication increases from back to front, with sensory processing mostly in back, control of your limbs in the middle, and planning and goal-setting in the front. If you ignored an ocean of evidence to the contrary, you might even agree. Let's not do that. There is no little person at the helm in your head, and every book that colors in a specific region for high-level processes is, at least at this point in the progress of neuroscience, full of shit. It's true that you plan up front, and your feelings and self-awareness have been linked to several separate regions in the front third of your brain, like your left and right insula just above your ears and behind your temples, but the regions are interconnected with every other part of your neocortex and have no clear-cut boundaries.

Every region that's related to how you assemble a unified self spends most of its time petting your inner puppy. Since your inner puppy creates most of the feelings on which you act, we could as accurately state that you are your puppy. In other words, you're a dog. Some folks might not appreciate this oversimplification.

On the other hand, the concept of lateral thought, the source of humor and novelty, the font of genius, is a metaphor that might be grounded in literal, lateral brain geometry.

10.2 OBSESSIVE PATTERN PREDICTORS NEED LOTS OF EDUCATION

Our survival as a species, as well as the survival of most of the other species that share this planet, depends on our ability to solve the problems that come from ten billion people trying to live in harmony on one big, wet rock. Solving these problems—our tendency to fight wars, blow shit up, destroy fertile fields, muck up the atmosphere, you know the list—requires innovation. Not just scientific and technological innovations, but innovations of economy, diplomacy, politics, culture, and so on. The one thing we know for certain about innovation and creativity is that they emerge when we carry concepts from one field into another and then blend them into something completely new. In our heads, this happens through lateral associations of seemingly unrelated concepts that emerge as whole new ideas.

Cutting arts programs in schools is as stupid as cutting science and mathematics programs. We need artists at the top of their games to help us understand and empathize, to feel the repercussions of political decisions. For scientists and engineers to help solve our technological problems, they need answer resolution fortified by literature, history, philosophy, arts, music, and social science. Fully educated people have a huge advantage no matter what challenges confront them.

We tend to innovate in layers of abstraction. Have you noticed how the progress of the World Wide Web follows the simplest model of abstraction layering? The first marketplace emerged about ten thousandyears ago so that communities could capitalize on specialization; eBay is nothing but an abstraction of the marketplace, a virtual flea market. Amazon is another layer of the department store. Facebook is a town square. You can predict everything that will come from the Internet by abstracting everything that came before it—I was serious about that Internet karaoke comment a couple of hundred pages back.

The occupants of this planet need the greatest possible answer resolution, the best tools for abstraction, and the widest and wisest perspectives.

10.3 THE NEUROSCIENCE ONION

When forced to answer what single point I hope to have made in these pages, I'd be tempted to say something about innovation, but that would make my marketing bullshit meter go off. The one theme that permeates neuroscience is that certain, seemingly obvious, aspects of the brain are not separable. Trying to separate talent and skill or any of the other dichotomies I've used as chapter titles is a loser's game. The brain is a system of feedback layers, a picture within a picture that can't be approximated by simple, general statements or "this" versus "that" arguments—it's damn near always this *and* that.

10.3.1 Neuroscience has issues

Will special, unique, mirror neurons be discovered, or will the process of mirroring or mentalizing or whatever you want to call it turn out to be a more subtle process? Will high-level processes like judgment and awareness be nailed down to specific isolated regions of the neocortex, or will they be mapped across dozens to thousands of processors? How will "thought" be defined, and how many different categories of thought will be distinguished? We never even talked about sleep. It probably has something to do with memory formation. Will dreams turn out to come from our top-down processors trying to make sense of whatever boils up from the night-shift work of the hippocampus? Will consciousness turn out to be a threshold of complexity or a spectrum ranging from probably unconscious trees to primarily conscious dogs to whatever consciousness is experienced by sperm whales to the higher-level consciousness of some woman meditating on a hill in Marin County? And what does that mean for the consciousness of beehives or billions of networked computing devices?

The answers are limited by experimental techniques. The primary tools of neuroscience, EEG, fMRI, and PET scans, along with methods from psychology and the behavioral sciences, will experience an incremental improvement in the next decade. And the answers to many of these questions will be unveiled. For each answer, scientists will formulate dozens of new questions aimed at peeling off the next layer. Curiosity tends to generate its own job security.

Scientific conclusions can also be used for corruption and propaganda.

Science has earned a great deal of respect for its ability to unravel complex systems. However, it has also been responsible for giant prejudicial mistakes, like eugenics—the presumption that only wealthy "successful" people should procreate. In the late nineteenth century, as achievements in science flowed into civilization, Darwin's theory of evolution was abused by politicians, businesses, institutions, and even scientists. Many of the European Arctic explorers believed that Inuit, Lapps, and Eskimos were a separate, inferior species.

The state of neuroscience now in the early twenty-first century could easily devolve into a similar pile of unjustified tripe if we're not careful. Gross observations about differences between men and women, different cultures or ethnicities, and even income levels can easily be misconstrued from correlation to cause.

Lie-detection technology could continue on its infamous path. Most people believe that polygraphs can reliably tell whether or not someone is lying. They can't, which is why polygraph results aren't admissible evidence in courts. Polygraphs aren't useless though. If you do a polygraph on someone who believes that they work, that person is far more likely to tell the truth when lying might be in their best interests.

We're headed down the polygraph path with fMRI imaging. A slick neuro-snake-oil dealer could easily convince people that his super-expensive, superconducting fMRI machine can tell when someone's lying: the more expensive, the more convincing; the more expensive, the greater the probability of corruption.

What if the dealer convinced you that her machine is 99 percent accurate? That should be good enough to sway a jury judging a case that's otherwise supported by a pile of circumstantial evidence. Without going into a lecture on statistics (and I'm tempted!), let me paint the picture: Say we have one hundred people who never lie. The 99 percent accurate test means that the odds are 50 percent that it will call someone in that sample of one hundred honest people a liar. Now apply the test to ninety-nine honest people and one liar. The odds are almost 50 percent that the test will turn up two possible liars: a 99 percent chance that it will identify the real liar and nearly a 50 percent chance that it will falsely accuse an honest person—a coin flip.

If that's good enough for you, I hope you're not on my jury.

10.3.2 Neuroscience's dark matter problems

It drives me crazy that we don't have a functional definition of thought.

Ideas and perceptions are like black holes without a definition of gravity. Someday neuroscience will define thought as an unambiguous function in terms that allow independent observers to determine whether or not a thought has occurred. Right now, it's possible to make a good guess when several different regions of the brain light up an fMRI or PET scan. These tests give us a hint of what the minimal, observable definition of a thought will look like. EEGs measure the currents that correlate to thoughts and can tell us if a brain is not thinking, but they don't provide that unambiguous measure: "Ding! She just had a thought. Whoa, there's another one. She's a frickin' genius!"

If a thought is defined as a pattern of neural associations, a minimum number of simultaneously active, coordinated neurons, a cusp of organization, then people can't be the only thinkers on the planet.

When information theory has sufficiently merged with neuroscience that we can measure the difference between the whole and the sum of its parts—really measure it with integrated information—then we might have an observational definition of consciousness and levels of awareness.

Here's another fun assault on what we're trying to do: Glial cells make up half the cells in your brain. They include the stuff that forms myelin and the insulation around axons, but they also include astrocytes, cells that transmit action potentials but lack synapses. How do you think neuroscience would differ if astrocytes were easier to study than neurons, or if the first few discoveries in the field had revolved around astrocytes instead of neurons? Maybe we'd be discussing the "strange neurons that thread throughout the brain, probably serving as no more than a net that holds the entire structure together while astrocytes do all the work."

10.3.3 Experimental difficulties

Functional magnetic resonance imaging, fMRI, has unleashed a torrent of observations about how brains work. To deny that fMRI plays a huge role in figuring out how we figure stuff out would be ridiculous, but no less ridiculous than failing to point out the technical limitations of fMRI.

Everything we've discovered about the mind can be traced back to electrical spikes propagating between neurons. So to figure out how everything works, all we have to do is track every one of these signals, map where they go and when—called a connectome, the neuroscience equivalent of genetics' genome—and, voila, we'll get a clue of why we do what we do, maybe even answer the ultimate question as to why some people listen to jazz and drink wine, while others listen to rock 'n' roll and swill beer.

The multicolored graphics obtained through fMRI brain scans sure look like maps of what's going on in there, don't they? That's kind of the problem with them: They look like what we're after, but they're not quite it.

The nuclear magnetic resonance imaged by fMRI scans is not directly caused by action potentials flowing from neuron to neuron. Instead of mapping the signals, fMRI measures water movement, which is to say, blood flow. Blood flows to cells that deplete their oxygen supply by burning energy. Regions of increased blood flow *correlate* to regions of increased electrical activity, but let's make this perfectly clear: fMRIs do not measure neuron signal transmission or reception; they track variations in blood supply.

Brain scans are capable of distinguishing activity in neighboring regions that are a fraction of an inch (several millimeters) apart, about the width of a pea. The changes in blood flow that they track occur over a couple of seconds. Neuron cell bodies are about 0.030 millimeters (30 microns) across and axons are about 0.001 millimeters (1 micron) in diameter. Neurons receive and process a signal and then transmit their responses in thousandths of a second (milliseconds). Adding it all up, each pixel of an fMRI scan indicates the blood flow required to support the actions of tens of thousands of separate neurons over a time period when those neurons can receive, process, and respond to thousands of signals.

In other words, judging the activity of a brain based on fMRI scans is like determining traffic conditions by sniffing car exhaust once an hour.

That such coarse, imprecise measurements have unveiled such a trove of information indicates just how new this field is and should wave a cautionary flag: Do not *conclude* anything on the basis of fMRI scans alone.

10.3.4 Skepticism is warranted

Good scientists tread warily among new results. Physicists don't accept a discovery unless the odds of random processes mimicking that discovery are worse than a million to one (5 sigma). In other words, if you report something new, but it's possible for random processes to show the same signal more than once in every million trials, they will read your paper, stroke their chins, nod and take it in. They might even buy you a beer, but they won't put out a press release until you get a stronger signal.

Typical neuroscience experiments are performed on too few people to draw statistically sound, decisive results. For example, in a test performed on sixteen people, the probability of mistaking a random fluctuation for a signal is about 25 percent, the statistical uncertainty; double the sample size to thirty-two, and the odds drop to 18 percent; double it again to sixty-four, and the odds drop to 12.5 percent. To get down to an uncertainty of 5 percent, you need a sample of four hundred. The results can be refined by applying rigorous statistical techniques to trends and correlations, but no matter how you add it up, these experiments have huge uncertainties. Now add the experimental bias caused by using university undergraduates—mostly healthy, well-educated people in the age range from eighteen to twenty-five—and the uncertainty goes up again. Most neuroscience results quote statistical significance but make no effort to estimate their entire experimental uncertainty. Estimating systematic bias is difficult and time-consuming, but it is certainly possible. The point is that neuroscience builds over many studies; don't invest too much value in one or two individual investigations.

Neuroscience excites people; we all want to peer into the picture within a picture and catch a glimpse of the camera that actually takes the picture. We all want to know the secret of how we are who we are. I hope that we also want accurate answers.

People like to be right. Sometimes people like to be considered right even when they're wrong. How many times have you argued with a blockhead long after his claims have been disproven? How many times have you been the blockhead?

I once asserted, "No, I did not leave that cabinet door open!" even as I stood before the open cabinet in a house where I had been the only occupant, the only cabinet-opening suspect, until the accuser arrived. Graham Greene's novel *The Quiet American* is a mystery with only one suspect, but it still works. I still maintain my innocence in the face of that cabinet-opening accusation!

In the interest of being correct, skepticism of any new claims is always warranted. Skepticism is what drives scientists into great piles of data until the results convince them one way or another.

Someday, some sort of scan, whatever succeeds fMRI, will have the spatial and temporal resolution required to watch individual axons and astrocytes in real people in real time. Meanwhile, we are a picture within a picture studying a picture that's out of focus.

10.4 SO HERE WE ARE

Your continued experience of this existence comes from the eighty to one hundred billion neurons in your head exchanging spikes of electrical energy. That seems to be it.

The neural cell body transmits a signal down an axon. The axon connects to thousands of dendrites, mostly those of other neurons, but it can also generate feedback to its own source. Groups of neurons process the data collected by our senses and feed their results up to other groups of neurons at ever-higher levels of abstraction, processors we've developed by virtue of our elastic, plastic, trainable brains. Each processor is like a recipe or an algorithm; they take signals in, modify them, and spit new things out. Neuroscience can't tell us yet how many distinct algorithms we can train, but rest assured that you're capable of training more than you're going to need in this lifetime—which is another way of saying that you won't live up to your potential, but it's okay. All your gray and white matter combines into webs of networks and, from those, well, here you are, looking good.

Since this is the last chapter, I feel compelled to say something deeply profound. To make it look even deeper, I put it in a table.

SOMETHING DEEPLY PROFOUND
"The continued flow of signals among neurons in your brain provides your experience of existence."

Table 2: Something deeply profound.

We've only been people gossiping, complaining, and laughing together for something like 250,000 years, not even fifteen thousand generations. We started out staring at the Moon and the stars. Eclipses scared the crap out of us. We feel love and awe, happiness and contentment, certainty and doubt, fear and surprise, anger and grief, boredom, engagement, and distraction—the truth is, we're packed with feelings. Are we sensitive? Yes, we can safely say that humans are sensitive. So we write poetry, make art, perform music, and dance. Everything we do is a dance of some form or another. We have family, friends, colleagues, and associates—we travel in tribes.

But I'm left with some questions.

How the hell did we go from fearing eclipses to postulating multiple universes? How did we go from telling stories around campfires to watching blockbuster movies and playing video games in virtual reality? How did we decide that tribes were so great that we should invent politics, economies, and militaries?

Which I guess boils down to one question: Why do we make things so damn complicated? I have an idea. Let's relax and put on some tunes. Get yourself a beer and, while you're up, grab one for me too.

11

BIBLIOGRAPHY

IN POPULAR SCIENCE WRITTEN FOR A LAY audience, like you and me, I don't like footnotes. When they're useful, they destroy narrative flow by forcing us to jump back and forth across the entire text to get to their nuggets of wisdom. If the nugget is so wise, then it should be built into the text. When they're not useful, just dangling citations, then why bother? Citations play important roles in refereed journal articles. In this book, whenever we hit a topic that wasn't all that well established, like Allan Snyder's idea of how to induce the savant phenomenon, or was someone's invention, like V. S. Ramachandran's rules of neuroaesthetics, I told you who the source was.

In any case, here's a list of books for you to check out that cover different aspects of what we've done here in greater detail. Most of them are written by practicing professional neuroscientists. I've marked my top-five, all-time favorite neuroscience books but listed them in alphabetical order.

11.1 RECOMMENDED RELATED READING

1. Robert Burton, *On Being Certain: Believing You Are Right Even When You're Not*, St. Martin's Press, 2008.
   One of my top-five, all-time favorite neuroscience books. Written in a curious, authentic tone by a neurologist, Bob guides us through the question of how we come to believe what we know.

2. Robert Burton, *A Skeptic's Guide to the Mind: What Neuroscience Can and Cannot Tell Us About Ourselves*, St. Martin's Press, 2013.
   In this one, Bob works through the holes in the data and warns us about what is and isn't on solid scientific ground.

3. Susan Cain, *Quiet: The Power of Introverts in a World That Can't Stop Talking*, Broadway Books, 2012.
   Cain includes lots of studies of how people operate individually and in groups. There's plenty of good stuff here, but she cherry-picks studies that support her argument that introverts kick extroverts' asses—as an introvert, I applaud this—and quotes studies with highly uncertain evidence that can mislead people who've never studied statistics.

4. Rita Carter, *Mapping the Mind*, University of California Press, updated edition, 2010.
   One of my top-five, all-time favorite neuroscience books. Rita Carter is a medical journalist and her books are big, colorful, and wonderfully illustrated works that describe every gyri and sulci.

She does her level best to identify processing centers in every instance where the field has provided evidence. If you want to know the anatomical details, this is the book for you.

5.   Mihaly Csikszentmihalyi, *Finding Flow*, Basic Books, 1997.

6.   Antonio Damasio, *Descartes' Error: Emotion, Reason, and the Human Brain*, Penguin Books, 1994; and *Self Comes to Mind: Constructing the Conscious Brain*, Vintage Books, 2010.
     Dr. Damasio did the pioneering research on the emotion-reason connection.

7.   Stanislaus Dehaene, *The Number Sense: How the Mind Creates Mathematics*, Oxford University Press, 2011.
     Dehaene makes the case that quantitative understanding is like a sense. If you're a teacher and want to understand why mathematics is difficult for so many people and figure out better ways to teach it, read this book.
          I particularly enjoyed the studies he referenced on how birds and animals (other than humans) count and estimate quantities.

8.   Paul Ekman, *Emotions Revealed: Recognizing Faces and Feelings to Improve Communication and Emotional Life*, second edition, Holt Paperbacks, 2007.

9.   Gerald M. Edelman, *Wider Than the Sky: The Phenomenal Gift of Consciousness*, Yale University Press, 2005.
     This is a little rough going, but if you have a background in science, reading this book is like sitting at the knee of a genius as he struggles with the questions that drive him.

10. Michael S. Gazzaniga, *Who's in Charge: Free Will and the Science of the Brain*, HarperCollins, 2011.
     Dr. Gazzaniga has done a great deal of work studying the comple-

mentary and collaborative functions of the left and right hemispheres and has written a pleasant, heartfelt, and readable book.

11.   Steven Jay Gould, *The Mismeasure of Man*, W.W. Norton, 1981.

12.   Jeff Hawkins, *On Intelligence: How a New Understanding of the Brain
      Will Lead to the Creation of Truly Intelligent Machines*, St. Martin's
      Press, 2004.
      Great food for thought about plasticity and how the brain
      develops algorithms and adapts to situations, all oriented toward
      the physical source of intelligence.

13.   Douglas Hofstadter, *I Am a Strange Loop*, Basic Books, 2007.
      This has lots of great stuff about nonlinearity, chaos, and feed-
      back loops.

14.   Steven Johnson, *Emergence: The Connected Lives of Ants, Brains,
      Cities, and Software*, Scribner, 2001.

15.   Eric R. Kandel, *The Age of Insight: The Quest to Understand the
      Unconscious in Art, Mind, and Brain*, Random House, 2012.
      One of my top-five, all-time favorite neuroscience books. I love
      this book! One of those rare cases when it's worth paying extra to
      get the hardcover version. Big, beautifully formatted, with tons of
      color pictures, and Dr. Kandel, Nobel laureate for his pioneering
      work in memory, writes in kind of an innocent, curious voice—
      he even includes a picture of his wife as an example of beauty.
          This book had a huge influence on how I approached the
      subject. I learned a great deal about value and empathy and the
      neural interactions of creators and beholders from *The Age of
      Insight*.

16.   Daniel Kahneman, *Thinking Fast and Slow*, Farrar, Straus, and
      Giroux, 2011.

Written by an economics Nobel laureate, this is an in-depth discussion of unconscious bottom-up processors and conscious top-down processors. Rather than use a metaphor, the way I did with unconscious thoughts boiling or percolating up into top-down consciousness, he simply calls them system 1 and system 2.

17. Christof Koch, *Consciousness: Confessions of a Romantic Reductionist*, MIT Press, 2012.
    One of my top-five, all-time favorite neuroscience books because of his forthcoming, personal writing style, or because he's a physicist and I speak his language, or maybe because we agreed on the topic of free will, so I was primed to love it.
    This book was a key source for the idea that consciousness could be a spectrum rather than a complexity threshold effect and how integrated information theory might be able to calculate the degree of consciousness of a system.

18. Matthew D. Lieberman, *Social: Why Our Brains are Wired to Connect*, Crown Publishers, 2013.
    Lieberman has a different view of human interaction than most researchers. For example, he expresses a lot of doubt about the existence of mirror neurons and offers less conventional ideas on topics like autism and theory of mind, and he is a proponent of mentalizing.

19. Iain McGilchrist, *The Master and His Emissary: The Divided Brain and the Making of the Western World*, Yale University Press, 2009.

20. Isaac Newton, *Philosophiae Naturalis Principia Mathematica*, 1687; in English, *Principia*, 1728.

21. Steven Pinker, *How the Mind Works*, W.W. Norton, 1997.

22. V. S. Ramachandran, *The Tell-Tale Brain: A Neuroscientist's Quest for What Makes Us Human*, W.W. Norton, 2011.
    Definitely one of my top-five, all-time favorite neuroscience books. He covers his rules of neuroaesthetics, the main topic of our chapter 8. While he tends to leap a bit before looking, that is, he doesn't quite require a preponderance of evidence before accepting a discovery, his ideas are wonderful, and he writes with curiosity and bemusement.

23. Sebastian Seung, *Connectome: How the Brain's Wiring Makes Us Who We Are*, Houghton Mifflin Harcourt, 2012.

24. David Shenk, *The Genius in All of Us: New Insights into Genetics, Talent, and IQ*, Anchor Books, 2010.

25. Mark Turner, *The Origin of Ideas: Blending, Creativity, and the Human Spark*, Oxford University Press, 2014.

11.2 OTHER STUFF THAT SHOWED UP HERE

26. Douglas Adams, *A Hitchhiker's Guide to the Galaxy*, Pan Books, 1979.

27. Chuck Berry, *Johnny B. Goode*, Chess Studios, 1958.

28. Elvis Costello and Paul McCartney, "Veronica," from the album *Spike*, Warner Brothers, 1989.

29. Richard Feynman, Robert Leighton, and Matthew Sands, *The Feynman Lectures on Physics*, Addison-Wesley, 1963.

30. Graham Greene, *The Quiet American*, William Heinemann, 1958.

31. Allen Ginsburg, *Howl and Other Poems*, City Lights Books, 1955.

32. Nick Hornby, *High Fidelity*, Riverhead, 1996.

33. Jack Kerouac, *On the Road*, Viking Press, 1957.

34. Tony Magee, *So You Want to Start a Brewery?: The Lagunitas Story*, Chicago Review Press, 2014; Lagunitas IPA, a twelve gang of twelves, Lagunitas Brewery, 2016; Lagunitas Dogtown Pale Ale, 12 oz. bottle, Lagunitas Brewery, 2016.

35. Monty Python, *Monty Python's Life of Brian*, Handmade Films, 1979.

36. Poison, "Every Rose Has Its Thorn," from the album *Open Up and Say...Ahhh!* Capitol, 1988.

37. Kim Stanley Robinson, *Galileo's Dream*, Spectra, 2009.

38. Shunryu Suzuki, *Beginner's Mind*, Shambhala Publications, 2006.

39. Mark Twain, *Following the Equator*, American Publishing, 1897.

FROM THE AUTHOR

Thank you for reading *The Left Brain Speaks, the Right Brain Laughs.* Thank you even more for buying it.

Before thanking everyone who helped make this book possible, I'd like to apologize for any wisecracks that might have offended you. If you crack enough wise, you're doomed to drop some boners, but I certainly don't intend offense. I'd also like to apologize for those instances when I've mistaken universal human traits with traits engendered by different cultures. Cultural errors are experimental biases that, in this field, have a sick legacy of providing the rationale for evil behavior.

You might have noticed the seemingly random way that I chose between "she" and "he" when referring to generic individuals. Let me confirm that I did indeed let a random number generator make the choice whenever one of these pronouns was needed.

ACKNOWLEDGMENTS

Now, in alphabetical order, here are the people who tried to help me correct my misunderstandings about neuroscience, music, art, history, biology, information theory, and chaos by combing through early drafts of the manuscript: Steve Allen, Bill Bonnet, Joshua Gibson, Brad Henderson, Robert Kennedy, and Lee Sawyer. The list of neuroscientists who provided answers and education is too long to list, even if I'd kept track well enough for it to be inclusive. The bibliography includes texts for laypeople that cover everything that showed up here.

I'd also like to thank legendary publisher Brenda Knight. One day in 2012, Brenda asked me about my second novel, *The Sensory Deception*, which I'd just finished. After describing the neuroscience basis for the "sensory saturation" virtual reality technology my characters develop to convert people into environmentalists, she said, "Hey, why don't you write a neuroscience book for me?" I said, "Huh?" And she said, "Sure, you're a scientist and a writer, it'd be awesome!" So I did and I enjoyed every second of it.

I'd also like to thank everyone at both the Berkeley and Jersey City versions of Viva Editions for creating the beautiful work that you hold in your hands and for tolerating me, especially Josephine Mellon, who combed through this draft with you in mind and warmth and affection in her heart.

And, of course, thanks to Karen, Professor Buckley, and Dear Abby because nothing happens without the support of your mate and your dogs.

NOTE TO YOU

It says on my business card that I'm a scientist, technologist, and novelist. So let me confess my personal reasons for writing this book: As a technologist, I'm acutely aware that the innovation necessary to solve big problems occurs when we take a concept from one field and apply it to another and I wanted to know how that works. As a novelist, I set out to understand the best techniques for developing characters and plots that engage readers, to really put them into my stories. As a veteran scientist, I wanted to understand the art of science; why we pursue elegant descriptions and why we study what we study. I hope that this book has helped you understand your innovative engine and that you can now squeeze out a bit more creative horsepower than you could before.

Books are capsules of thought and reading one is akin to reading the author's mind. It's an intimate experience that ought to breed familiarity. To that end, it's only fair that you share your thoughts with me. Please send me a note: ransom@ransomstephens.com.

My website is www.ransomstephens.com. It has links to my science articles and to my other books. My first novel, *The God Patent* (47North, 2010), is set in the culture war between science and religion, the story of a laid-off engineer who gets caught between science and religion in a battle over the origin of the universe and the existence of the soul; plus, you'll get an easy-to-swallow dose of quantum physics. *The Sensory Deception* (47North, 2013) is about three scientists and a venture capitalist who set out to save the environment by putting people in the minds of endangered animals; you'll get a ride in Moby Dick's head as well as a tour of Silicon Valley tech development and a visit with Somali pirates. My next two novels, *The 99% Solution* (coming in 2017) and *Too Rich to Die* (probably 2018) are thought provoking and funny international inter-dimensional thrill rides.

Should it ever be relevant, and I hope it will be, I prefer beer to wine, tea to coffee, hard rock to jazz, and I find solace in yelling obscenities at Oakland Raiders home games. See you in the Black Hole.

Ransom Stephens, Ph.D.
Petaluma, California, March 2016